A-Z KINGSTON

G000298309

CONTENTS

Key to Map Pages	2-3
Large Scale City Centre	4-5
Map Pages	6-59
In...	
V...	
selected Places of Interest	

REFERENCE

A Road	A1034	Car Park (selected)	P
Under Construction		Park & Ride	Walton St. P+
B Road	B1231	Church or Chapel	†
Dual Carriageway		Cycleway	
One-way Street	→	Fire Station	■
Traffic flow on A Roads is also indicated by a heavy line on the driver's left.	→	Hospital	H
Restricted Access		House Numbers Selected Roads	245 32
Pedestrianized Road		Information Centre	i
Track / Footpath		National Grid Reference	505
Residential Walkway		Police Station	▲
		Post Office	★

Toilet:
without facilities for the Disabled ▽
with facilities for the Disabled ▽
for exclusive use by the Disabled ▽

Railway — Station, Level Crossing, Tunnel	
Built-up Area — VICTOR ST.	
Viewpoint	
Educational Establishment	
Local Authority Boundary	— · — · —
Hospital, Hospice or Health Centre	
Posttown Boundary	———
Industrial Building	
Postcode Boundary within Posttown	— — —
Leisure or Recreational Facility	
Place of Interest	
Map Continuation 16 Large Scale City Centre 4	
Public Building	
Shopping Centre or Market	
Other Selected Buildings	

SCALE

Map Pages 6-59 1:15840	Map Pages 4-5 1:7920
0 ¼ ½ Mile	0 ⅛ ¼ Mile
0 250 500 750 Metres	0 100 200 300 Metres
4 inches (10.16 cm) to 1 mile 6.31 cm to 1 km	8 inches (20.32 cm) to 1 mile 12.63 cm to 1 km

Copyright of Geographers' A-Z Map Company Ltd.

Head Office:
Fairfield Road, Borough Green, Sevenoaks, Kent TN15 8PP
Telephone: 01732 781000 (Enquiries & Trade Sales)
01732 783422 (Retail Sales)

www.a-zmaps.co.uk

Ordnance Survey® This product includes mapping data licensed from Ordnance Survey® with the permission of the Controller of Her Majesty's Stationery Office.

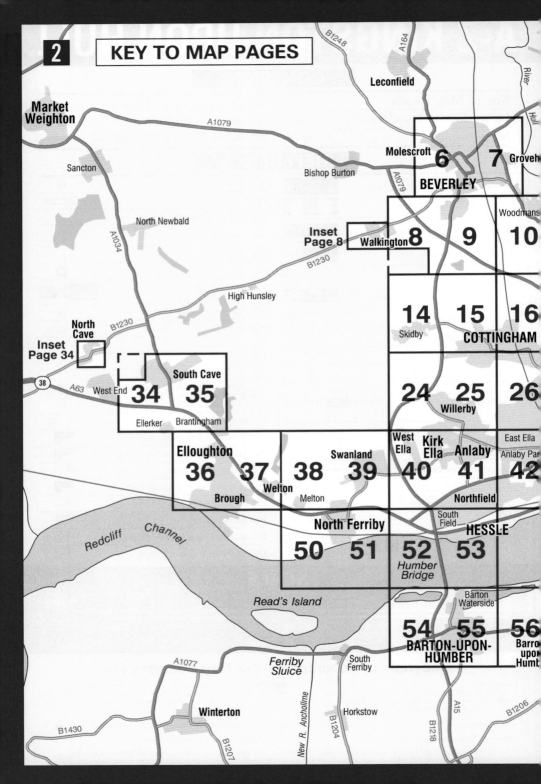

Leconfield

Market Weighton

A1079

Sancton

Bishop Burton

Molescroft **6** **7** Grove

BEVERLEY

Woodmans

North Newbald

A1034

Inset Page 8 Walkington **8** **9** **10**

B1230

High Hunsley

14 **15** **16**

Skidby **COTTINGHAM**

North Cave

B1230

Inset Page 34

(38)

A63 West End **34** **South Cave 35**

Ellerker Brantingham

24 **25** **26**

Willerby

West Ella Kirk Ella Anlaby

East Ella

Anlaby Par

Elloughton 36 **37** **38** **Swanland 39** **40** **41** **42**

Welton

Brough Melton

Northfield

South Field **HESSLE**

North Ferriby

50 **51** **52** **53**

Humber Bridge

Redcliff Channel

Read's Island

Barton Waterside

54 **55** **56**

BARTON-UPON- HUMBER

Barro upon Humb

A1077

Ferriby Sluice

South Ferriby

Winterton

Horkstow

New R. Ancholme

B1204

B1218

A15

B1206

B1430

B1207

River Hull

B1248

A164

A179

A1079

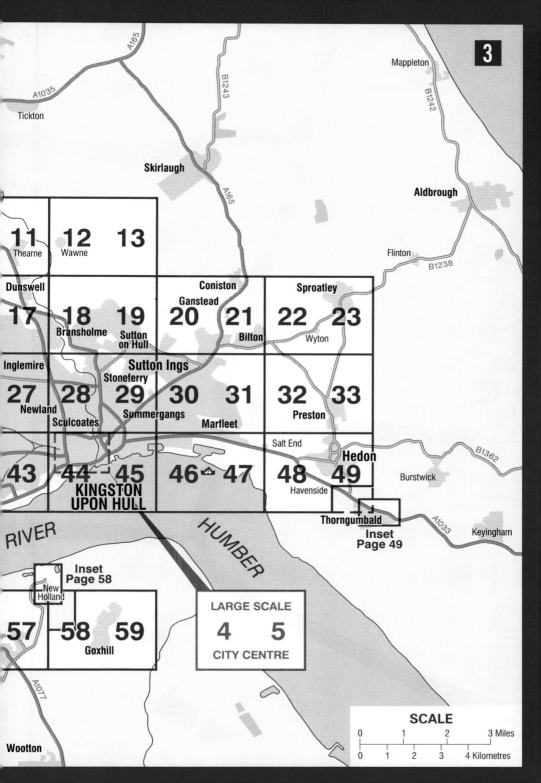

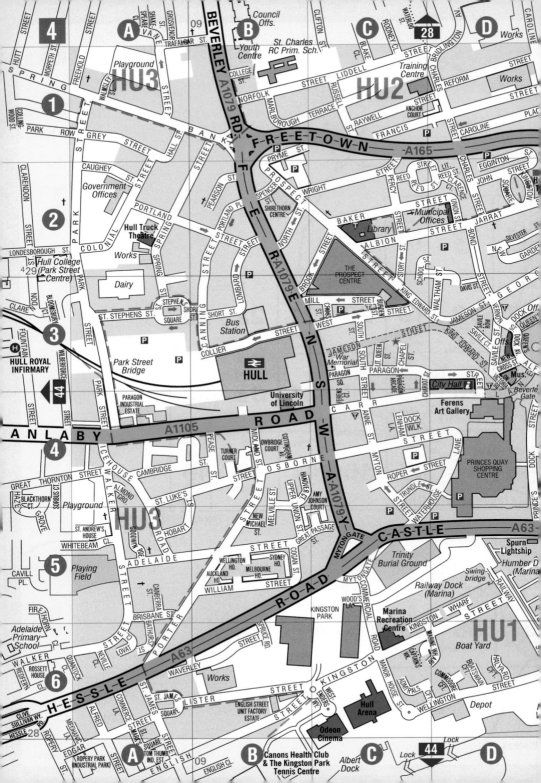

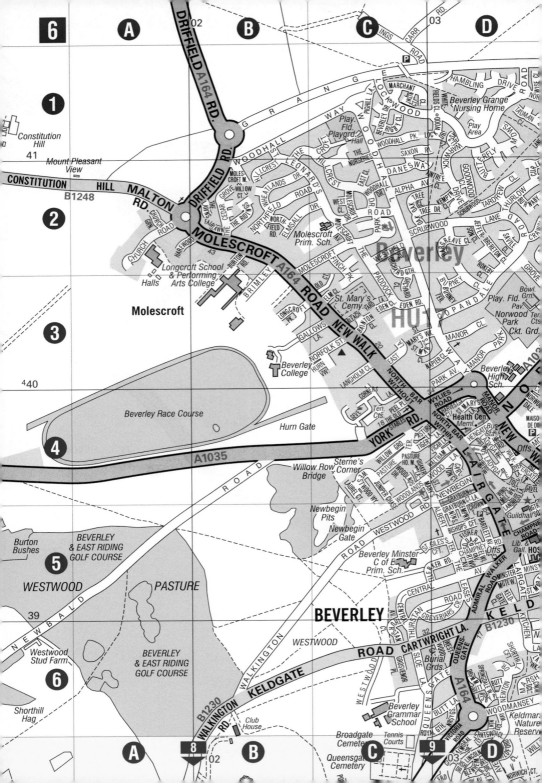

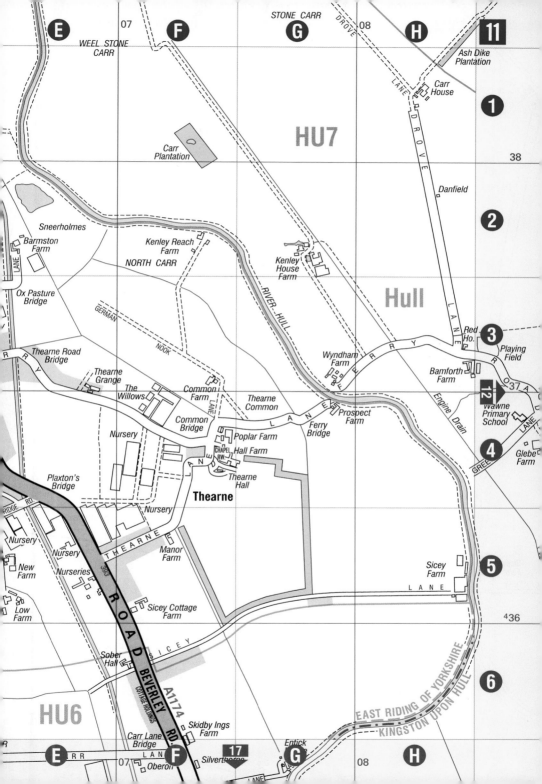

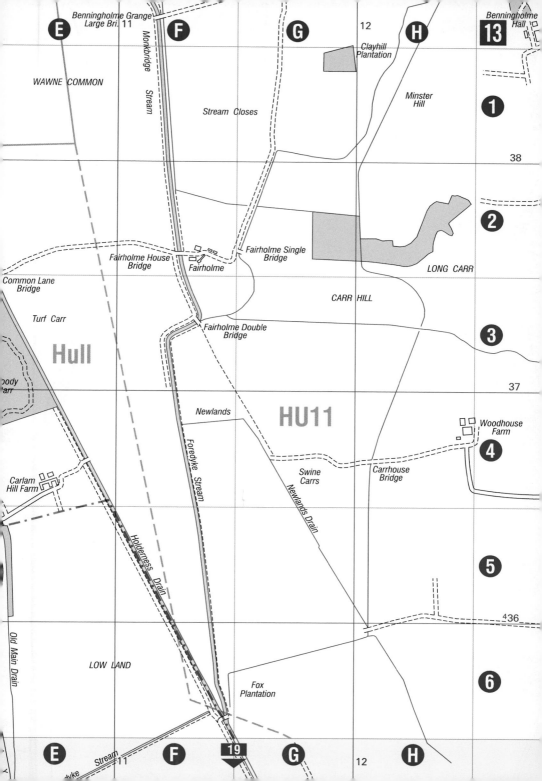

E Benningholme Grange
Large Bri. 11 **F** **G** 12 **H** Benningholme
Hall **13**

Monkbridge
Stream

Clayhill
Plantation

WAWNE COMMON

Minster
Hill

1

Stream Closes

38

2

Fairholme Single
Bridge

Fairholme House
Bridge

LONG CARR

Fairholme

Common Lane
Bridge

CARR HILL

3

Turf Carr

Hull

oody
arr

37

Newlands

HU11

4

Woodhouse
Farm

Foredyke Stream

Swine
Carrs

Carrhouse
Bridge

Carlam
Hill Farm

Newlands Drain

Holderness Drain

5

436

Old Main Drain

LOW LAND

6

Fox
Plantation

E **F** **19** **G** 12 **H**

Dyke Stream 11

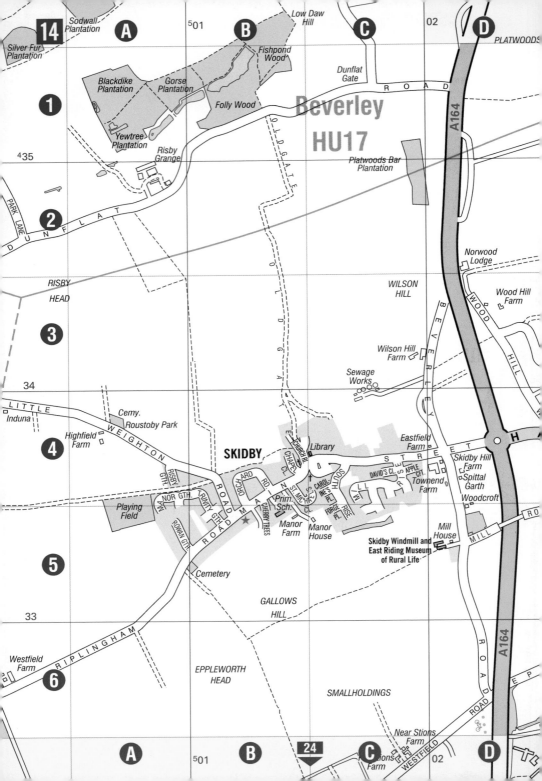

14

A ⁵01 **B** Low Daw Hill **C** 02 **D**

Sodwall Plantation

Silver Fur Plantation

PLATWOODS

Fishpond Wood

Blackdike Plantation

Gorse Plantation

Folly Wood

Dunflat Gate

Beverley

HU17

1

Yewtree Plantation

Risby Grange

R O A D

A164

Platwoods Bar Plantation

⁴35

2

PARK LANE

D U N F L A T

OLD GATE

Norwood Lodge

WILSON HILL

Wood Hill Farm

RISBY HEAD

3

Wilson Hill Farm

W O O D   H I L L

34

LITTLE

Induna

WEIGHTON

Cemy. Roustoby Park

Sewage Works

Eastfield Farm

B E V E R L E Y

4

Highfield Farm

SKIDBY

CHURCH RI

CHAPEL CL

Library

S T R E E T

S T

Skidby Hill Farm

Spittal Garth

DAVID'S CL. APPLE CFT.

Townend Farm

Woodcroft

RISBY GTH

ORCHARD RD

NOR GTH.

TRINITY GTH

ROWAN GTH

R O A D

Prim. Sch.

ST MICH CL

CHERRY TREES

Playing Field

Manor Farm

Manor House

CAROL INE'S CL

S O U T H

FORGE PL

HILL MT

RISE

Mill House

Skidby Windmill and East Riding Museum of Rural Life

MILL ROAD

5

Cemetery

A164

33

GALLOWS HILL

RIPLINGHAM

Westfield Farm

EPPLEWORTH HEAD

SMALLHOLDINGS

R O A D

EP

6

Near Stions Farm

...ions Farm

WESTFIELD

A ⁵01 **B** **24** **C** 02 **D**

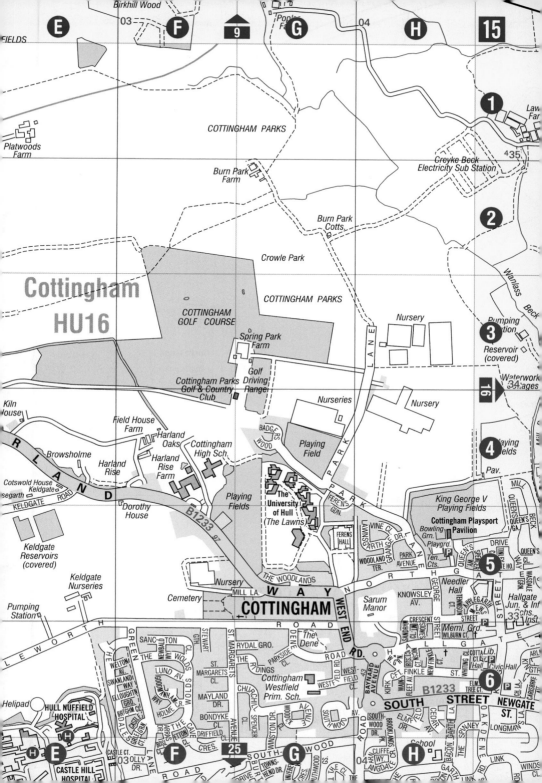

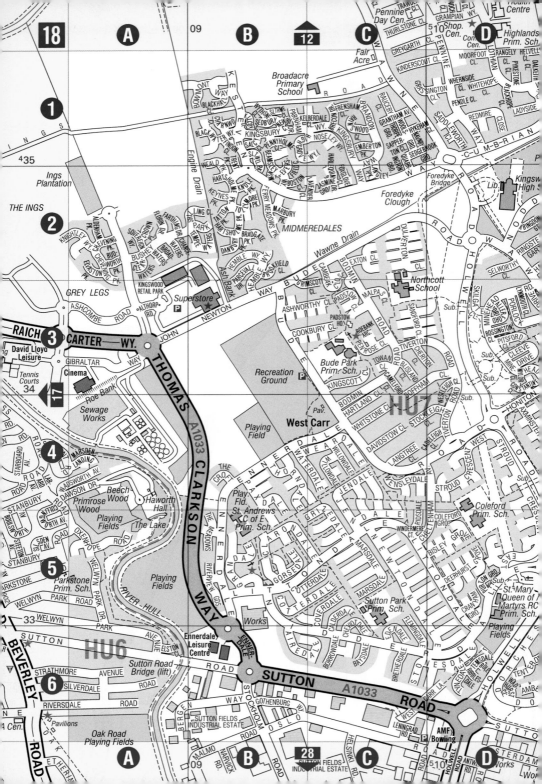

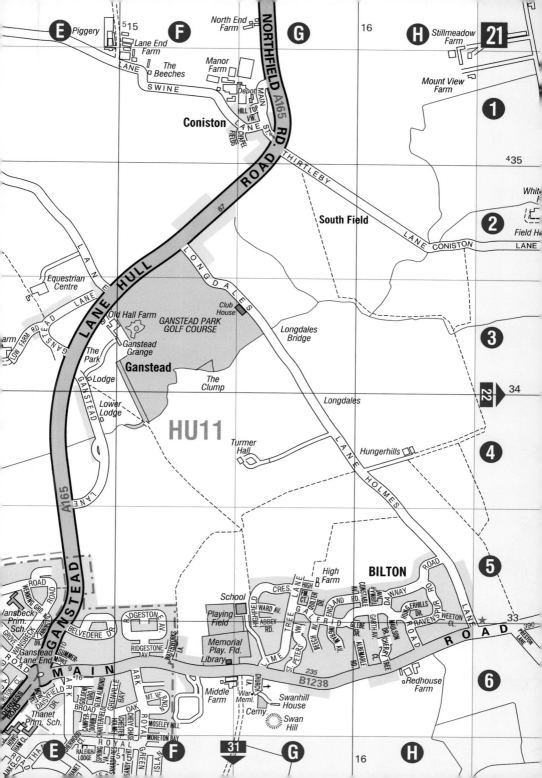

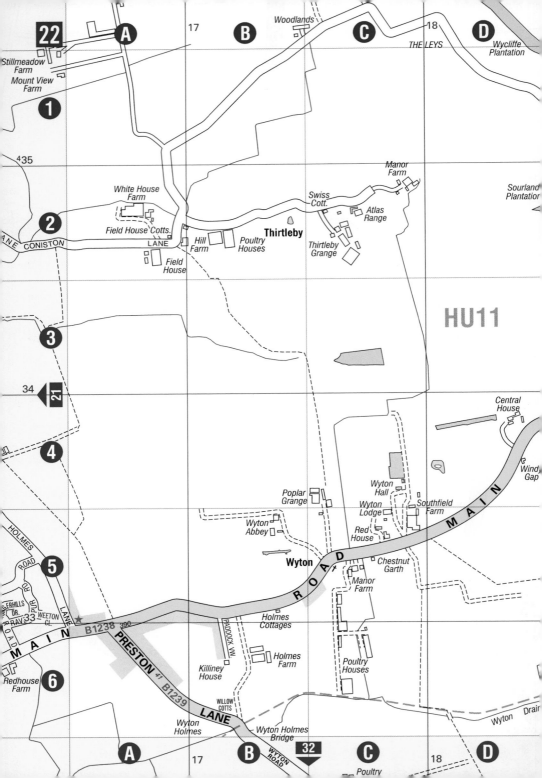

22

A 17 **B** Woodlands **C** 18 **D**

Stillmeadow Farm

Mount View Farm

THE LEYS

Wycliffe Plantation

1

435

White House Farm

Swiss Cott.

Manor Farm

Sourland Plantation

2 CONISTON LANE LANE

Field House Cotts.

Hill Farm

Poultry Houses

Thirtleby

Atlas Range

Thirtleby Grange

LANE

Field House

3

HU11

34 **21**

Central House

4

Poplar Grange

Wyton Hall

Wind Gap

Wyton Lodge

Southfield Farm

HOLMES ROAD

5

Wyton Abbey

Red House

MAIN ROAD

SUMMERHILLS DR.

WEETON CL.

Wyton

Manor Farm

Chestnut Garth

RAV... 33

B1238 390

Holmes Cottages

LANE

PADDOCK VW.

Poultry Houses

MAIN ROAD

PRESTON 41 B1239

Killiney House

Holmes Farm

6 Redhouse Farm

WILLOW COTTS

LANE

Wyton Holmes

Wyton Holmes Bridge

A 17 **B** WYTON ROAD **32** **C** 18 **D**

Wyton Drain

Poultry

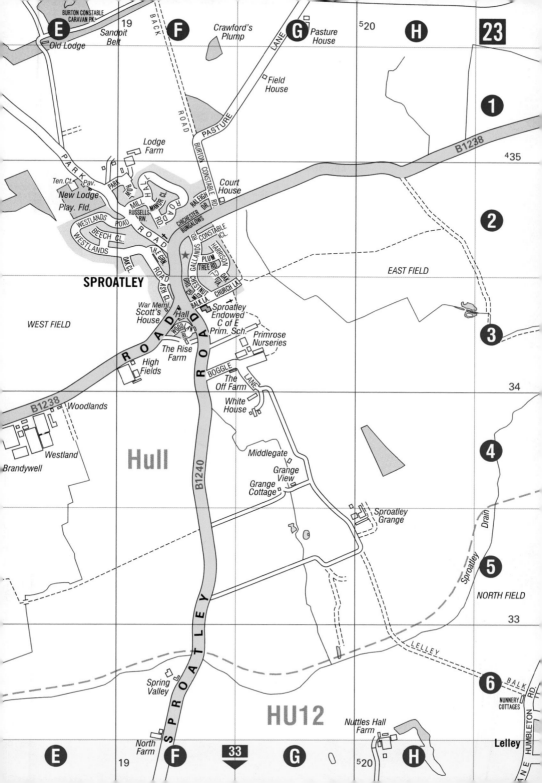

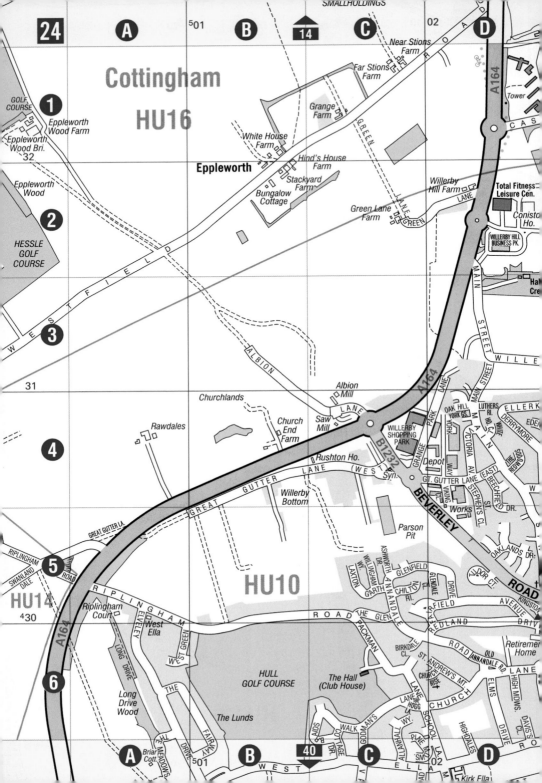

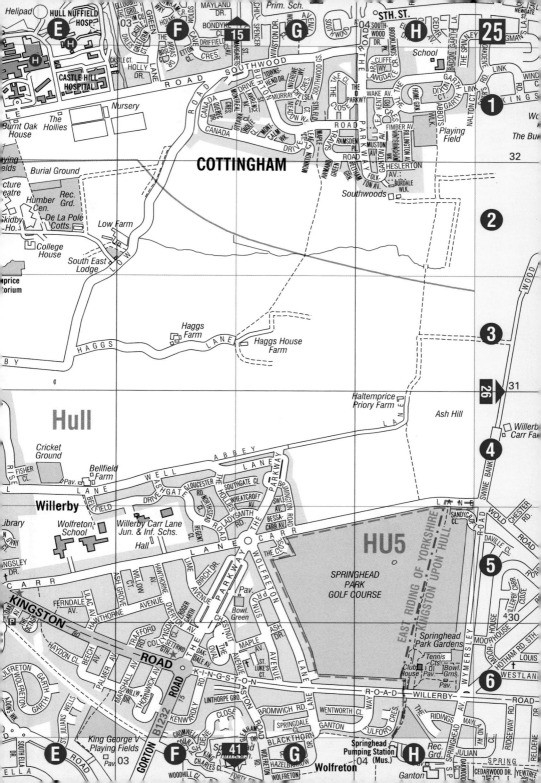

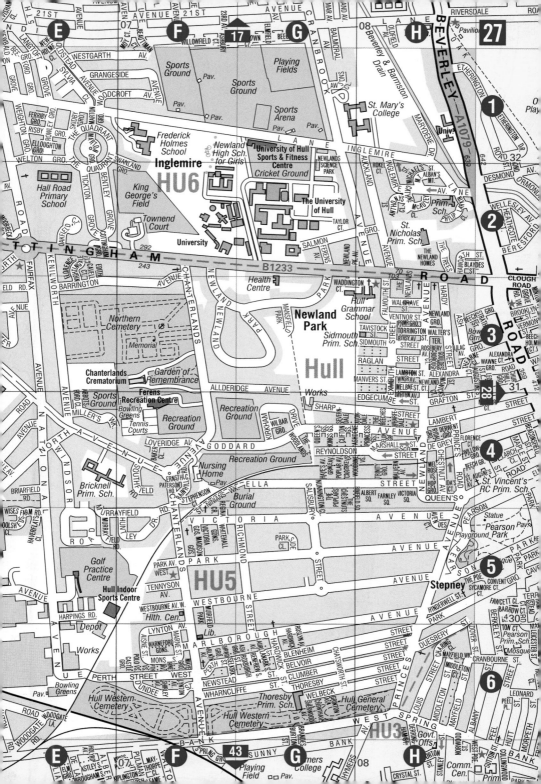

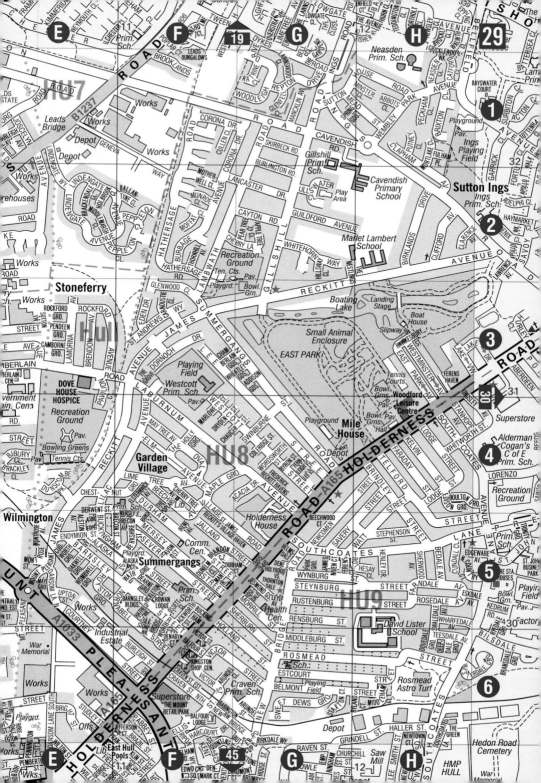

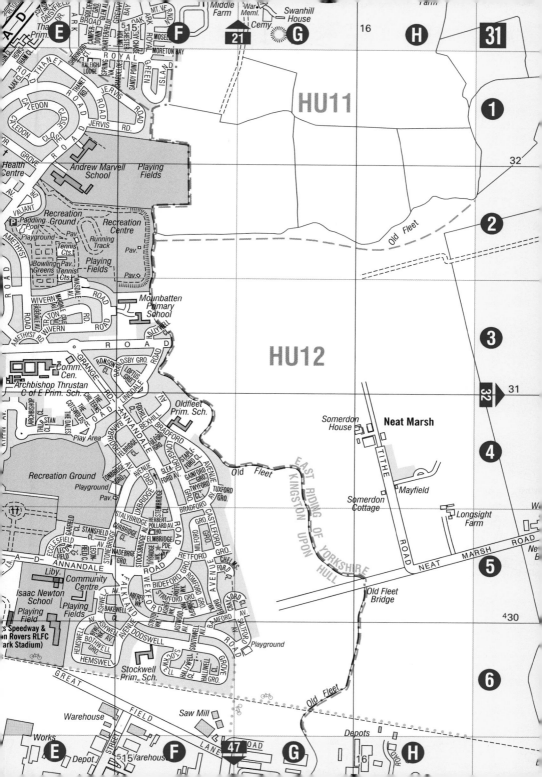

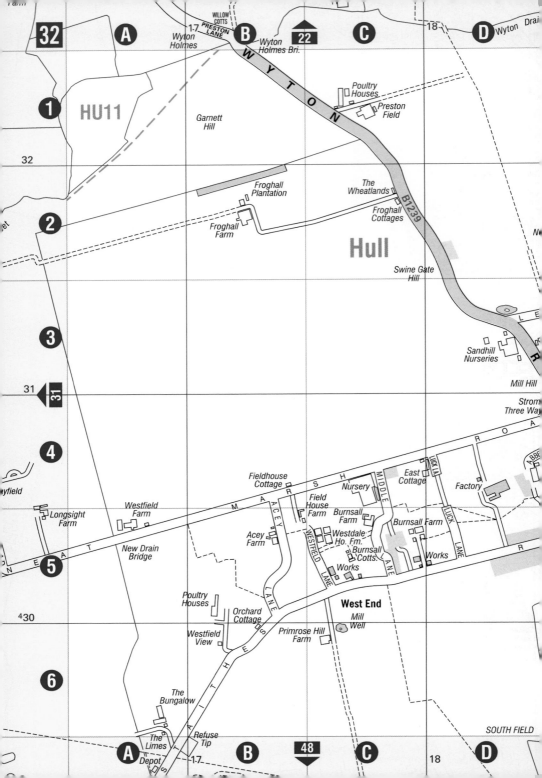

32

A

B

C

D

1

HU11

Farm

WILLOW COTTS

PRESTON LANE

1·7

Wyton Holmes

Wyton Holmes Bri.

22

18

Wyton Drai

Garnett Hill

Poultry Houses

Preston Field

WYTON

2

Froghall Plantation

The Wheatlands

Froghall Cottages

N

Froghall Farm

Hull

B1239

Swine Gate Hill

et

3

LE

Sandhill Nurseries

R

Mill Hill

31

31

Strom Three Wa

4

Fieldhouse Cottage

Nursery

East Cottage

Factory

R O A

ayfield

Westfield Farm

M A R S H

Field House Farm

Burnsall Farm

MIDDLE LANE

Burnsall Farm

LUCK LA.

BBF

Longsight Farm

ACEY

Acey Farm

WESTFIELD LANE

Westdale Ho. Fm.

Burnsall Cotts.

LUCK LANE

Works

R

New Drain Bridge

E A T

5

Works

West End

N

Poultry Houses

Orchard Cottage

S LITHE LANE

Primrose Hill Farm

Mill Well

6

Westfield View

The Bungalow

SOUTH FIELD

A

48

B

C

D

The Limes

Depot

Refuse Tip

1·7

18

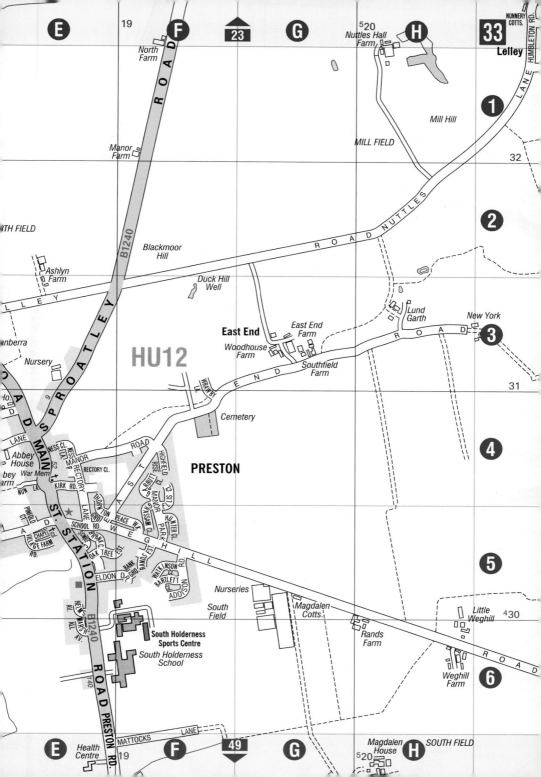

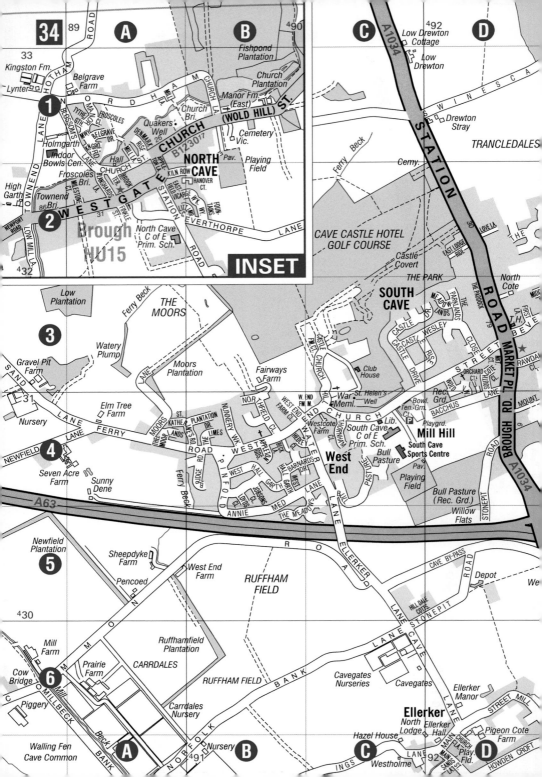

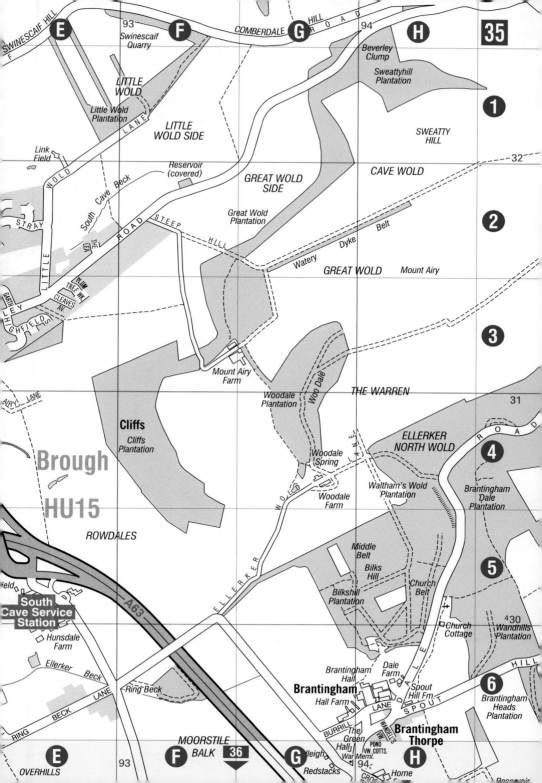

SWINESCAIF HILL

E · 93 · F · COMBERDALE · G · HILL · ROAD · 94 · H · **35**

Swinescaif Quarry

Beverley Clump

Sweattyhill Plantation

LITTLE WOLD

Little Wold Plantation

1

LITTLE WOLD SIDE

SWEATTY HILL

Link Field

Reservoir (covered)

GREAT WOLD SIDE

CAVE WOLD · 32

WOLD LANE

South Cave Beck

ROAD STEEP HILL

Great Wold Plantation

Dyke Belt

2

STRAY

THE LEA

LITTLE

Watery

GREAT WOLD · Mount Airy

PLUM TREE WK.

CLEAVES AV.

BARTLEY HIGHFIELD

3

Mount Airy Farm

Woo Dale

THE WARREN · 31

AIRY LANE

Cliffs

Cliffs Plantation

Woodale Plantation

ELLERKER NORTH WOLD

ROAD

4

Brough

Woodale Spring

Waltham's Wold Plantation

Brantingham Dale Plantation

HU15

Woodale Farm

ELLERKER WOLD

ROWDALES

Middle Belt

Bilks Hill

Church Belt

5

South Cave Service Station

A63

Bilkshill Plantation

Church Cottage

⁴30 Wandhills Plantation

Hunsdale Farm

Ellerker Beck

Ring Beck

RING BECK LANE

ELLERKER LANE

Brantingham Hall

Dale Farm

Spout Hill Fm.

SPOUT HILL

6

Brantingham Heads Plantation

Brantingham

Hall Farm

DALE LANE

MOORSTILE BALK · **36**

BURRILL LANE

The Green Hall

WANDELLS LANE

PTN.

POND

IW. COTTS.

War Meml.

Brantingham Thorpe

E · OVERHILLS · 93 · F · G · ⸱leigh ⸱ Redstacks · 94 · H · Home

CROSS

36

A 93 **B** 35 **C** **D** 94

Ellerker

Pigeon C Farm

Street Mill Hill Ring Beck Howden Croft Hill

1 White House Farm

OVERHILLS

29

LANE

2

WHIN MOOR

Whinneymoor Farm

MOORSTILE BALK

Hall Farm LANE SPOUT

Burrill The Green VW.COTTS. PON D War Meml. VW.

Woodleigh Redstacks

Brantingham Thorpe

Hall

Home Farm

CROOK HILL

Thorpe Cottage

CROOK

A63

NEW ROAD

OUTGANG U BRANTINGHAM

Brantingh

Branti Thorp Par

3

BRANTINGHAM COMMON

Brantingham Drain

SAND FIELD

THE CAVE

Trinity House Land

Nurseries

Depot

STOCKBRIDGE

Osier Beds

Rugby Ground

Club House

PINDLEWOOD

St. MARY'S CL.

Cemy CHURCH

Hall Prim Sch

Vic. LA.

VICARAGE

CGE GS

CH. VW

ST MARY'S

28

Brantingham Grange

Stockbridge Plantations

Stock Bridge

SANDS

ORCH

ERS RISE

ROAD

Depo

4

BRANTINGHAM SANDS

Avenue Plantation

Monument

BROUGH GOLF COURSE

WEST

LANE

Mill Hill

MILL LANE

LANE

MAIN

Ellerker Drain

MILL LANE

Glenrock Cottage

Glenrock

GLENROCK PK.

ELLOUGHTON

Larchmont Cl.

WESTFIELD CL.

WESTFIELD PARK

Westfield Park

BIRCH

CT.

CHANTR

5

ELLERKER SANDS

Club House

BROUGH GOLF COURSE

GOLF LINKS DR.

ROAD

HUNTE

Playgrd.

Hall

Lib.

JEFFERSON

ATKINSON DR.

DRIVE

Brough Prim. Sch

TRE

4 27

Reservoir

PETUARIA CL.

BRENTWOOD CL.

STATION RD

HAVEN AV.

GRANGE PARK

JEFFERSON

ELLOUGHTON LANE

WELTON

ROAD

WELTON

Superstore

PRESCOTT

CENTUR

6

RIVER

HUMBER

Ellerker Foreshore

Sawmills

Ellerker Clough

Ellerker Haven

Works

HAVEN GARTH

FERRY CL.

STATION RD

THE

Works

GRASSDALE PK.

The Burrs

SALTGROUNDS

WRYGARTH AV.

CAVENDISH PARK

RANDSFIELD AV.

AV. Bowl. Grns.

BLACKBURN

Pav. Ten. Cts.

Brough Sand

A 93 **B** **C**

Nab End

Brough Haven

KING EDWARDS

TER.

SALTGROUNDS ROAD

Works

94

MARLE

PABE

SKILLINGS

COURT

BUCCANEE WY.

D

INGS LANE

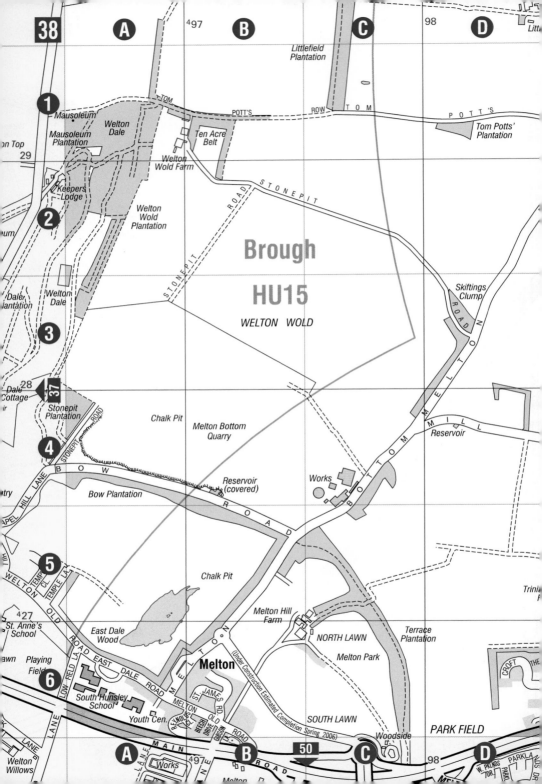

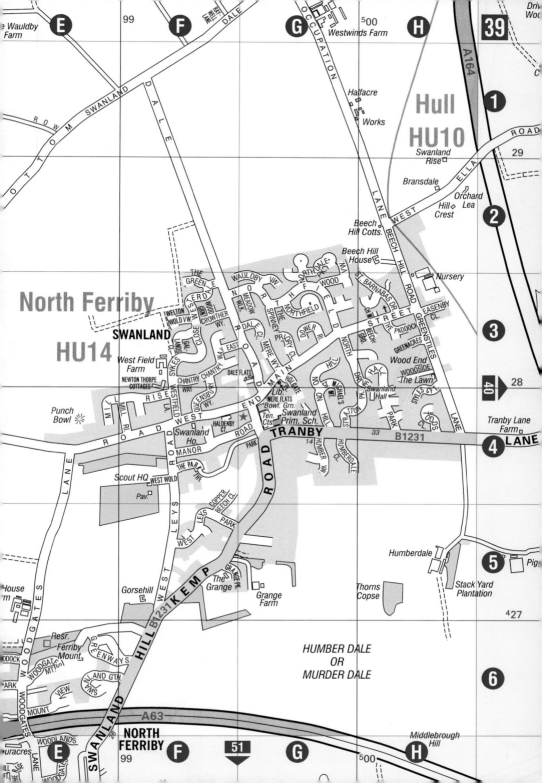

North Ferriby

HU14

SWANLAND

Hull

HU10

Wauldby Farm

Westwinds Farm

Halfacre

Works

Swanland Rise

Bransdale

Orchard Lea

Hill Crest

Beech Hill Cotts.

Beech Hill House

Nursery

West Field Farm

Newton Thorpe Cottages

Punch Bowl

Swanland Ho.

Scout HQ

West Wold

Pav.

Gorsehill

The Grange

Grange Farm

Resr.
Ferriby Mount

House Farm

Woodacres

NORTH FERRIBY

Wood End

Woodside
The Lawn

Swanland Hall

Tranby Lane Farm

TRANBY

B1231 LANE

Humberdale

Stack Yard Plantation

Pig

Thorns Copse

HUMBER DALE
OR
MURDER DALE

Middlebrough Hill

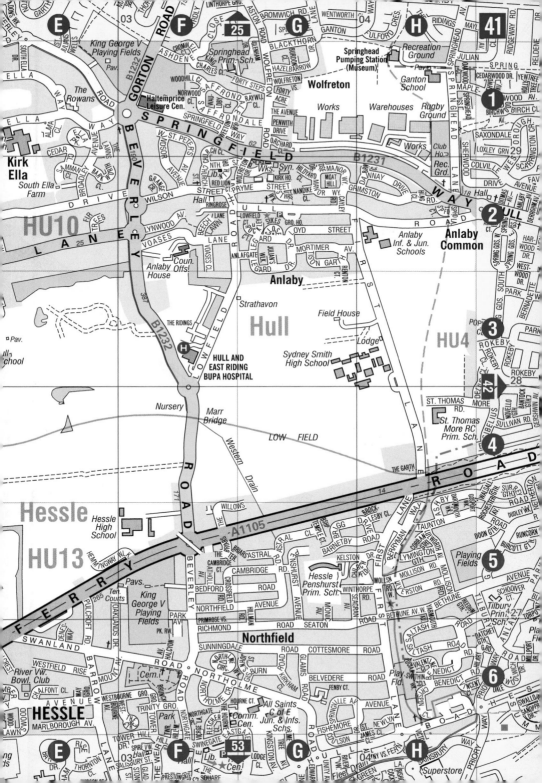

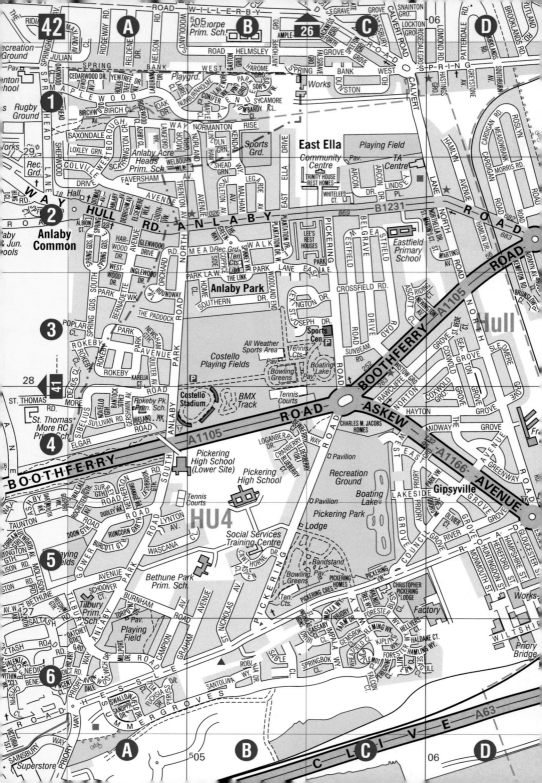

KINGSTON UPON HULL

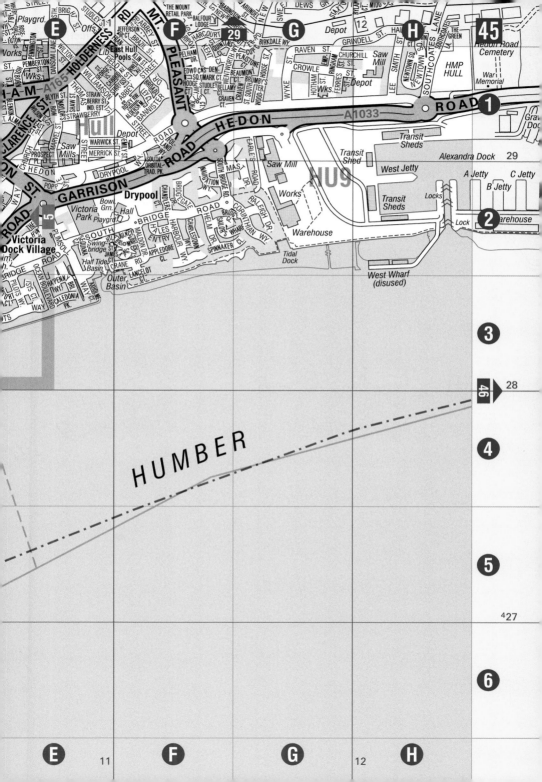

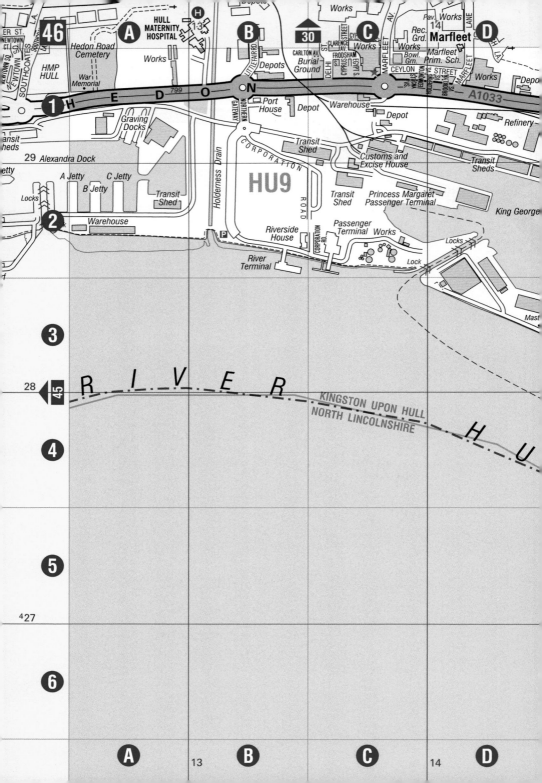

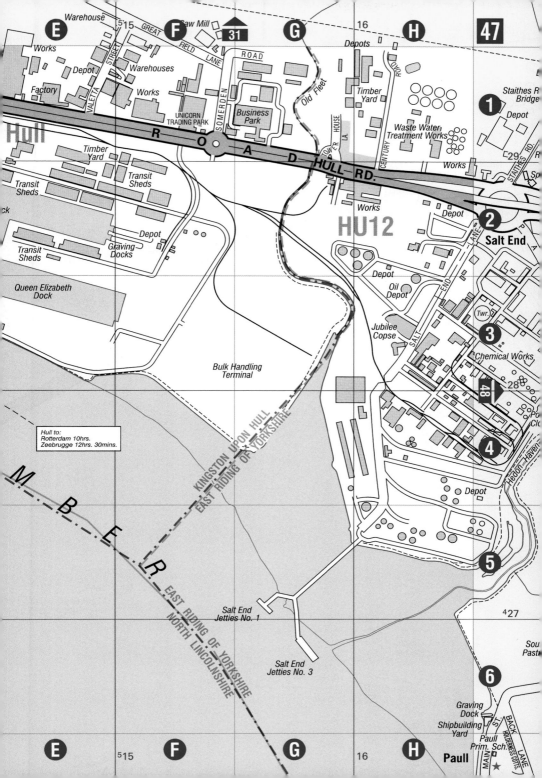

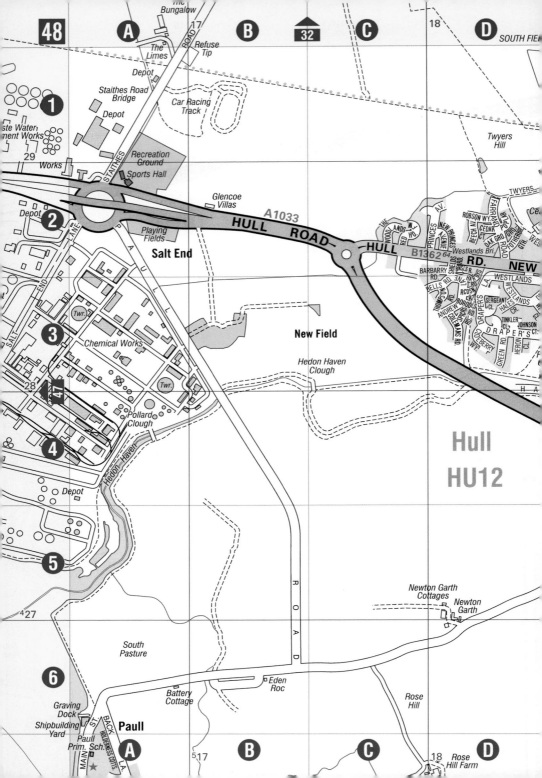

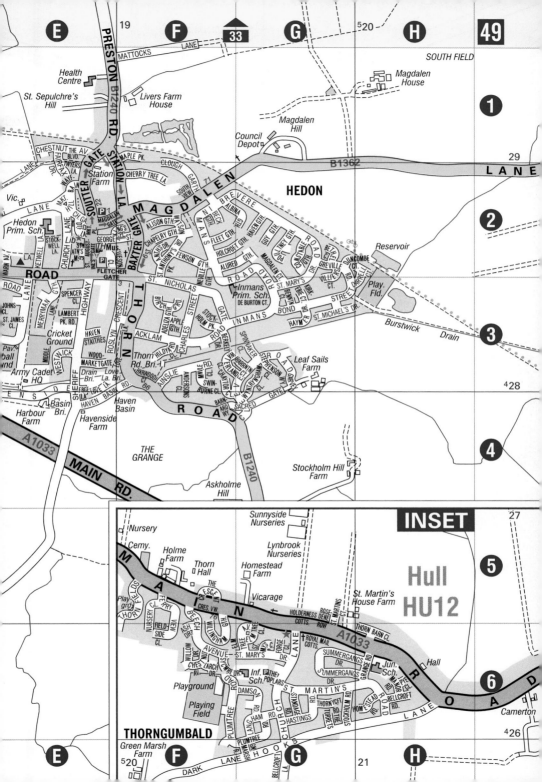

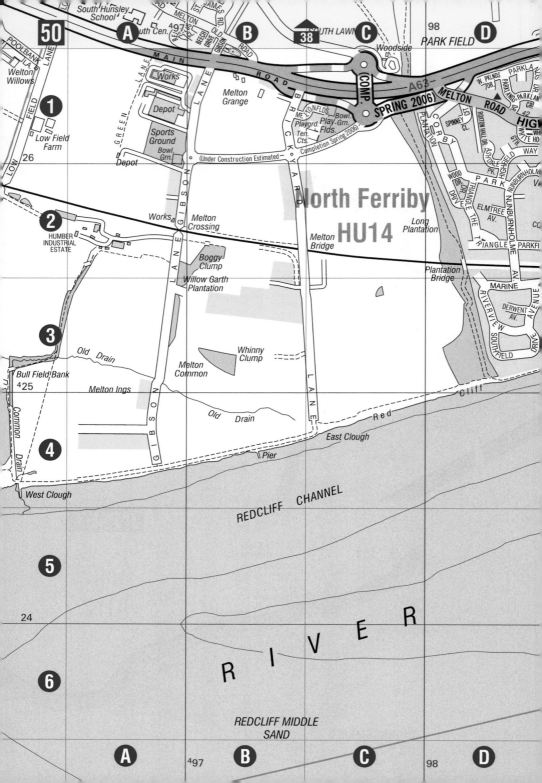

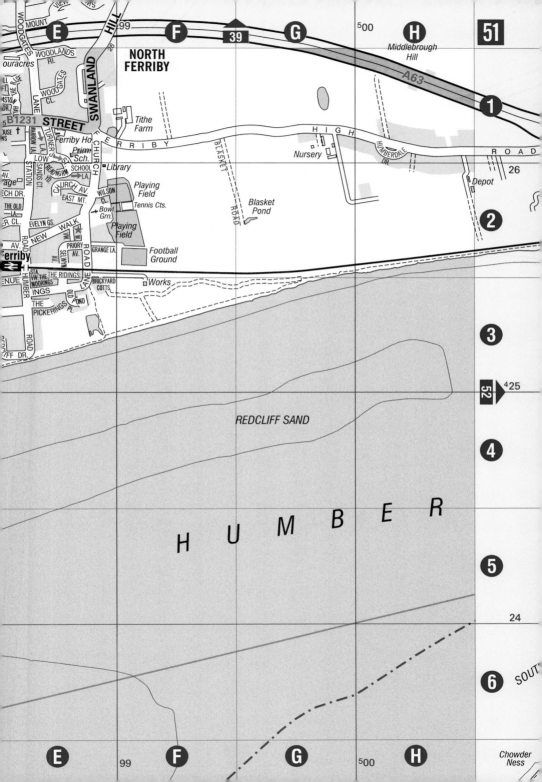

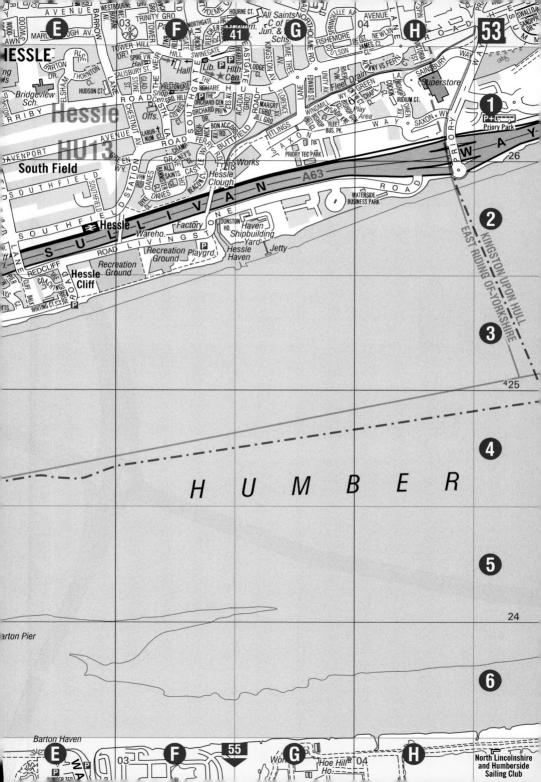

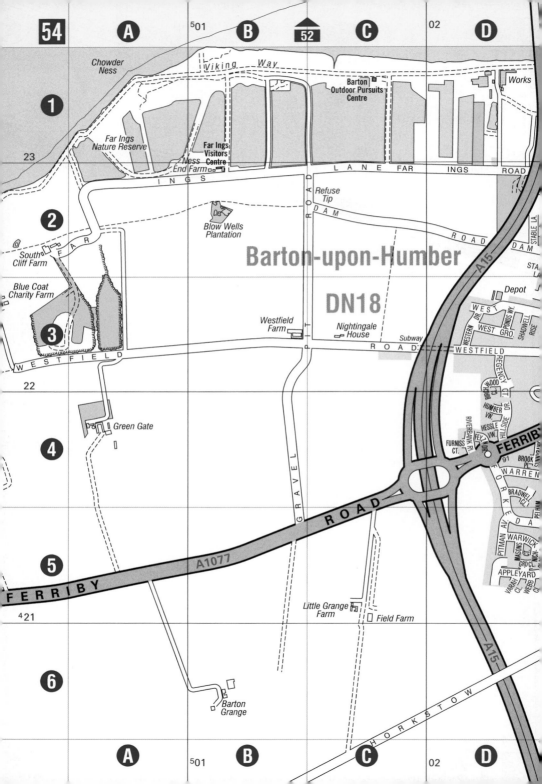

54

1

Chowder Ness

Viking Way

Barton Outdoor Pursuits Centre

Works

23

Far Ings Nature Reserve

Far Ings Visitors Centre

Ness End Farm

I N G S   L A N E   FAR   INGS   ROAD

R O A D   D A M

Refuse Tip

2

Blow Wells Plantation

D A M   R O A D

South Cliff Farm

STABLE LA.

Barton-upon-Humber

STA.
LA.

Blue Coat Charity Farm

DN18

Westfield Farm

Nightingale House

Depot

WEST

3

Subway

WEST   GRO.

SHADWELL

RISE

WESTERN DR.

ROAD   WESTFIELD

22

W E S T F I E L D

WESTFIELD

REGENCY

BIRCHWOOD CL.

HUMBER VW.

HESSLE VW.

RIVERBANK RD.

HILLSIDE DR.

4

Green Gate

FURNISS CT.

FERRIB

91   BROOK

WARREN

BRADWELL CL.

PELHAM

GRAVEL

R O A D

PITMAN AV.

WARWICK

MASONS CL.

GRD CL.

VARAH CL.

WEBB CL.

NICH-

A15

5

A1077

APPLEYARD

F E R R I B Y

⁴21

Little Grange Farm

Field Farm

6

Barton Grange

H O R K S T O W

A15

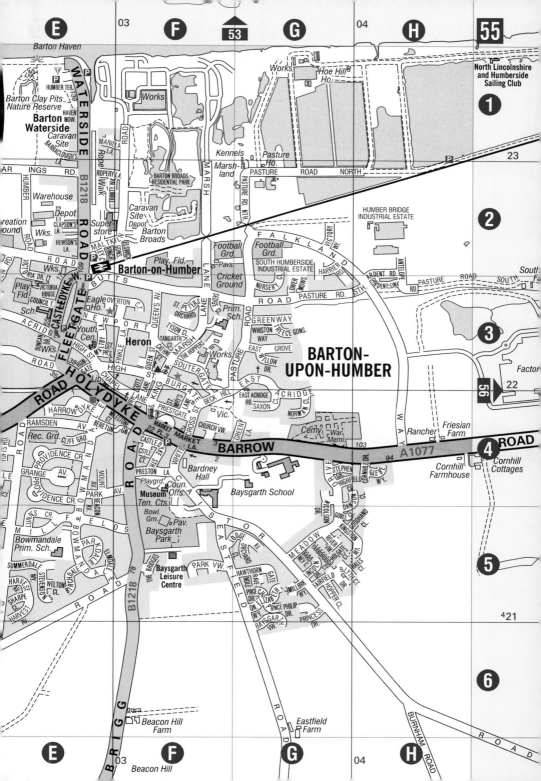

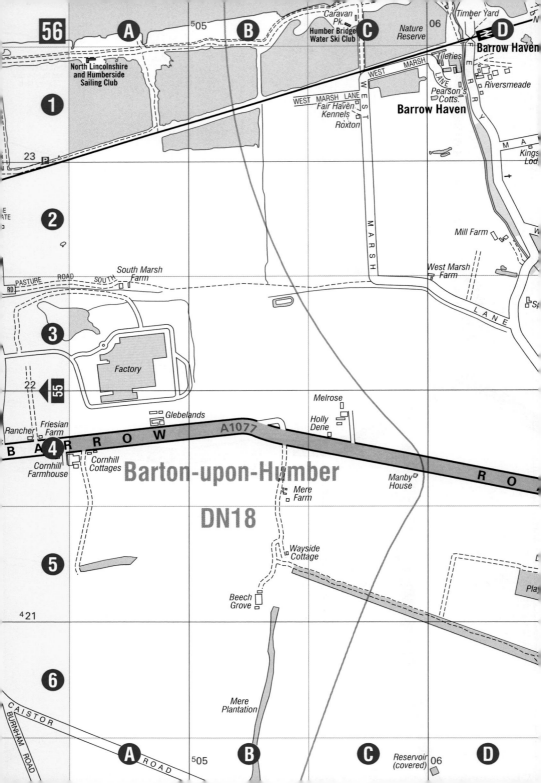

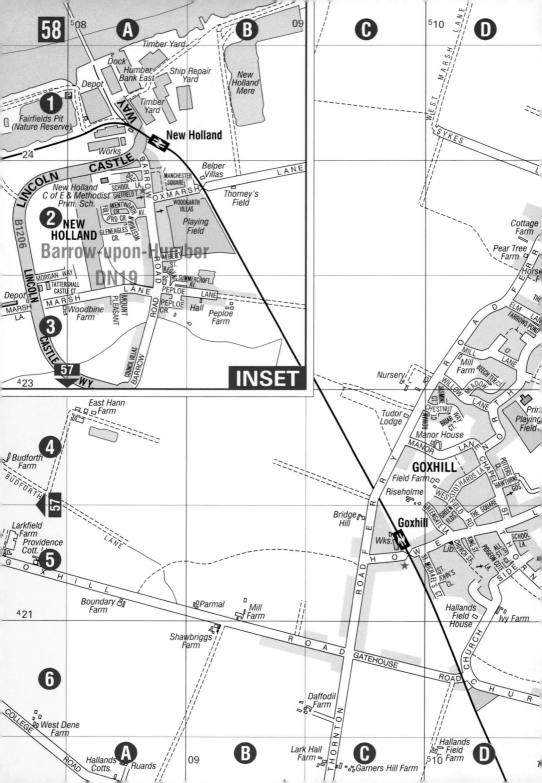

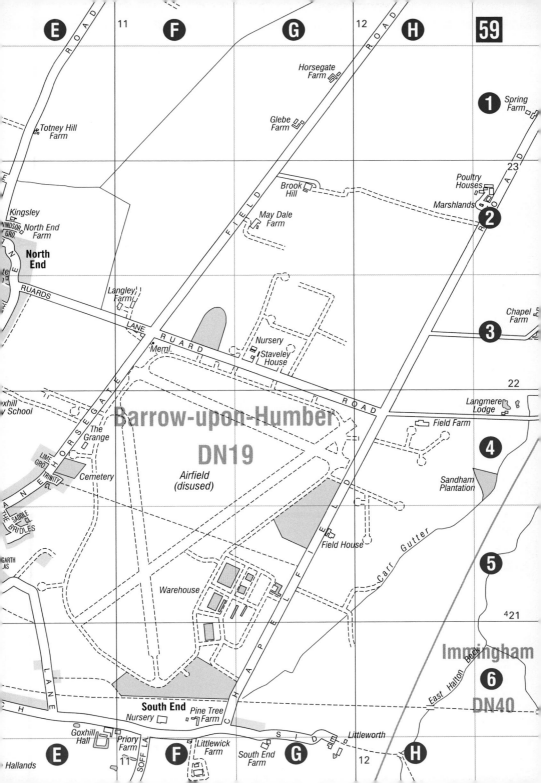

ROAD

Horsegate
Farm

1 Spring
Farm

Glebe
Farm

23

Totney Hill
Farm

Brook
Hill

Poultry
Houses
Marshlands

2

Kingsley

WINDSOR
GRO.

North End
Farm

May Dale
Farm

**North
End**

RUARDS

Langley
Farm

Chapel
Farm

3

LANE

RUARD

Nursery
Meml.
Staveley
House

22

oxhill
y School

ROAD

Langmere
Lodge

HORSEGATE

The
Grange

Barrow-upon-Humber

DN19

Field Farm

LIME
GRO.

TRINITY CL.

N E CL.

THE SADDLE CL.

BRIDLES

Cemetery

Airfield
(disused)

FIELD

Sandham
Plantation

4

Field House

Carr Gutter

5

Warehouse

CHAPEL FIELD

4 21

LANE

Immingham

South End
Nursery

Pine Tree
Farm

SIDE

East Halton Beeling

6

DN40

Goxhill
Hall

Priory
Farm

SOFF LA.

Littlewick
Farm

Littleworth

Hallands

INDEX

Including Streets, Places & Areas, Hospitals & Hospices, Industrial Estates,
Selected Flats & Walkways, Stations and Selected Places of Interest.

HOW TO USE THIS INDEX

1. Each street name is followed by its Postal District and then by its Locality abbreviation(s) and then by its map reference; e.g. **Abbey La.** HU10: Will . . . .4F **25** is in the Hull 10 Postal District and the Willerby Locality and is to be found in square 4F on page **25**. The page number is shown in bold type.

2. A strict alphabetical order is followed in which Av., Rd., St., etc. (though abbreviated) are read in full and as part of the street name; e.g. **Abbotsford Cl.** appears after **Abbots Cl.** but before **Abbots Wlk.**

3. Streets and a selection of flats and walkways too small to be shown on the maps, appear in the index with the thoroughfare to which it is connected shown in brackets; e.g. **Aigburth Av.** *HU3: Hull. . . .3F **43** (off St George's Rd.)*

4. Addresses that are in more than one part are referred to as not continuous.

5. Places and areas are shown in the index in BLUE TYPE and the map reference is to the actual map square in which the town centre or area is located and not to the place name shown on the map; e.g. **ANLABY. . . .2G 41**

6. An example of a selected place of interest is Barton Clay Pits Nature Reserve. . . . 1E 55

7. An example of a station is **Barrow Haven Station (Rail).** Included are Rail **(Rail)** and Park and Ride **(Park and Ride)**

8. An example of a hospital or hospice is CASTLE HILL HOSPITAL. . . .1E 25

9. Map references shown in brackets; e.g. **Adelaide St.** HU1: Hull . . . .3B **44** (5B **4**) refer to entries that also appear on the large scale pages **4 & 5.**

GENERAL ABBREVIATIONS

All. : Alley	**Flds.** : Fields	**Nth.** : North
Arc. : Arcade	**Gdn.** : Garden	**Pde.** : Parade
Av. : Avenue	**Gdns.** : Gardens	**Pk.** : Park
Blvd. : Boulevard	**Gth.** : Garth	**Pl.** : Place
Bri. : Bridge	**Ga.** : Gate	**Ri.** : Rise
Bldgs. : Buildings	**Gt.** : Great	**Rd.** : Road
Bungs. : Bungalows	**Grn.** : Green	**Shop.** : Shopping
Bus. : Business	**Gro.** : Grove	**Sth.** : South
Cvn. : Caravan	**Hgts.** : Heights	**Sq.** : Square
Cen. : Centre	**Ho.** : House	**Sta.** : Station
Chu. : Church	**Ind.** : Industrial	**St.** : Street
Circ. : Circle	**Info.** : Information	**Ter.** : Terrace
Cl. : Close	**La.** : Lane	**Trad.** : Trading
Cotts. : Cottages	**Lit.** : Little	**Up.** : Upper
Ct. : Court	**Mans.** : Mansions	**Va.** : Vale
Cres. : Crescent	**Mkt.** : Market	**Vw.** : View
Cft. : Croft	**Mdw.** : Meadow	**Vs.** : Villas
Dr. : Drive	**Mdws.** : Meadows	**Wlk.** : Walk
E. : East	**M.** : Mews	**W.** : West
Ent. : Enterprise	**Mt.** : Mount	**Yd.** : Yard
Est. : Estate	**Mus.** : Museum	

LOCALITY ABBREVIATIONS

Anla : **Anlaby**	Gox : **Goxhill**	Skid : **Skidby**
Bar H : **Barrow-upon-Humber**	Hed : **Hedon**	S'th C : **South Cave**
Bart H : **Barton-upon-Humber**	Hess : **Hessle**	Sproat : **Sproatley**
Bev : **Beverley**	Hull : **Hull**	Swan : **Swanland**
Bil : **Bilton**	King : **Kingswood**	Swin : **Swine**
Brans : **Bransholme**	Kir E : **Kirk Ella**	Thorn : **Thorngumbald**
Brant : **Brantinghamthorpe**	Mole : **Molescroft**	Tick : **Tickton**
Brou : **Brough**	New H : **New Holland**	Walk : **Walkington**
Burt C : **Burton Constable**	N'th C : **North Cave**	Waw : **Wawne**
Coni : **Coniston**	N'th F : **North Ferriby**	Welt : **Welton**
Cott : **Cottingham**	Paul : **Paull**	Will : **Willerby**
Elle : **Ellerker**	Prest : **Preston**	Wood : **Woodmansey**
Ello : **Elloughton**	Salt : **Saltend**	

1st Av. HU6: Hull 6G **17**	**32nd Av.** HU6: Hull. 5E **17**	**Acorn Way** HU13: Hess 5C **40**
2nd Av. HU6: Hull 5G **17**	**33rd Av.** HU6: Hull. 5E **17**	**Acton Cl.** HU8: Hull 1A **30**
4th Av. HU6: Hull 5G **17**	**34th Av.** HU6: Hull. 6E **17**	**Ada Holmes Circ.** HU6: Hull 5F **17**
5th Av. HU6: Hull 6E **17**	**36th Av.** HU6: Hull. 5E **17**	**Adas Av.** HU3: Hull 2G **43**
6th Av. HU6: Hull 5F **17**	**37th Av.** HU6: Hull. 6D **16**	**Adderbury Cres.** HU5: Hull 4A **28**
7th Av. HU6: Hull 6G **17**	**38th Av.** HU6: Hull. 5E **17**	**Adderbury Gro.** HU5: Hull 4A **28**
8th Av. HU6: Hull 4F **17**	**40th Av.** HU6: Hull. 5E **17**	**Addison Gdns.** HU8: Hull 3G **29**
9th Av. HU6: Hull 6G **17**		**Addison Rd.** HU12: Prest. 5F **33**
10th Av. HU6: Hull 5G **17**		**Adelaide St.** HU1: Hull 3B **44** (5B **4**)
11th Av. HU6: Hull 6G **17**		HU3: Hull 3A **44** (5A **4**)
12th Av. HU6: Hull 5F **17**	## A	**Adeliza Gth.** HU12: Hed 3F **49**
14th Av. HU6: Hull 5F **17**		**Adelphi Cl.** HU8: Hull 2A **30**
15th Av. HU6: Hull 5F **17**	**Abbeygarth Vs.** DN19: Gox 5E **59**	**Admirals Cft.** HU1: Hull 3B **44** (6C **4**)
16th Av. HU6: Hull 5F **17**	**Abbey La.** HU10: Will 4F **25**	**Admiral Walker Rd.**
17th Av. HU6: Hull 5F **17**	HU12: Prest. 4D **32**	HU17: Bev 5D **6**
18th Av. HU6: Hull 5F **17**	**Abbey Ri.** DN19: Bar H 5G **57**	**Aigburth Av.** *HU3: Hull. 3F **43***
19th Av. HU6: Hull 5F **17**	**Abbey Rd.** HU11: Bil 5G **21**	*(off St George's Rd.)*
20th Av. HU6: Hull 5F **17**	**Abbey St.** HU9: Hull 6F **29**	**Ainshaw** HU6: Hull 4D **16**
21st Av. HU6: Hull 6E **17**	**Abbots Cl.** HU8: Hull 1H **29**	**Ainslie Rd.** HU12: Hed 3F **49**
22nd Av. HU6: Hull 5F **17**	**Abbotsford Cl.** HU5: Hull 4E **27**	**Ainthorpe Gro.** HU5: Hull 1B **42**
23rd Av. HU6: Hull 6F **17**	**Abbots Wlk.** HU16: Cott 1H **25**	**Aintree Cl.** HU17: Bev 2D **6**
24th Av. HU6: Hull 5F **17**	**Aberdeen St.** HU9: Hull 3A **30**	**Aire Cl.** HU15: Brou 6F **37**
25th Av. HU6: Hull 5F **17**	**Aberdovey Cl.** HU7: Brans 5D **12**	**Airedale** HU7: Brans 6B **18**
26th Av. HU6: Hull 5E **17**	**Aberford Wlk.** HU9: Hull 5F **31**	**Airlie St.** HU3: Hull 3G **43**
27th Av. HU6: Hull 6F **17**	**Abingdon Gth.** HU7: Brans 2D **18**	**Airmyn Av.** HU3: Hull 2D **42**
28th Av. HU6: Hull 5E **17**	**Acacia Dr.** HU8: Hull 4G **29**	**Air St.** HU5: Hull 4C **28**
29th Av. HU6: Hull 6E **17**	**Acadia Gro.** HU13: Hess 1G **53**	**Aisne St.** HU5: Hull 6F **27**
30th Av. HU6: Hull (not continuous). 5E **17**	**Acey La.** HU12: Prest 5B **32**	**Ajax Cl.** HU9: Hull 1E **31**
31st Av. HU6: Hull 6E **17**	**Acklam Rd.** HU12: Hed 3F **49**	**Akester Cl.** HU17: Bev 5G **7**
	Ackworth St. HU8: Hull 5F **29**	**Alandale** HU5: Hull (off Goddard Av.) 4G **27**
	Acland St. HU3: Hull 2F **43**	**Alandale** HU3: Hull 2E **43**
	Acorn Gro. HU8: Hull. 4H **19**	**Alaska Ct.** HU8: Hull 5F **29**
	Acorn Ind. Est. HU17: Bev 4H **7**	**Alaska St.** HU8: Hull 5E **29**

Alaska Vs. *HU8: Hull (off Barnsley St.)* 5E **29**
Albany St. HU3: Hull 6H **27**
Albany Vs. HU13: Hess 1H **53**
Albemarle Cl. HU15: Brou 6C **36**
Albemarle Rd. HU11: Bil 6H **21**
Albemarle St. HU3: Hull 3G **43**
Albert Av. *HU3: Hull (off Mayfield St.)* *6H 27*
  HU3: Hull (Spring Bank W.) 1E **43**
  HU3: Hull (Wellsted St.) 3H **43**
  HU3: Hull (off Rhodes St.) *3F 43*
  HU3: Hull (Boulevard) 4G **43**
  HU9: Hull (off Middleburg St.) *6G 29*
Albert Gro. HU3: Hull 4F **43**
Albert Sq. *HU5: Hull (off Ella St.)* *4H 27*
Albert St. DN19: New H 2A **58**
Albert Ter. HU7: Hull 6G **19**
  HU17: Bev 5D **6**
Albina Gth. HU12: Hed 2F **49**
Albion Av. HU3: Hull 2E **43**
Albion Ct. HU4: Anla 2A **42**
  HU17: Bev 4G **7**
Albion Gro. HU3: Hull 3G **43**
Albion La. HU10: Will (not continuous) 3B **24**
Albion St. HU1: Hull 1B **44** (2C **4**)
Aldborough Gro. HU9: Hull 4B **30**
Aldbro' St. HU2: Hull 6C **28** (1E **5**)
Aldenham Pk. HU7: King 2A **18**
Alder Cl. HU3: Brou 6E **37**
Alder Hey Dr. HU8: Hull 1B **30**
Alderson M. HU9: Hull 1F **45**
Aldwych Ct. HU5: Hull 6D **26**
Alexandra Av. *HU3: Hull* *6H 27*
                                       (off Mayfield St.)
  HU5: Hull *3H 27*
                                      (off Alexandra Rd.)
Alexandra Ct. HU5: Hull 3A **28**
Alexandra Dr. HU17: Bev 2D **8**
Alexandra Rd. HU5: Hull 3H **27**
Alexandra St. HU3: Hull 1A **44**
Alfonso St. HU3: Hull 3G **43**
Alfred Av. HU3: Hull 4F **43**
Alfred Gelder St. HU1: Hull 2C **44** (3D **4**)
Alfred St. HU3: Hull 3A **44** (6A **4**)
Alfriston Cl. HU7: Brans 6E **19**
Alison Gth. HU12: Hed 2F **49**
Allanhall Way HU10: Kir E 1C **40**
Allanson Dr. HU16: Cott 1C **26**
Allan Vale *HU9: Hull* *6G 29*
                                      (off Estcourt La.)
Alldridge Av. HU5: Hull 3F **27**
Allendale *HU9: Hull* *6G 29*
                                 (off Middleburg St.)
Allerford Dr. HU7: Brans 3D **18**
Allerthorpe Cres. HU15: Brou 6G **37**
All Hallows Rd. HU17: Walk 5B **8**
Alliance Av. HU3: Hull 1E **43**
Alliance La. HU3: Hull 1E **43**
Alloa Cl. HU6: Hull 4G **17**
All Saint's Cl. DN19: Gox 5D **58**
All Saints Cl. HU13: Hess 2F **53**
All Saints St. HU3: Hull 6A **28**
Alma Av. *HU5: Hull* *4B 28*
                                      (off Folkstone St.)
Alma Cl. HU10: Kir E 1E **41**
Alma St. HU9: Hull 1E **45** (2H **5**)
Almond Gro. HU3: Hull 2A **44** (4A **4**)
Alpha Av. HU17: Bev 2C **6**
Alston Av. HU5: Hull 5E **29**
Althorp Rd. HU7: King 3A **18**
Alured Gth. HU12: Hed 2F **49**
Alwoodley Cl. HU8: Hull 1C **30**
Amanda Cl. HU6: Hull 6E **17**
Amberley Cl. HU7: Brans 6D **18**
Amethyst Rd. HU9: Hull 2D **30**
AMF Bowling Kingston Upon Hull 6D **18**
Ampleforth Gro. HU5: Hull 6B **26**
Amsterdam Rd. HU7: Hull 1D **28**
Amy Johnson Ct. HU1: Hull 4C **4**
Amy's Gro. *HU3: Hull* *3E 43*
                                        (off Pretoria St.)
Ancaster Av. HU5: Hull 3D **26**
Anchor Ct. HU2: Hull 1C **4**
Anchor Rd. HU6: Hull 4H **17**
Ancourt HU6: Hull 6D **16**
Andersons Cl. HU12: Hed 3F **49**
Andrew La. HU12: Hed 3D **48**
Andrew Marvell Ho. HU1: Hull 4E **5**
ANLABY 2G **41**
Anlaby Av. HU4: Hull 2A **42**
ANLABY COMMON 2H **41**
ANLABY PARK 2B **42**
Anlaby Pk. Rd. Nth. HU4: Hull 6C **42**
Anlaby Pk. Rd. Sth. HU4: Hull 6A **42**
Anlaby Rd. HU1: Hull 2A **44** (4A **4**)
  HU3: Hull 2B **42** (4A **4**)
  HU4: Hull 2B **42**
Anlafgate HU10: Anla 2G **41**
Annandale Rd. HU9: Hull 4F **31**
  HU10: Kir E 5C **24**
Anne St. HU1: Hull 2B **44** (4C **4**)
Annie Med La. HU15: S'th C 5B **34**
Annie Reed Ct. HU17: Bev 5H **7**
Annie Reed Rd. HU17: Bev 5H **7**
Ann Watson St. HU7: Hull 2D **28**

Anson Rd. HU9: Hull 3C **30**
Antelope Rd. DN18: Bart H 2H **55**
Antholme Cl. HU7: Hull 6F **19**
Antwerp Rd. HU7: Hull 1D **28**
Apollo Wlk. HU8: Hull 2A **30**
Appin Cl. HU7: Brans 6D **12**
Appledore Cl. HU9: Hull 2F **45**
Apple Gth. HU12: Hed 3F **49**
Applegarth M. HU16: Cott 5H **15**
Applegarth Rd. HU8: Hull 1D **44** (1G **5**)
Appleton Gdns. HU15: S'th C 4B **34**
Appleton La. HU15: N'th C 1A **34**
Apple Tree Cl. HU8: Hull 4D **26**
Apple Tree Wlk. HU16: Cott 6C **16**
Appleyard Dr. DN18: Bart H 5D **54**
Archbishop Cl. HU9: Hull 4E **31**
Arcon Dr. HU4: Hull 2C **42**
Arctic Corsair 2D **44** (3G **5**)
Arden Cl. HU5: Hull 4B **26**
Arden Rd. HU17: Bev 3F **7**
Ardent Link DN18: Bart H 3H **55**
Ardent Rd. DN18: Bart H 3H **55**
Ardmore Cl. HU8: Hull 2C **30**
Argent Cl. HU6: Hull 4G **17**
Argyle Av. *HU9: Hull* *6G 29*
                                      (off Middleburg St.)
Argyle St. HU3: Hull 1H **43**
Arkley Cl. HU15: Brou 6D **36**
Ark Royal HU11: Bil 6E **21**
Arlington Av. *HU5: Hull (off Perth St.)* *6F 27*
  HU16: Cott 6A **16**
Arlington St. HU3: Hull 2A **44**
Armstrong Cl. HU17: Bev 5F **7**
Arncliffe Dr. HU7: Brans 6C **12**
Arncliffe Way HU16: Cott 1H **25**
Arnold La. HU5: Hull 2G **43**
Arnold St. HU3: Hull 2H **43**
Arram Gro. HU6: Hull 1D **26**
Arran Cl. HU7: Hull 2B **30**
Arras Dr. HU16: Cott 1F **25**
Arreton Cl. HU8: Hull 6E **21**
Arthur Lucan Ct. HU9: Hull 5D **30**
Arthur St. HU3: Hull 3F **43**
Arundel Ct. HU9: Hull 6F **29**
Arundel St. HU9: Hull 6G **29**
Ascott Cl. HU4: Hull 3C **42**
  HU17: Bev 1D **6**
Asenby Wlk. *HU5: Hull (off Dent Rd.)* *3C 26*
Ash Av. HU15: Ello 5E **37**
Ashbourne Gro. *HU3: Hull (off Greek St.)* *3F 43*
Ashbrook *HU8: Hull* *5E 29*
                                    (off Buckingham St.)
Ashbury Ct. HU6: Hull 6F **17**
Ashby Cl. HU4: Hull 1A **42**
Ashby Rd. HU4: Hull 5H **41**
Ash Cl. HU11: Sproat 3F **23**
  HU13: Hess 5D **40**
  HU17: Bev 2E **7**
Ashcombe Rd. HU7: King 3A **18**
Ashdale Lodge HU3: Hull 2E **43**
Ashdale Pk. HU14: N'th F 1D **50**
Ashdene *HU5: Hull (off Goddard Av.)* *4H 27*
  HU17: Walk 2C **8**
Ash Dene Cl. HU10: Will 1F **41**
Ashdene Vs. *HU8: Hull (off Brecon St.)* *5E 29*
Ash Dr. HU10: Will. 6G **25**
  HU12: Thorn 6F **49**
Ashendon Dr. HU8: Hull 4D **28**
Ashford Wlk. HU9: Hull 5F **31**
Ashgate Rd. HU10: Will 4F **25**
Ash Gro. *HU3: Hull (off Perth St.)* *3E 43*
  HU3: Hull (off De La Pole Av.) *1E 43*
  HU5: Hull (Perth St.) 6G **27**
  HU5: Hull (Beverley Rd.) 3H **27**
  HU10: Will 5F **25**
Ashington Wlk. HU8: Hull 5D **20**
Ashmole Wlk. HU17: Bev 3F **7**
Ashthorpe HU6: Hull 4E **17**
Ashton Cl. HU6: Hull 4E **17**
Ashwell Av. HU9: Hull 5E **31**
Ashworth Dr. HU10: Kir E 5C **24**
Ashworthy Cl. HU7: Brans 3B **18**
Aske M. HU5: Hull 3C **26**
Askew Av. HU4: Hull 4C **42**
Askrigg Wlk. *HU5: Hull* *3C 26*
                                        (off Dent Rd.)
Aspall Wlk. HU8: Hull 5D **20**
Aspen Cl. HU4: Hull 5B **42**
Aspen Wlk. HU15: Brou 6F **37**
Assaby Cl. HU4: Hull 6C **42**
Astley St. HU3: Hull 1E **43**
Aston Hall Dr. HU14: N'th F 1E **51**
Aston Rd. HU10: Will 6G **25**
Astoria Cres. HU4: Hull 2A **30**
Astral Cl. HU7: Brans 5G **19**
  HU13: Hess 5G **41**
Astral Gdns. HU7: Brans 5F **19**
Astral Rd. HU13: Hess 5G **41**
Astral Way HU7: Brans 5G **19**
Astwood Av. HU9: Hull 5F **31**
Athelstan Rd. HU17: Bev 3E **7**
Athens Cl. HU3: Hull 3E **43**

Athletic Gro. HU3: Hull 3G **43**
Athlone Grn. HU8: Hull 1D **30**
Atholl Av. HU13: Hess 5F **41**
Athol St. HU3: Hull 3E **43**
Atkinson Dr. HU15: Brou 5D **36**
Atlanta Cl. HU8: Hull 1C **30**
Atwick Ct. HU9: Hull 5C **30**
Auburn Cl. HU9: Hull 5D **30**
Auckland Av. HU6: Hull 2H **27**
Auckland Ho. HU1: Hull 3B **44** (5B **4**)
Audley St. HU3: Hull 6B **28**
Augusta Cl. HU8: Hull 6C **20**
Augustine's Ct. HU5: Hull 3A **28**
Augustus Dr. HU15: Brou 6E **37**
Autherd Gth. HU17: Walk 6C **8**
Avenue Cres., The *HU3: Hull* *3G 43*
                                        (off Albermarle St.)
Avenue Halcyon HU13: Hess 6F **41**
Avenues Ct. HU5: Hull 5H **27**
Avenue, The HU3: Hull 3F **43**
  HU4: Hull *5D 42*
                                        (off Hampshire St.)
  HU7: Hull. 6H **19**
  HU10: Anla 1G **41**
  HU10: Kir E 1D **40**
  HU16: Cott 6H **15**
                                        (off Crescent St.)
Avondale HU4: Hull 6A **42**
  HU5: Hull. *4H 27*
                                        (off Goddard Av.)
  HU9: Hull. *6G 29*
                                      (off Rustenburg St.)
Avondale Cres. *HU5: Hull* *6F 27*
                                       (off Perth St. W.)
Avon St. HU5: Hull 5F **29**
Avon Vale *HU9: Hull* *6H 29*
                                      (off Estcourt St.)
Awmand Grn. HU16: Cott 2G **25**
Axdane HU6: Hull 5D **16**
Axholme Cl. HU9: Hull 3E **45**
Axminster Cl. HU7: Brans 4D **18**
Aylesbury Gro. HU16: Cott 6C **26**
Aylesford St. HU3: Hull 3G **43**
Aysgarth Av. HU6: Hull 2D **26**

B

Babington Row HU9: Hull 6F **29**
Bacchus La. HU15: S'th C 4D **34**
Bacheler St. HU3: Hull 3G **43**
Back La. HU12: Paul 6A **48**
Back Rd. HU11: Burt C 1F **23**
Bacon Gth. La. HU16: Cott 1H **25**
                                        (not continuous)
Baden Cl. HU4: Hull 4A **28**
Badgers Wood HU16: Cott 4G **15**
Bagby M. HU5: Hull. 3C **26**
Bailey La. HU16: Cott 4C **16**
Bainbridge Av. HU9: Hull 4E **31**
Bainton Cl. HU17: Bev 3C **6**
Bainton Gro. HU6: Hull 1D **26**
Baker St. HU2: Hull 1B **44** (2C **4**)
Bakewell Cl. HU9: Hull 5E **31**
Balfour Lodge HU9: Hull 6F **29**
Balfour St. HU9: Hull 6F **29**
Balham Av. HU8: Hull 6H **19**
Balk La. HU11: Sproat 3F **23**
Balk M. HU5: Hull 3C **26**
Ballantyne Cl. HU7: Hull 2F **29**
Ballathie Cl. HU6: Hull 3G **17**
Balmoral Av. HU6: Hull 6G **17**
Balmoral Dr. HU17: Bev 1F **9**
Bamford Av. HU9: Hull 5F **31**
Bankside HU5: Hull 4C **28**
Bankside Ind. Est. HU5: Hull 3C **28**
Bannister St. HU13: Hess 2F **53**
Bannister Cl. HU9: Hull 1F **45**
Bantock Gth. HU4: Anla 4A **42**
Barbarry Rd. HU12: Hed 2D **48**
Barberry Cl. HU3: Hull 3H **43**
  HU15: Brou 6E **37**
Bardney Cl. DN18: Bart H 5G **55**
Bardshaw HU6: Hull 4E **17**
Bargate Gro. HU5: Hull 6C **26**
Barham Rd. HU9: Hull 3D **30**
Barkers Mill HU17: Bev 5G **7**
Barking Cl. HU8: Hull 1B **30**
Barkworth Cl. HU10: Anla 2E **41**
Barleigh Cl. HU9: Hull 3D **30**
Barleigh Rd. HU9: Hull 3B **30**
Barmouth Cl. HU7: Brans 5G **7**
Barmston Cl. HU17: Bev 3G **7**
Barmston La. HU17: Wood 3D **10**
Barmston Rd. HU17: Bev 3G **7**
Barmston Gro. HU6: Hull 6C **28**
Barnards Dr. HU15: S'th C 4B **34**
Barnard Way HU12: Hed 4F **49**
Barnes Cl. HU17: Bev 4G **7**
Barnetby Rd. HU13: Hess 5G **41**
Barnet Cl. HU8: Hull 1B **30**
Barnsley Bldgs. HU8: Hull 5F **29**
Barnsley St. HU8: Hull. 5E **29**

Barnstaple Rd. HU7: Brans 5E 19
Baroness Cl. HU6: Hull 4G 17
Barra Cl. HU8: Hull 6A 20
Barraclough's La. DN18: Bart H . . 1E 55
Barrick Cl. DN19: Bar H. 5F 57
Barrington Av. HU5: Hull 3E 27
Barrow Ct. HU3: Hull 5A 28
BARROW HANN 3G 57
BARROW HAVEN 1D 56
Barrow Haven Station (Rail) . . . 1D 56
Barrow Lane HU13: Hess 6E 41
Barrow Rd. DN18: Bar H, Bart H . . 4G 55
    DN19: Bar H 4G 55
    DN19: New H. 2A 58
BARROW-UPON-HUMBER 5F 57
Bartlett Av. HU17: Bev. 5D 6
Bartlett Cl. HU12: Prest 5F 33
Barton Broads Residential Pk. DN18: Bart H . . 2F 57
Barton Clay Pits Nature Reserve . . 1E 55
Barton Dr. HU13: Hess 1E 53
Barton La. DN19: Bar H 5E 57
Barton-on-Humber Station (Rail) . . 2E 55
Barton Outdoor Pursuits Cen. . . 1C 54
Barton St. DN19: Bar H 4F 57
BARTON-UPON-HUMBER 3F 55
BARTON WATERSIDE 1E 55
Bartrams HU15: Welt. 5G 37
Basil Dr. HU17: Bev. 6D 6
Bathurst St. HU3: Hull . . . 3A 44 (6A 4)
Batley Cl. HU9: Hull 4D 30
Battersea Cl. HU8: Hull 1A 30
Baxter Ga. HU12: Hed 2F 49
Bay Ct. HU17: Bev 2E 9
Baynard Av. HU16: Cott. 6H 15
Baysdale HU7: Brans. 6C 18
Baysgarth House Mus. 4F 55
Baysgarth Leisure Cen. 5F 55
Baysgarth Vw. DN18: Bart H . . . 5G 55
Bayswater Ct. HU8: Hull 1A 30
Beacon Av. DN18: Bart H 4E 55
Beacon Cl. HU13: Hess 2F 53
Beaconsfield Gdns. HU5: Hull . . . 3H 27
    (off Raglan St.)
Beaconsfield St. HU5: Hull . . . 4A 28
Beaconsfield Vs. HU9: Hull . . . 6F 29
    (off Holland St.)
Beadlam M. HU5: Hull 2D 26
Beamsley Way HU7: King 1B 18
Bearwood Cl. HU8: Hull 6C 20
Beaufort Cl. HU3: Hull 3A 44
Beaulieu Cl. HU9: Hull 3B 30
Beaumont Ct. HU9: Hull 1G 45
Beautiman Ct. HU6: Hull 6F 17
Beaver Rd. HU17: Bev 4G 7
Beccles Cl. HU8: Hull 6C 20
Beck Bank HU16: Cott 6A 16
Beckdale HU7: Brans 6D 18
Beck Gth. HU12: Hed 2F 49
Beck Hill HU12: Bart H 4F 55
Beckhole Cl. HU3: Hull 2F 43
Beckington Cl. HU8: Hull 5D 20
Beck La. DN19: Bar H 4F 57
    HU15: S'th C 4B 34
    HU15: Welt 5G 37
Beckside HU15: Welt. 5G 37
    HU17: Bev 5F 7
Beckside Cl. HU4: Hull 5G 17
Beckside Nth. HU17: Bev 5G 7
Beck Vw. Rd. HU17: Bev. 5H 7
Bedale Av. HU9: Hull 5H 29
Bedford Rd. HU13: Hess 5F 41
Bedford St. HU8: Hull 5D 28
Bedford St. Cvn. Site HU8: Hull . . 5D 28
Beech Av. HU8: Hull 4F 29
    HU10: Will 6E 25
    HU11: Bil. 6G 21
    HU12: Hed. 2D 48
    HU12: Thorn 5F 49
    HU17: Bev 2E 7
Beechcliffe Av. HU6: Hull 5H 17
Beech Cl. HU3: Hull 3H 43
    HU11: Sproat. 2E 23
Beechdale HU16: Cott 6B 16
Beech Dr. HU14: N'th F 2E 51
    HU14: Welt 6B 38
Beeches, The HU5: Hull 3H 27
    (off Sidmouth St.)
    HU5: Hull. 4H 27
    (off Goddard Av.)
Beechfield HU6: Hull 6G 17
Beechfield Dr. HU10: Will 4D 24
Beech Gth. DN19: Bar H 6E 57
Beech Gro. HU3: Hull 3E 43
    (Ringrose St.)
    HU3: Hull. 3H 43
    (Wellsted St.)
    HU5: Hull. 6G 27
    (off Perth St.)
Beech Gro. HU5: Hull (Strath St.) . . 3H 27
    HU5: Hull (off Reynoldson St.) . . 4H 27
    HU5: Hull (Prince's Rd.) . . 4H 27
    HU8: Hull (off Lorraine St.) . . 3D 28
    HU13: Hess 5D 40
    HU14: Swan 3H 39

Beech Hill Rd. HU14: Swan 2H 39
Beech Holme Cl. HU5: Hull 3A 28
Beech Lawn HU10: Anla 2F 41
Beech Rd. HU15: Ello 4D 36
Beech Tree Cl. HU17: Bev 1E 7
Beech Vw. HU17: Walk 5C 8
Beechwood Cl. HU9: Hull 5G 29
Beeford Gro. HU6: Hull 1E 27
Beilby St. HU3: Hull. 3E 43
Belfry Ct. HU8: Hull 6C 20
Belgrave Dr. HU4: Hull 2C 42
    HU15: N'th C 1A 34
Bellamy Ct. HU9: Hull 1F 45
Bell Cl. HU7: Hull 6G 19
Bellcroft La. HU12: Thorn 6G 49
Bellcroft Rd. HU12: Thorn 6G 49
Belle-Vue HU9: Hull 6G 29
    (off Middleburg St.)
Bellfield Av. HU8: Hull 6H 19
Bellfield Dr. HU10: Will 4E 25
Bells Rd. HU12: Hed 3D 48
Belmont Farm HU13: Hess (off Cliff Rd.) . . 3E 53
Belmont St. HU9: Hull 6G 29
Belphrin Rd. HU17: Bev 3G 7
Beltham Grn. HU16: Cott 2G 25
Belton Cl. HU8: Hull 1C 30
Belvedere Dr. HU11: Bil. 6E 21
Belvedere Rd. HU5: Hull 6G 41
Belvoir St. HU5: Hull 6G 27
Bempton Gro. HU5: Hull 6C 26
Benedict Rd. HU4: Hull 6H 41
Bennington Cl. HU12: Hed 3G 49
BENTLEY 6D 8
Bentley Ct. HU3: Hull 3F 43
Bentley Gro. HU6: Hull 2E 27
Berberis Cl. HU3: Hull 3H 43
Beresford Av. HU6: Hull 2A 28
    HU9: Hull (off Middleburg St.) . . 6G 29
Beretun Grn. DN18: Bart H 4E 55
Bergen Way HU7: Hull. 6A 18
Berkeley Dr. HU17: Bev 1F 9
Berkeley St. HU3: Hull 5A 28
Berkely Dr. HU12: Hed. 3F 49
Berkshire Cl. HU17: Bev 2F 9
Berkshire St. HU8: Hull 5F 29
Bermondsey Dr. HU5: Hull 6D 26
Bernadette Av. HU4: Anla 3A 42
Berryman Way HU13: Hess. . . . 5H 41
Bessacarr Av. HU10: Will 5G 25
Bessingby Gro. HU9: Hull 4C 30
Beta Vs. HU3: Hull (off Mayfield St.) . . 6H 27
Bethel Cl. HU12: Hed 2G 49
Bethune Av. HU4: Hull 5H 41
Bethune Av. W. HU4: Hull 5H 41
Betula Ct. HU8: Hull 5H 19
BEVERLEY 4F 7
Beverley Dr. HU17: Bev. 1C 6
Beverley Leisure Cen. 5F 7
Beverley Minster 5E 7
Beverley Parklands HU17: Bev . . 6F 7
Beverley Race Course 4A 6
Beverley Rd. HU3: Hull . . . 3A 28 (1B 4)
    HU5: Hull. 3A 28
    HU6: Hull, Wood (not continuous) . . 6F 11
    HU10: Anla, Hess, Kir E, Will. . . 4C 24
    HU13: Hess 1F 41
    HU15: S'th C 3D 34
    HU16: Skid 3D 14
Beverley Road Baths 5A 28
Beverley Station (Rail) 4E 7
Beverley Swimming Pool 4E 7
Bewick Gro. HU9: Hull 4A 30
Bibury Cl. HU8: Hull 4E 29
Bickerton Cl. HU8: Hull 5E 17
Bickleigh Gro. HU8: Hull 6D 20
Bideford Gro. HU9: Hull 5F 31
Bielby Dr. HU17: Bev. 5G 7
Biggin Av. HU7: Brans 4E 19
Bilsdale Gro. HU9: Hull 6A 30
BILTON. 5H 21
Bilton Gro. HU9: Hull. 5C 30
Binbrook Gth. HU7: Brans 2E 19
Binfield Sq. HU5: Hull (off Ella St.) . . 4H 27
Birch Cl. HU15: Ello 1A 42
    HU13: Hess 5C 40
    HU15: Brou 6E 37
    HU17: Bev 2E 7
Birch Cft. HU15: Ello 5D 36
Birchdale DN18: Bart H 5E 55
Birch Dr. HU10: Will. 5F 25
Birch Lea HU17: Walk 5A 8
Birch Leigh HU3: Hull 2H 43
Birchwood Av. HU5: Hull 1A 42
Birchwood Cl. DN18: Bart H . . . 3D 54
Birdforth M. HU5: Hull 3C 26
Birdsall Av. HU5: Hull 4B 26
Birdsall Av. HU16: Cott 1F 25
Birkby Gro. HU9: Hull 4D 30
Birkdale Cl. HU10: Kir E 6C 24
Birkdale Way HU9: Hull 6G 29
Birklands Dr. HU8: Hull 2H 29
Bishop Alcock Rd. HU5: Hull . . . 3C 26
Bishop Blunt Cl. HU13: Hess . . . 1G 53

Bishop Cockin Cl. HU13: Hess . . . 1H 53
Bishop Gurdon Cl. HU13: Hess . . 1G 53
Bishop Kempthorne Cl. HU13: Hess. . 1G 53
Bishop La. HU1: Hull . . . 2D 44 (4F 5)
Bishop La. Staith HU1: Hull . . 2D 44 (4F 5)
Bishops Cft. HU17: Bev. 5D 6
Bishop Temple Cl. HU13: Hess. . . 5G 41
Bisley Gro. HU7: Brans 5D 18
Bittern Cl. HU4: Hull 6C 42
Blackburn Av. HU15: Brou. . . . 6D 36
Blackfriargate HU1: Hull . . . 3D 44 (5F 5)
Blackhall Cl. HU7: King. 1B 18
Blackhope Cl. HU7: Brans 1D 18
Blackthorn La. HU10: Will. . . . 1G 41
Blackthorn Ct. HU3: Hull . . . 2A 44 (4A 4)
Blackwater Way HU7: King 1B 18
Bladons Wlk. HU10: Kir E. . . . 6E 25
Blaides Staithe HU1: Hull . . . 1D 44 (3G 5)
Blake Cl. HU2: Hull. . . . 6B 28 (1C 4)
Blandford Cl. HU7: Brans 6E 19
Blanket Row HU1: Hull. . . 3C 44 (5E 5)
Blanshards La. HU15: N'th C . . . 2A 34
Blasket Rd. HU14: N'th F. 1F 51
Blaycourt HU6: Hull. 6D 18
Blaydes St. HU6: Hull 2H 27
Bleach Yard La. HU17: Bev 3C 6
Blenheim Rd. HU17: Bev. 1F 9
Blenheim St. HU5: Hull 6G 27
Blenkin St. HU9: Hull . . . 1E 45 (1H 5)
Blisland Cl. HU7: Brans 3C 18
Bloomfield Av. HU5: Hull. . . . 6B 26
Bloomsbury Ct. HU3: Hull . . . 2A 44 (3A 4)
Blossom Gro. HU8: Hull 4G 19
Blossom's La. HU15: N'th C . . . 1A 34
Blucher La. HU7: Brans 5F 7
Blue Ball Entry HU12: Hed 2E 49
    (off George St.)
Blueberry Ct. HU4: Hull 4B 42
Blundell Cl. HU2: Hull 6B 28
Blyth Ct. DN18: Bart H 5G 55
Blythorpe HU6: Hull 4E 17
Blyth St. HU9: Hull . . . 1E 45 (1H 5)
Boatswain Cft. HU9: Hull . . 3C 44 (6D 4)
Bobbers Staith HU3: Hull 4A 44
Bodmin Rd. HU7: Brans 2C 18
Boggle La. HU11: Sproat. . . . 3F 23
Boltby M. HU3: Hull 3D 26
Bon Accord Rd. HU13: Hess . . . 1F 53
Bondane HU6: Hull. 5D 16
Bond St. HU1: Hull . . . 1C 44 (2D 4)
    HU12: Hed. 3G 49
Bondyke Cl. HU16: Cott 6F 15
Bontoft Av. HU5: Hull 5D 26
Boothferry Rd. HU3: Hull. 3C 42
    HU4: Hull. 6D 40
    HU13: Hess, Hull 1C 52
Borella Gro. HU3: Hull 4F 43
Borodales Rd. HU12: Hed 3D 48
Borrowdale HU7: Brans. 6C 18
Borthwick Cl. HU7: Brans 6D 12
Borwick Dr. HU17: Bev 4H 7
Bossington Cl. HU7: Brans 3D 18
Boston Ct. HU7: King. 2B 18
Bothwell Gro. HU9: Hull 6E 31
Boulevard HU3: Hull 2G 43
Boulevard, The HU12: Hed 1E 49
Boulevard Unit Factory Est.
    HU3: Hull. 4H 43
Boulsworth Av. HU6: Hull 5H 17
Boulton Gro. HU9: Hull 4H 29
Bournemouth St. HU5: Hull 4B 28
Bourne St. HU2: Hull . . . 1C 44 (1E 5)
Bowes Wlk. HU5: Hull. 3D 26
    (off Bishop Alcock Rd.)
    HU5: Hull. 3D 26
    (off Dent Rd.)
Bowlalley La. HU1: Hull . . . 2C 44 (4E 5)
Bowl Circ. HU9: Hull 3A 30
Bowmandale DN18: Bart H 4E 55
Bowmont Way HU7: King 1B 18
Bow Rd. HU14: Welt 4A 38
    HU15: Welt 4A 38
Boxtree Wlk. HU5: Hull 3H 43
BP Av. HU3: Hull (off Clyde St.) . . 3E 43
Brackendale Cl. HU7: Hull 2E 29
Brackley Cl. HU8: Hull 4E 29
Bradford Av. HU3: Hull 4F 31
Bradgate Pk. HU7: King 2B 18
Bradwell Cl. DN18: Bart H 4D 54
Braemar Av. HU6: Hull 6G 17
Braid Hill Way HU7: Brans 3G 19
Braids Wlk. HU10: Kir E 6C 24
Bramble Gth. HU17: Bev 1E 7
    HU17: Bev. 6A 8
Bramble Hill HU17: Bev. 1F 9
Brambles, The HU9: Hull 5E 57
Brandesburton St. HU3: Hull . . . 6G 27
Brandon Ct. HU4: Hull 5F 29
Brandon Way HU7: King 1C 18
Brandsby Gro. HU9: Hull 3F 31
Bransdale Gro. HU9: Hull 6A 30
BRANSHOLME (Bransholme Rd.) . . 1G 19
    (Goodhart Rd.) 4E 19

Bransholme Rd. HU7: Brans 2E 19
BRANTINGHAM 6G 35
Brantingham Cl. HU16: Cott 6F 15
Brantingham Rd. HU15: Ello 1C 36
BRANTINGHAM THORPE 1D 36
Brantingham Wlk. HU5: Hull 4B 26
Brazil St. HU9: Hull .6F 29
Brecon Av. HU8: Hull 5F 29
Brecon Dr. HU7: King 1C 18
Brecon St. HU8: Hull 3E 29
Brendon Av. HU8: Hull 6C 20
Brent Av. HU8: Hull .6C 20
Brentwood Av. *HU5: Hull* 6G 27
  (off Hardwick Av.)
  HU9: Hull 6F 29
  (off Brazil St.)
Brentwood Cl. HU15: Brou 6C 36
Brentwood Vs. *HU3: Hull* 2G 43
  (off Perry St.)
  HU5: Hull 4H 27
  (off Reynoldson St.)
Brereton Cl. HU17: Bev 2D 6
Bretherdale HU7: Brans 6C 18
Brevere Rd. HU12: Hed 2F 49
Brewery Ho. M. *HU17: Bev* 4D 6
  (off Walkergate)
Briar Ct. DN19: Gox 4D 58
Briarfield Rd. HU5: Hull 4E 27
Briars, The HU13: Hess 5F 41
Bricknell Av. HU5: Hull 2C 26
Brickyard Cotts. HU14: N'th F 3E 51
Brickyard La. HU14: N'th F 1B 50
Bridgegate Dr. HU9: Hull 2F 45
Bridgeman Ho. HU6: Hull 4F 17
Bridge Rd. HU15: S'th C 4B 34
Bridges, The DN18: Bart H 5F 55
Bridles, The DN19: Gox 5E 59
Bridlington Av. HU2: Hull 5B 28 (1D 4)
Bridport Cl. HU7: Brans 5F 19
Brigg Dr. HU13: Hess 5G 41
Brigg Rd. DN18: Bart H 6F 55
Brigham Ct. *HU17: Bev* 3E 7
  (off Cooper St.)
Brigham Gro. HU9: Hull 5C 30
Brighton Rd. Ind. Est. HU3: Hull 5E 43
Brighton St. HU3: Hull 5E 43
  HU4: Hull 5E 43
Bright St. HU8: Hull .6E 29
Brimington Rd. HU10: Will 4G 25
Brimley HU5: Mole 3B 6
Brindley St. HU9: Hull 4H 29
Brisbane St. HU3: Hull 3A 44 (5A 4)
Bristol Rd. HU5: Hull 5B 26
Britannia Gdns. HU5: Hull 4B 28
Brixham Ct. HU3: Hull 3F 43
Brixton Cl. HU8: Hull 1H 29
Broadacre Pk. HU15: Ello 6F 37
Broadgate HU17: Walk 2B 8
Broadland Dr. HU9: Hull 2B 30
Broad La. HU16: Cott 5A 16
Broadley Av. HU10: Anla 2E 41
Broadley Cl. HU9: Hull 1F 45
Broadley Cft. HU15: Brou 6F 37
Broadley Way HU5: Brou 6F 37
Broad Oak HU11: Bil 6E 21
Broadstairs Cl. HU8: Hull 5H 19
Broadstone Cl. HU7: Brans 6F 19
Broadwaters HU7: King 2A 18
Broadway Dr. HU9: Hull 3B 30
Broadway, The HU9: Hull 3A 30
Brockenhurst Av. HU16: Cott 1C 26
Brocklebank Ct. HU12: Prest 5E 33
Brocklesby Cl. HU13: Hess 5H 41
Brockley Cl. HU8: Hull 6H 19
Brockton Cl. HU8: Hull 3D 42
Brodsworth St. HU8: Hull 6F 29
Bromley St. HU2: Hull 6C 28
Brompton Cl. HU5: Hull 4D 26
  HU10: Anla 2H 41
Brompton Ct. HU3: Hull 5A 28
Bromwich Rd. HU10: Will 6G 25
Bronte Ct. HU6: Hull 5H 17
Brookfield Cl. HU7: King 2B 18
Brooklands HU7: Hull 1F 29
Brooklands Cl. HU17: Bev 2F 7
Brooklands Pk. HU16: Cott 6H 15
Brooklands Rd. HU5: Hull 6D 26
Brooklyn Av. *HU5: Hull* 3A 28
  (off Brooklyn St.)
  HU5: Hull 6G 27
  (off Perth St.)
Brooklyn St. HU5: Hull 3A 28
Brooklyn Ter. HU5: Hull 3A 28
Brooklyn Vs. HU5: Hull 1D 46
Brookside HU15: Welt 5G 37
Brook St. HU2: Hull 1B 44 (3B 4)
Brook Ter. HU15: N'th C 2A 34
Broomhead Cl. HU8: Hull 5H 19
BROUGH 6D 36
Brough Cl. HU9: Hull 1E 43
Brough Rd. HU15: S'th C 4D 34
Brough Station (Rail) 6C 36
Broughton Cl. HU9: Hull 3B 30

Browning Cl. HU3: Hull 6A 28
Browns Yd. Ind. Est. HU17: Bev 2E 9
Brucella Gro. HU3: Hull 4F 43
Brudenell Way HU6: Hull 3D 16
Brumby's Ter. HU9: Hull 1G 45
Brumfield Ct. HU17: Bev 3F 7
Brunslow Cl. HU3: Hull 3D 42
Brunswick Av. HU2: Hull 6B 28
  HU9: Hull 1F 45
  (off Franklin St.)
Brunswick Gro. HU13: Hess 6F 41
Brunswick Ter. *HU13: Hess* 5F 29
  (off Durham St.)
Buccaneer Way HU15: Brou 6D 36
Buckingham St. HU8: Hull 5E 29
  (not continuous)
Buckland Cl. HU8: Hull 5D 20
Bude Rd. HU7: Brans 3B 18
Budforth La. DN19: Bar H 4H 57
Budworth Pk. HU7: King 2A 18
Bull Pasture HU15: S'th C 4C 34
Burbage Av. HU8: Hull 2F 29
Burcott Gth. HU4: Hull 5A 42
Burdale Cl. HU9: Hull 3C 30
Burdale Wlk. HU16: Cott 2H 25
Burden Cl. HU17: Bev 3F 7
Burden Rd. HU17: Bev 3E 7
Burden St. HU1: Hull 2B 44 (3C 4)
  HU2: Hull 2B 44 (3C 4)
Burdon Cl. HU10: Will 1G 41
Burgate DN18: Bart H 3F 55
Burgess Ct. *HU17: Bev* 3E 7
  (off Goths La.)
Burleigh St. HU8: Hull 6F 29
Burlington Rd. HU8: Hull 1G 29
Burma Dr. HU9: Hull .6C 30
Burnaby Cl. HU17: Bev 2D 6
Burnby Cl. HU5: Hull .4B 26
Burney Cl. HU17: Bev 3D 6
Burnham Rd. DN18: Bart H 6H 55
Burnsalls Rd. HU5: Hull 5A 42
Burniston Rd. HU5: Hull 4D 26
Burnsalls Rd. HU12: Hed 2D 48
Burrill La. HU15: Brant 6G 35
Burrill M. HU5: Hull .3D 26
Burrs, The HU15: Brou 6C 36
Burslem St. HU2: Hull 6B 28
Burton Constable Cvn. Pk. HU11: Burt C 1E 23
Burton Constable Rd. HU11: Sproat 1F 23
Burton Rd. HU16: Cott 1G 25
  HU17: Mole 2B 6
Bush Cl. HU4: Hull 5C 42
Bushey Pk. HU7: King 2A 18
Butcher Row HU17: Bev 4E 7
Buttercup Cl. HU9: Hull 6G 29
Butterfly Mdws. HU17: Bev 2D 6
Butt Field Rd. HU13: Hess 1F 53
Butt La. HU17: Bev (not continuous) 6D 6
Butts Rd. DN18: Bart H 3E 55
Buxton Vs. *HU9: Hull* 6G 29
  (off Rosmead St.)
Bylands Ct. HU9: Hull 6H 29
Byron St. HU8: Hull .4G 29
Bywell Wlk. HU9: Hull 6E 31

C

Cadeleigh Cl. HU7: Brans 4D 18
Cadogan Av. *HU3: Hull (off Cadogan St.)* 3G 43
Cadogan Gro. HU3: Hull 3G 43
Cadogan St. HU3: Hull 3G 43
Caistor Rd. DN18: Bart H 4F 55
Caldane HU6: Hull 4D 16
Caldberg M. HU5: Hull 3D 26
Calderdale HU7: Brans 5C 18
Calder Gro. HU8: Hull 6D 20
Calder Sq. HU15: Brou 6F 37
Caledon Cl. HU9: Hull 1E 31
Caledonia Pk. HU9: Hull 3E 45 (5H 5)
Carlow Hill Dr. HU7: Brans 3G 19
Calthorpe Gdns. *HU3: Hull* 3E 43
  (off Newington St.)
Calthorpe St. HU3: Hull 3G 43
Calvert La. HU4: Hull 1C 42
Calvert Rd. HU5: Hull 6C 26
Cambeak Cl. HU7: Brans 2C 18
Camberwell Way HU8: Hull 1B 30
Camborne Gro. HU8: Hull 3E 29
Cambrian Av. *HU9: Hull* 6G 29
  (off Holland St.)
Cambridge Ct. HU13: Hess 5F 41
Cambridge Gro. HU9: Hull 5A 30
Cambridge Rd. HU13: Hess 5A 30
Cambridge St. HU3: Hull 2A 44 (4A 4)
Camden St. HU3: Hull 3G 43
Camelford Cl. HU7: Brans 3C 18
Cameron Gro. HU8: Hull 4A 30
Cam Gro. HU8: Hull .6D 20
Camilla Cl. HU9: Hull 3D 44 (5G 5)
Campbell Ct. HU3: Hull 4B 30
  HU13: Hess 6F 41
  (off Hourne, The)

Campbell St. HU3: Hull 3A 44
Camperdown HU11: Bil 6E 21
Campion Av. HU4: Hull 6A 42
Canada Dr. HU16: Cott 1F 25
Canberra St. HU3: Hull 3A 44 (5A 4)
Canning St. HU2: Hull 2B 44 (3B 4)
Cannon St. HU2: Hull 6C 28
Canongate HU16: Cott 5A 16
Canons Health Club 4B 44 (6B 4)
Canon Tardrew Ct. HU13: Hess 1G 53
Canopias Cl. HU3: Hull 4F 43
Canterbury Cl. HU17: Bev 1E 9
Canterbury Dr. HU8: Hull 5H 19
Capital Pk. HU7: Hull 4H 7
Capstan Rd. HU6: Hull 4H 17
Captain's Wlk. HU1: Hull 3B 44 (6C 4)
Carden Av. HU9: Hull 4D 30
Cardigan Av. *HU3: Hull* 1E 43
  (off De La Pole Av.)
  HU5: Hull 5B 28
  (off Fenchurch St.)
Cardigan Rd. HU3: Hull 1D 42
Carew St. HU3: Hull .1E 43
Carisbrooke Av. *HU3: Hull* 1E 43
  (off De La Pole Av.)
  HU5: Hull 3H 27
  (off Manvers St.)
  HU8: Hull 5E 29
  (off Montrose St.)
  HU16: Cott 6A 16
Carisbrooke Vs. *HU5: Hull* 4G 27
  (off Reynoldson St.)
Carlam La. HU7: Waw 5C 12
Carlisle Av. HU3: Hull 3G 43
Carlton Av. *HU5: Hull* 4G 27
  (off Reynoldson St.)
  HU9: Hull 1B 46
Carlton Ct. HU17: Bev 4D 6
Carlton Ri. HU17: Bev 2F 9
Carlton St. HU3: Hull 4E 43
Carlton Vs. *HU3: Hull (off Greek St.)* 3F 43
  HU5: Hull (off Goddard Av.) 4H 27
Carnaby Gro. HU6: Hull 1D 26
Carnegie St. HU3: Hull 2F 43
Carnoustie Cl. HU3: Hull 3F 29
Carol Dickson Ct. HU3: Hull 3H 43
Caroline Pl. HU2: Hull 1C 44 (1D 4)
Caroline's Pl. HU16: Skid 4C 14
Caroline St. HU2: Hull 6C 28 (1D 4)
Carperby M. HU5: Hull 3C 26
Carr Cl. HU17: Bev 4F 7
Carrington Av. *HU3: Hull* 1E 43
  (off De La Pole Av.)
  HU5: Hull 3H 27
  (off Manvers St.)
  HU16: Cott 6A 16
Carrington St. HU3: Hull 5B 28
Carr La. HU1: Hull 2B 44 (4C 4)
  HU10: Will 5E 25
Carroll Pl. HU2: Hull 1D 44 (2F 5)
Carr Rd. HU17: Mole 1C 6
Carr St. HU2: Hull 6C 28
Carter Dr. HU17: Bev 1D 6
Cartmell Ct. HU9: Hull 4D 30
Cartwright La. HU17: Bev 6C 6
Castle Ct. DN18: Bart H 4F 55
  HU16: Cott 1E 25
Castle Dr. HU15: S'th C 3C 34
Castledyke Sth. DN18: Bart H 4F 55
Castledyke W. DN18: Bart H 3E 55
Castle Farm Ct. HU15: S'th C 3C 34
Castleford Gro. HU3: Hull 5F 31
Castle Grn. HU16: Cott 6F 15
Castle Gro. *HU5: Hull* 6F 27
  (off Perth St. W.)
Castle Hall HU7: Brans 3E 19
CASTLE HILL HOSPITAL 1E 25
Castlehill Rd. HU7: Brans (not continuous) . . .4F 19
Castle Ri. HU15: S'th C 3C 34
Castle Rd. HU16: Cott 1D 24
Castle St. HU1: Hull 3C 44 (5C 4)
Castle Way HU13: Hess 2F 53
Castltton Av. HU5: Hull 3D 26
Catford Cl. HU8: Hull 1H 29
Cathedral Cl. HU17: Bev 1F 9
Catherine Gro. *HU3: Hull* 3G 43
  (off Carrington St.)
Catherine McAuley Cl.
  HU6: Hull 2H 27
  HU2: Hull 6C 28 (1E 5)
Catherine St. DN18: Bart H 3F 55
Catterick M. HU5: Hull 3C 26
Caughey St. HU3: Hull 1A 44 (2A 4)
Caukeel La. HU16: Cott (not continuous) 5A 16
Causeway, The HU17: Bev 4E 7
Cautley M. *HU12: Hed* 2E 49
  (off St Augustine's Ga.)
Cave By-Pass HU15: S'th C 5D 34
Cave Cres. HU16: Cott 6F 15
Cave La. HU15: Elle .6C 34
Cavendish Dr. HU17: Bev 1F 9
Cavendish Pl. HU15: Brou 6D 36
Cavendish Rd. HU8: Hull 1G 29
Cavendish Sq. HU3: Hull 5A 28

Cave Rd. HU15: Brou 3B **36**
Cave St. HU5: Hull 5A **28**
Cavill Pl. HU3: Hull 3A **44** (5A **4**)
Cawdale Av. HU9: Hull. 3E **31**
Cawood Av. HU9: Hull 1F **45**
Cawthorne Dr. HU4: Hull 5B **42**
Cayley Rd. HU10: Anla 2G **41**
Cayton Rd. HU8: Hull 2G **29**
Cecil St. HU3: Hull 3E **43**
Cedar Av. HU5: Cott 6H **15**
Cedar Cl. HU10: Anla. 1E **41**
Cedar Ct. HU12: Hed 2D **48**
Cedar Gro. HU3: Hull. 3E **43**
   HU9: Hull (off Estcourt St.) 6G **29**
Cedar Gro., The HU17: Bev 2B **6**
Cedars, The HU5: Hull 3H **27**
                      (off Sidmouth St.)
Cedarwood Dr. HU5: Hull 1A **42**
Celandine Cl. HU5: Hull 5C **26**
Central Av. HU17: Bev 5C **6**
Central Pk. Ind. Est. HU8: Hull 5E **29**
Central St. HU2: Hull 5C **28**
Centurion Way HU15: Brou 6D **36**
Century Rd. HU12: Salt 1H **47**
Ceylon St. HU9: Hull 1C **46**
Chadcourt HU6: Hull 6D **16**
Chalfont Cl. HU13: Hess 6E **41**
Chamberlain Bus. Cen. HU8: Hull 3E **29**
Chamberlain Cl. HU7: Hull 6G **19**
Chamberlain Gdns. HU8: Hull 3F **29**
Chamberlain Rd. HU8: Hull 3D **28**
Chamberlain St. HU7: Hull 6G **19**
Champney Gdns. HU17: Bev 5D **6**
                   (off Champney Rd.)
Champney Rd. HU17: Bev 5D **6**
Champney's Cl. HU13: Hess 1F **53**
Chancery Cl. HU5: Hull 6D **26**
Chancewaters HU7: King 2A **18**
Chandlers Ct. HU9: Hull 2F **45**
Chanterlands Av. HU5: Hull 2F **27**
Chanterlands Crematorium HU5: Hull 3E **27**
Chantry La. HU17: Bev 5E **7**
Chantrys Dr. HU15: Ello 5D **36**
Chantry Way HU14: Swan 3F **39**
Chantry Way E. HU14: Swan 3F **39**
Chapel Cl. DN19: Bar H 6F **57**
   HU12: Prest. 5E **33**
   HU13: Hess 1H **53**
   HU16: Skid 4B **14**
Chapelfield Rd. DN19: Gox 6G **59**
Chapel Flds. HU11: Coni 1G **21**
Chapel Hill HU15: Welt 5H **37**
Chapel Hill La. HU15: Welt 5H **37**
Chapel La. DN18: Bart H 3E **55**
   HU1: Hull 2D **44** (3F **5**)
   HU7: Waw 4A **12**
   HU10: Kir E 1A **40**
Chapel La. Staith HU1: Hull 2D **44** (3F **5**)
Chapel M. HU15: Ello 4D **36**
Chapel Row HU17: Wood 4F **11**
Chapelry Gth. HU12: Hed 2F **49**
Chapel St. DN19: Gox 4D **58**
   HU1: Hull 2B **44** (3C **4**)
Chapman St. HU2: Hull 6D **28**
   HU8: Hull. 6D **28**
Chapman St. Ind. Est. HU8: Hull 5E **29**
Charing Cl. HU3: Hull 6H **27**
Chariot St. HU1: Hull 2B **44** (4C **4**)
Charles Brady Ct. HU9: Hull 1D **30**
Charles M Jacobs Homes HU4: Hull 4C **42**
Charles St. HU2: Hull 1C **44** (1D **4**)
   HU12: Hed 3F **49**
Charlestown Way HU9: Hull 2F **45**
Charlotte St. HU1: Hull 1D **44** (2F **5**)
Charlotte St. M. HU1: Hull 1C **44** (2E **5**)
Charlton Vs. HU9: Hull 6H **29**
                    (off Estcourt St.)
Charnock Av. HU9: Hull 2B **30**
Charnwood Cl. HU7: King 1B **18**
Charterfield HU11: Bil 6E **21**
Charterhouse La. HU1: Hull 1D **44** (1F **5**)
Charterhouse, The HU2: Hull 1C **44** (1F **5**)
Chatham Av. HU5: Hull 3H **27**
                  (off Manvers St.)
Chatham St. HU3: Hull 1E **43**
Chatsworth Av. HU5: Hull 6G **27**
Chatsworth Cl. HU17: Bev 1F **9**
Chatsworth St. HU5: Hull 6G **27**
Chaucer St. HU3: Hull 4F **29**
Chaytor Cl. HU12: Hed. 3F **49**
Cheadle Cl. HU4: Hull 6B **28**
Chelmer Rd. HU8: Hull 6C **20**
Chelmsford Cl. HU9: Hull 5F **31**
Chelsea Cl. HU8: Hull 1A **30**
Chelsea Ct. HU16: Cott 1G **25**
Cheltenham Av. HU7: Brans 3C **18**
Cheriton Cl. HU7: Brans 5D **18**
Cherry Gth. HU17: Hull 3F **43**
   HU17: Bev 4F **7**
Cherry Hinton Cl. HU5: Hull 4B **26**
Cherry La. DN19: Bar H 4F **57**
Cherry Tree Av. HU8: Hull 4F **29**
Cherry Tree Cl. HU11: Bil 6H **21**

Cherry Tree La. HU12: Hed 2F **49**
   HU17: Bev 4E **7**
Cherry Trees HU16: Skid 5B **14**
Cherry Tree Ter. HU17: Bev 4F **7**
Cheshire Cl. HU5: Hull 5C **26**
Chesnut Av. HU5: Hull 4H **27**
Chester Av. HU5: Hull (off Manvers St.) 3H **27**

   HU5: Hull (off Fenchurch St.) 5B **28**
Chester Gro. HU3: Hull (off Albermarle St.) 3G **43**
Chesterholme HU11: Bil 6F **21**
Chester Rd. HU5: Hull 5A **26**
Chestnut Av. HU3: Hull 3E **43**
   HU8: Hull (off Montrose St.) 5E **29**
   HU10: Will 6F **25**
   HU12: Hed 1E **49**
   HU12: Thorn 6F **49**
   HU13: Hess 1F **53**
   HU17: Bev 2E **7**
Chestnut Cl. HU17: Bev 2E **7**
Chestnut Gro. HU8: Hull 4E **29**
   HU11: Sproat. 3F **23**
Chestnut Ri. HU9: Bar H 5E **57**
Chestnuts, The HU5: Hull (off Ella St.) 4G **27**
Chestnut Way DN19: Gox 4D **58**
Chevening Pk. HU7: King 2A **18**
Cheviotdale HU7: Brans 5D **18**
Chevy Chase HU11: Bil 6F **21**
Chichester Bungs. HU11: Sproat. 2F **23**
Chilterns, The HU9: Hull 4E **31**
Chiltern St. HU3: Hull 3G **43**
Chilton Ri. HU10: Kir E 5C **24**
Chingford Wlk. HU3: Hull 5F **31**
Cholmley St. HU3: Hull 3G **43**
Christopher Pickering Lodge HU4: Hull 5C **42**
Church All. HU1: Hull 2D **44** (4F **5**)
Church Av. HU14: N'th F 2E **51**
Church Cl. HU7: Hull 6G **19**
   HU10: Anla. 2F **41**
Church Cres. HU7: Waw 4A **12**
Church Field HU13: Hess 5H **41**
Church Ga. HU12: Hed 2E **49**
Church Grn. HU17: Mole 2A **6**
Church Hill HU15: S'th C 3C **34**
Churchill Av. HU3: Hull 1E **43**
   HU16: Cott 6G **15**
Churchill Gro. HU5: Hull 3A **28**
Churchill St. HU9: Hull 1G **45**
Churchill Vs. HU9: Hull (off Holland St.) 6G **29**
Church La. HU9: Hull 6D **30**
   HU10: Kir E 6D **24**
   HU11: Bil. 6G **21**
   HU11: Sproat. 3F **23**
   HU12: Hed 2E **49**
   HU12: Thorn 6G **49**
   HU15: Elle 6D **34**
   HU15: Ello 3D **36**
   HU15: N'th C 1B **34**
   HU16: Cott. 6A **16**
Church La. Staith HU1: Hull 2D **44** (4F **5**)
Church Mt. HU7: Hull 6G **19**
   HU11: Sproat. 3F **23**
Church Ri. HU16: Skid 4B **14**
Church Rd. HU7: Waw 4A **12**
   HU14: N'th F 1E **51**
   HU17: Mole 2A **6**
Church Row HU8: Hull. 6D **28**
Church Side DN19: Bar H 5F **57**
   DN19: Gox. 6D **58**
Church St. DN19: Gox. 5D **58**
   HU7: Hull. 5G **19**
   HU9: Hull 1E **45** (3H **5**)
   HU10: Anla. 2F **41**
   HU15: Ello 3D **36**
   HU15: N'th C 2A **34**
   HU15: S'th C 4C **34**
   HU15: Welt 5G **37**
Church Vw. DN18: Bart H 4F **55**
   HU15: Ello 3D **36**
Church Vw. Cl. HU17: Bev 4F **7**
Church Wlk. HU17: Walk 5B **8**
Circle, The HU13: Hess 6F **41**
Citadel Ct. HU17: Bev 4E **7**
Citadel Trading Pk. HU9: Hull 2D **44** (3H **5**)
Citadel Way HU9: Hull 2D **44** (4G **5**)
Cladshaw HU6: Hull. 4E **17**
Clairbrook Cl. HU3: Hull 3F **43**
Clanthorpe HU6: Hull. 4E **17**
Clapham Av. HU8: Hull 1H **29**
Clapson's La. DN18: Bart H 2E **55**
Clare Ct. HU17: Bev 4G **7**
Clare Gro. HU9: Hull 5B **30**
Claremont Av. HU5: Hull 4G **27**
                (off Reynoldson St.)
   HU5: Hull. 6G **27**
                   (off Selkirk St.)
   HU8: Hull. 2A **28**
Clarence Av. HU8: Hull 2H **29**
   HU9: Hull. 6C **30**
Clarence Ct. HU2: Hull 1C **44** (2D **4**)
Clarence St. HU9: Hull 2D **44** (3G **5**)
Clarendon Av. HU5: Hull 3H **27**
                  (off Manvers St.)

Clarendon St. HU3: Hull 1A **44** (2A **4**)
Clarondale HU7: Brans 5B **18**
Clay St. HU8: Hull 3D **28**
Clearview Cl. HU8: Hull 6A **20**
Clearwaters HU7: King 2A **18**
Cleaves Av. HU15: S'th C 3E **35**
Cleeve Dr. HU7: Brans 3D **18**
Cleeve Rd. HU12: Hed 4G **49**
Clements Way HU9: Hull. 4A **30**
Cleminson Hall HU16: Cott 1B **26**
Cleveland St. HU8: Hull 6D **28**
Cliff Balk HU13: Hess 3E **53**
Cliff Cotts. HU13: Hess 3D **52**
Cliff Gro. DN18: Bart H 4E **55**
Cliff Ho. Dr. HU13: Hess 2D **52**
Clifford Av. HU8: Hull 2H **29**
Cliff Rd. HU13: Hess 3D **52**
CLIFFS 4F **35**
Cliff Top La. HU13: Hess 2D **52**
Clifton Gdns. HU3: Hull 3F **43**
   HU5: Hull (off Goddard Av.) 4G **27**
Clifton St. HU2: Hull 6B **28** (1C **4**)
Clifton Ter. HU5: Hull 5B **28**
Clinton Av. HU5: Hull (off Manvers St.) 3H **27**
Clivedale Av. HU5: Hull 3H **27**
                (off Edgecumbe St.)
Clive Sullivan Way HU3: Hull. 6C **42** (6A **4**)
   HU4: Hull. 6C **42**
   HU13: Hess 2B **52**
   HU14: Hess 2B **52**
Clive Vale HU9: Hull (off Estcourt St.) 6H **29**
Cloeberry Way HU12: Hed 3D **48**
Cloisters, The HU17: Bev 5E **7**
                     (off Eastgate)
Close, The DN19: Gox. 3D **58**
   HU7: Hull. 6G **19**
   HU10: Will. 5G **25**
   HU16: Cott 1G **25**
Clough Gth. HU12: Hed 2F **49**
Clough Rd. HU5: Hull 3A **28**
   HU6: Hull 3A **28**
Cloughton Gro. HU5: Hull 4D **26**
Clovelly Av. HU3: Hull 1E **43**
                (off De La Pole Av.)
   HU5: Hull. 3H **27**
                (off Edgecumbe St.)
Clovelly Gdns. HU5: Hull 5B **28**
Clover Bank Vw. HU6: Hull 3H **17**
Clowes Bldgs. HU2: Hull 1C **44** (1E **5**)
Clowes Ct. HU13: Hess 1F **53**
Clumber St. HU5: Hull 6G **27**
Clydesdale Av. HU3: Hull. 3E **43**
                    (off Clyde St.)
Clyde St. HU3: Hull 3E **43**
Coachings, The HU13: Hess 3E **53**
Cobblestone Pk. HU8: Hull 5D **28**
Cobden St. HU3: Hull 1E **43**
Cober Gro. HU8: Hull 5D **20**
Cockpit Cl. HU10: Kir E 2D **40**
Cockpit Row HU11: Sproat (off Ash Cl.) 3F **23**
Coelus St. HU9: Hull 1D **44** (2G **5**)
Cogan St. HU1: Hull 3B **44** (5B **4**)
Cohort Cl. HU15: Brou 6D **36**
Coldstream Cl. HU8: Hull 1D **30**
Coleford Gro. HU7: Brans 5D **18**
Colemans Rd. HU12: Hed 3D **48**
Colenso Av. HU9: Hull (off Holland St.) 6G **29**
Colenso St. HU3: Hull 3F **43**
Colenso Vs. HU8: Hull (off Barnsley St.) 5E **29**
Coleridge Gro. HU8: Hull 4G **29**
Coleridge Rd. HU16: Cott 5A **30**
College Rd. DN19: Bar H 5G **57**
College St. HU3: Hull 1B **44** (1B **4**)
   HU7: Hull. 6G **19**
Colleridge Gro. HU17: Bev 2D **8**
Collier Cl. HU14: N'th F 2D **50**
Collier St. HU1: Hull. 2B **44** (3B **4**)
Collin Av. HU9: Hull 4D **30**
Collinson Cl. HU10: Will 6F **25**
Colonial St. HU2: Hull 1A **44** (2A **4**)
Colt Bus. Pk. HU8: Hull 5G **43**
Coltman Av. HU17: Bev 2E **7**
Coltman Cl. HU17: Bev 1E **7**
COLTMAN STREET DAY HOSPITAL 3H **43**
Colville Av. HU4: Hull 2A **42**
Colwall Av. HU5: Hull 4C **26**
Colwyn Cl. HU7: Brans 5D **18**
Commerce La. HU3: Hull 3A **44** (6A **4**)
Commercial Rd. HU1: Hull 3B **44** (5C **4**)
Commodore Cft. HU1: Hull 3C **44** (6D **4**)
Common La. HU7: Waw 4B **12**
   HU15: Brou 6G **37**
Common Rd. HU15: S'th C 6A **34**
Commonwealth Homes HU5: Hull 4D **26**
Compass Rd. HU6: Hull 4H **17**
Conduit St. HU3: Hull 2D **44** (4G **5**)
Conifer Cl. HU5: Hull 1B **42**
Conington Av. HU17: Bev 4G **7**
CONISTON 1G **21**
Coniston Gro. HU9: Hull 4A **30**
Coniston Ho. HU3: Hull 2H **43**
Coniston La. HU11: Coni 2H **21**
   HU11: Swin 1D **20**

Consort Ct. HU9: Hull 3E **45** (5H **5**)
Constable Av. HU11: Bil 5H **21**
Constable Cl. HU11: Sproat. 2F **23**
Constable Gth. HU12: Hed 2G **49**
Constable St. HU3: Hull 3H **43**
Constantine Cl. HU7: Brans 3D **18**
Constitution Hill HU17: Mole 2A **6**
Convent Ct. HU5: Hull 5A **28**
Convent La. HU3: Hull 2A **44**
Conway Cl. HU3: Hull 3G **43**
Cookbury Cl. HU7: Brans 3B **18**
Coombs Yd. HU17: Bev 4D **6**
(off Nth. Bar Within)
Cooper St. HU2: Hull 6C **28**
HU17: Bev 3E **7**
Copandale Rd. HU17: Bev 3D **6**
Copenhagen Rd. HU1: Hull 1C **28**
Copper Beech Cl. HU14: Swan 5F **39**
Coppice Side HU4: Hull 2B **42**
Coppleflat La. HU17: Walk . . . . . . 1A **8** & 6D **8** & 5C **8**
Copse, The HU17: Bev 5G **7**
Corbridge Cl. HU9: Hull 5F **31**
Corby Pk. HU14: N'th F 1D **50**
Cordella Cl. HU3: Hull 3F **43**
Coriander Cl. HU7: Brans 6D **6**
Corinthian Way HU9: Hull 2G **45**
Cormorant Cl. HU7: Brans 4G **19**
Cornhill Dr. DN18: Bart H 4H **55**
Cornwall Gdn. HU3: Hull 3H **43**
Cornwall Gdns. HU5: Hull (off Raglan St.) . . 3H **27**
Cornwall St. HU8: Hull 5D **28**
HU16: Cott. 5B **16**
Corona Dr. HU8: Hull 1F **29**
Coronation Av. HU9: Hull 5G **29**
(off Rustenburg St.)
Coronation Cl. HU17: Bev 3F **7**
Coronation Rd. Nth. HU5: Hull 4B **26**
Coronation Rd. Sth. HU5: Hull 5A **26**
Coronet Cl. HU6: Hull 4G **17**
Corporation Rd. HU9: Hull (not continuous) . . 1B **46**
HU17: Bev 4D **6**
Corporation Workshops HU3: Hull. 3E **43**
Corran Gth. HU4: Hull 5H **41**
Corsair Gro. HU7: Brans 4F **43**
Cosford Gth. HU7: Brans 2E **19**
Costello Stadium 4A **42**
Costello Stadium Sports Cen. 3C **42**
Cotswolds, The HU9: Hull 4E **31**
Cotta Ct. HU16: Cott 6A **16**
Cottage Dr. HU10: Kir E 6C **24**
Cottage Holdings HU6: Wood 6F **11**
Cottage La. DN18: Bart H 3F **55**
Cottage M. HU17: Bev 4E **7**
Cottam Wlk. HU16: Cott 1H **25**
(off Winteringham Wlk.)
Cotterdale HU7: Brans. 5B **18**
Cottesmore Rd. HU13: Hess 6G **41**
COTTINGHAM 6A **16**
Cottingham Av. HU1: Hull 2B **44** (4B **4**)
Cottingham Gro. HU6: Hull 2E **27**
Cottingham Playsport Pavilion 5H **15**
Cottingham Rd. HU5: Hull 2D **26**
HU6: Hull. 2D **26**
Cottingham Station (Rail) 6B **16**
Coulson Dr. HU13: Hess 1G **53**
Coultas Ct. HU3: Hull 2F **43**
Council Av. HU4: Hull 5C **42**
Council Ter. DN18: Bart H 3E **55**
Council Vs. DN19: New H 3A **58**
Countess Cl. HU6: Hull 4G **17**
County Rd. Nth. HU5: Hull 5C **26**
County Rd. Sth. HU5: Hull 6B **26**
Coupland Gdns. HU5: Hull 4B **28**
Courtland Rd. HU6: Hull 5D **16**
Courtney St. HU8: Hull 5E **29**
Courtpark Rd. HU6: Hull 6D **16**
Courtway Rd. HU6: Hull 5D **16**
Coventry Rd. HU5: Hull 5B **26**
Coverdale HU7: Brans 5C **18**
Covert, The HU16: Cott 1B **26**
Covington HU15: Ello 5E **37**
Cowden Gro. HU9: Hull 4B **30**
Cowgate HU15: Welt 5G **37**
Coxwold Gro. HU4: Hull 3D **42**
Crab Tree Wlk. HU17: Bev 5F **7**
Cradley Rd. HU5: Hull 3B **26**
Cragdale Cl. HU8: Hull 5H **19**
Crake Wells HU17: Walk 5C **8**
Cranberry Way HU4: Hull 4B **42**
Cranbourne St. HU5: Hull 4B **28**
(off Fenchurch St.)
Cranbourne St. HU3: Hull 6A **28**
Cranbrook Av. HU6: Hull 6G **17**
Crane Rd. HU9: Hull 2F **45**
Cranham Gro. HU7: Brans 5D **18**
Cranswick Gro. HU9: Hull 5C **30**
Crathorne Rd. HU17: Bev 3F **7**
Craven Ct. HU9: Hull 1F **45**
Craven Pk. Stadium 6D **30**
Craven St. Est. HU9: Hull 6F **29**
Craven St. Nth. HU9: Hull 6F **29**
Craven St. Sth. HU9: Hull 1G **45**
Crawshaw Av. HU17: Bev 2D **6**
Crayford Cl. HU9: Hull 5F **31**

Crescent St. HU16: Cott 5H **15**
Crescent, The HU3: Hull 3F **43**
HU12: Thorn 5F **49**
HU15: Welt 5G **37**
Crescent Vw. HU12: Thorn 5F **49**
Cresswell Cl. HU2: Hull 6B **28**
Creyke Cl. HU16: Cott 5A **16**
Creyke St. HU15: Welt. 5G **37**
Cricklewood Wlk. HU8: Hull 6H **19**
Crinan Dr. HU6: Hull 4G **17**
Crispin Cl. HU8: Hull 6H **41**
Croft Dr. HU10: Anla 3D **40**
Croft Ent. Pk. HU2: Hull 1C **44** (1E **5**)
Crofters Dr. HU16: Cott 1B **26**
Crofton Av. HU8: Hull 6D **28**
(off Egton St.)
Croft Pk. HU14: N'th F 6D **38**
Croft, The HU7: Brans 4B **18**
HU17: Bev 1B **6**
Croft Vw. HU7: Brans 5F **19**
HU10: Anla 2D **40**
Cromarty Cl. HU9: Hull 3B **30**
Cromer St. HU5: Hull. 4B **28**
Crompton Vs. HU9: Hull 6H **29**
(off Estcourt St.)
Cromwell Cl. HU3: Hull 6A **28**
Cromwell Cl. HU10: Will 6F **25**
Crook Hill HU15: Brant 1D **36**
Cropton Rd. HU5: Hull 4D **26**
Crossfield Rd. HU4: Hull 3C **42**
HU13: Hess 5F **41**
Cross Hill DN19: Bar H 5E **57**
Cross Hill Vw. DN19: Bar H 5E **57**
(off Barton La.)
Crosshill Vw. DN19: Bar H 5F **57**
Crosskill Cl. HU17: Bev 3F **7**
Crossland Av. HU9: Hull 6G **29**
(off Holland St.)
Cross St. DN19: Bar H 4F **57**
HU2: Hull 2B **44** (3C **4**)
HU17: Bev 5D **6**
Crosswood Cl. HU7: Brans 5D **12**
Crowland Cl. HU8: Hull 5D **20**
Crowle St. HU9: Hull 1G **45**
Crown Ter. HU17: Bev 5D **6**
Crowther Cl. HU17: Bev 2F **7**
Crowther Way HU14: Swan 3F **39**
Croyland Av. HU9: Hull 6G **29**
(off Holland St.)
Crusoe Ct. HU5: Hull 4D **26**
Crystal St. HU3: Hull 1H **43**
Cudworth Gro. HU8: Hull 5E **29**
Cullen Cl. HU8: Hull 1F **29**
Cullingworth Av. HU6: Hull 5H **17**
Cumberland St. HU2: Hull 5C **28**
Cumberland Vs. HU8: Hull 1G **5**
Cumbrian Way HU7: Brans 5C **12**
Cundall Cl. HU9: Hull 5H **29**
Curlew Cl. HU7: Brans 4G **19**
HU17: Bev 2D **6**
Curzon St. HU3: Hull 1E **43**
Cuthbert Av. HU3: Hull (off Airlie St.) 3G **43**
Cyprus St. HU3: Hull 1C **46**
Cyprus Wlk. HU9: Hull 6C **30**

D

Dagger La. HU1: Hull 2C **44** (5E **5**)
DAIRYCOATES 5G **43**
Dairycoates Av. HU3: Hull 4F **43**
Daisyfield Dr. HU11: Bil. 6E **21**
Dalby Gro. HU9: Hull 4C **30**
Dale Cl. HU14: Swan 3G **39**
Dale Flats HU14: Swan 3G **39**
Dalehouse Dr. HU10: Anla 2G **41**
Dale Rd. HU14: Swan 1F **39**
HU15: Brant 6H **35**
HU15: Ello 3E **37**
HU15: Welt 5H **37**
Dale Royal Ct. HU16: Cott (off South St.) . . 6A **16**
Dales Fitness Cen., The 6C **12**
Dales Lodge HU7: Brans 6C **12**
Dales, The HU9: Hull 4E **31**
HU16: Cott. 6E **15**
Dalesway HU10: Kir E 1C **40**
Dalkeith Cl. HU7: Brans 1D **18**
Dalsetter Ri. HU8: Hull 6H **19**
Dalton St. HU8: Hull 5D **28**
Daltry St. HU3: Hull 4A **44**
Dalwood Cl. HU7: Brans 4E **19**
Dam Green La. HU15: Ello 3E **37**
Dam Rd. DN18: Bart H (not continuous) . . . 2C **54**
Damson Rd. HU12: Thorn 6G **49**
Danbury Pk. HU7: King 2B **18**
Danby Cl. HU8: Hull 5H **19**
Dane Pk. Rd. HU6: Hull 4D **16**
Danes Dr. HU13: Hess 2F **53**
Danesgate DN19: New H 2A **58**
Danesway HU17: Bev 2C **6**
Dansom La. Nth. HU8: Hull 5E **29**
Dansom La. Sth. HU8: Hull 1E **45** (1H **5**)
Danson Cl. DN18: Bart H 4H **55**

Danthorpe Gro. HU9: Hull 4A **30**
Danube Rd. HU5: Hull 5B **26**
Dark La. HU12: Thorn 6F **49**
Darnholm Ct. HU8: Hull 5H **19**
Darrell Ct. HU12: Hed 3H **49**
Darrismere Vs. HU3: Hull 3F **43**
Dartford Wlk. HU9: Hull 5F **31**
Dart Gro. HU8: Hull 1C **30**
Dartmouth Wlk. HU4: Hull 5H **41**
Datchet Gth. HU4: Hull 6A **42**
Davenport Av. HU13: Hess 1E **53**
David Lloyd Leisure 3H **17**
David's Cl. HU6: Skid 4C **14**
Davidstow Cl. HU7: Brans 4C **18**
David Whitfield Cl. HU3: Hull 3E **43**
Daville Cl. HU5: Hull 5A **26**
Davis's Cl. HU10: Kir E 6D **24**
Davis St. HU1: Hull 2C **44** (3D **4**)
Dawnay Dr. HU10: Anla. 2H **41**
Dawnay Rd. HU11: Bil. 5H **21**
Dawson Dr. HU4: Hull 4A **18**
Dawson Wlk. HU10: Anla (off Hull Rd.) 2G **41**
Dayton Rd. HU5: Hull 5B **26**
Deal Cl. HU8: Hull 4H **19**
Dean Pk. Ind. Est. HU17: Bev 4H **7**
Deans Dr. HU9: Hull 2A **30**
Dearne Cl. HU15: Brou 6F **37**
Dearne Gro. HU8: Hull 5F **29**
Debden Gro. HU8: Hull 5D **20**
De Burton Ct. HU12: Hed 3G **49**
Deepdale Gro. HU9: Hull 5H **29**
Deep, The 3D **44** (6F **5**)
Deerhurst Gro. HU7: Brans 5D **18**
Deer Pk. Way HU17: Bev 2F **9**
Dee St. HU3: Hull 4G **43**
De Grey St. HU5: Hull 4H **27**
De La Pole Av. HU3: Hull 1E **43**
Delaware Av. HU3: Hull 1E **43**
Delhi St. HU9: Hull 1C **46**
Delius Cl. HU4: Anla 4A **42**
Dell, The HU17: Bev 6G **7**
Denaby Cl. HU8: Hull 6F **29**
Dene Cl. HU6: Wood 2F **17**
Dene Pk. Sports Club 2G **17**
Dene Rd. HU16: Cott. 6G **15**
Dene St. HU9: Hull 5G **29**
Denesway HU13: Hess 6E **41**
Denholme Av. HU6: Hull 5H **17**
Denmark Ct. HU9: Hull 1F **45**
Denmark Ri. HU15: N'th C 1A **34**
Dennett Rd. HU17: Bev 3G **7**
Denton St. HU17: Bev 5G **7**
Dent Rd. HU5: Hull 3C **26**
Derby St. HU3: Hull 6A **28**
Derringham Av. HU4: Hull 2A **42**
Derringham St. HU3: Hull 6H **27**
Derrymore Rd. HU10: Will 4D **24**
Derwent Av. HU3: Hull 3G **43**
(off Alfonso St.)
HU4: Hull. 5D **42**
(off Hampshire St.)
HU14: N'th F 3D **50**
Derwent Cl. HU16: Cott. 6C **16**
Derwent Gro. HU5: Hull 4H **27**
Derwent St. HU8: Hull 4E **29**
Desmond Av. HU6: Hull 2A **28**
Devon Gro. HU5: Hull 4B **28**
(off Folkstone St.)
Devonport Av. HU3: Hull 3E **43**
(off Pretoria St.)
Devonshire Vs. HU3: Hull 4H **43**
(off Wellsted St.)
Devon St. HU4: Hull 5E **43**
HU16: Cott. 5B **16**
Dewberry Ct. HU4: Hull 4B **42**
Diadem Gro. HU9: Hull 1D **30**
Dibsdane HU6: Hull 4D **16**
Didscourt HU6: Hull 6D **16**
Digby Gth. HU7: Brans 2E **19**
Dill Dr. HU17: Bev 6E **7**
Dingley Cl. HU6: Hull 6G **17**
Distaff La. HU12: Hed 2E **49**
Ditmans Av. HU16: Cott 2A **42**
Division Rd. HU3: Hull 4G **43**
Dixon Ct. HU16: Cott. 1H **25**
Dock Office Row HU1: Hull. 1D **44** (2F **5**)
Dock St. HU1: Hull 2C **44** (3D **4**)
Dodswell Gro. HU9: Hull 6F **31**
Dodthorpe HU6: Hull 4F **17**
Dog & Duck La. HU17: Bev (off Walkergate) . . 4D **6**
Doldron M. HU5: Hull 3C **26**
Dominican Wlk. HU17: Bev 5E **7**
Doncaster St. HU3: Hull 2G **43**
Doongarth HU4: Hull 5A **42**
Dorado Cl. HU3: Hull 3F **43**
Dorchester Rd. HU7: Brans 6D **18**
Doris Va. HU3: Hull 3G **43**
Dorking Cl. HU8: Hull 2B **30**
Dorothy Gro. HU3: Hull 3E **43**
Dorset St. HU4: Hull 5E **43**
Dorsey Way HU15: Ello 3E **37**
Douglas Rd. HU8: Hull 6D **20**
Dovedale Gro. HU9: Hull 6H **29**

DOVE HOUSE HOSPICE 3E 29
Dover Cres. HU5: Hull 4B 28
     (off Folkstone St.)
Dover St. HU3: Hull 6H 27
Dower Ri. HU14: Swan 3G 39
Downfield Av. HU6: Hull 3G 17
Downhill Dr. HU7: Brans 3F 19
Downing Gro. HU9: Hull 5B 30
Downs Cres. HU5: Hull 4C 26
Drake Ho. HU6: Hull 4F 17
Draper's La. HU12: Hed 3D 48
Drayton Cl. HU8: Hull 1D 30
Dressay Gro. HU8: Hull 6A 20
Driffield Cl. HU16: Cott 6F 15
Driffield Rd. HU17: Bev, Mole 1A 6
Dringshaw HU6: Hull 4E 17
Drove La. HU7: Waw 1G 11
Drovers Ri. HU15: Ello 3D 36
Drummond Ct. HU7: Brans 3F 19
Drydales HU10: Kir E 2D 40
Dryden St. HU8: Hull 4F 29
DRYPOOL 2F 45
Drypool Way HU9: Hull 2E 45
Duddon Gro. HU8: Hull 6C 20
Dudley Av. HU3: Hull 6H 27
     (off Mayfield St.)
Dudley Wlk. HU4: Hull 5A 42
Duesbery St. HU5: Hull 6H 27
Duesbur Ct. HU17: Bev 3D 6
Dulverton Cl. HU7: Brans 2C 18
Dumbarton Av. HU3: Hull (off Clyde St.) . . 3E 43
Dumfries Wlk. HU8: Hull 5D 20
Dunblane Cl. HU3: Hull 2E 43
Duncan Dr. DN18: Bart H 3E 55
Duncan's Pl. HU1: Hull 3E 5
     (off Manor St.)
Duncombe Ct. HU12: Hed 2G 49
Dundee St. HU5: Hull 6F 27
Dunelm Cl. HU8: Hull 5F 29
     (off Durham St.)
Dunflat Rd. HU17: Walk 2A 14
Dunkeld Dr. HU6: Hull 4G 17
Dunlin Cl. HU7: Brans 4G 19
Dunmow Cl. HU8: Hull 1D 30
Dunnock Cl. HU8: Hull 5G 19
Dunscombe Pk. HU8: Hull 4E 29
Dunston Dr. HU13: Hess 1E 53
Dunston Ho. HU13: Hess 2F 53
Dunston Rd. HU13: Hess 1C 42
DUNSWELL 1F 17
Dunswell Cl. HU6: Hull 5F 17
Dunswell La. HU6: Wood 1C 16
Dunswell Rd. HU16: Cott 1B 16
Dunvegan Rd. HU8: Hull 5A 20
Durban St. HU8: Hull 1D 44 (1G 5)
Durham Cl. HU8: Hull 5G 29
Durham M. HU17: Bev 6D 6
Durham St. HU8: Hull 4F 29
Durham Vs. HU9: Hull 6G 29
     (off Middleburg St.)
Dyer La. HU17: Bev 4D 6
Dyke Cl. HU13: Hess 2F 53
Dykes Ho. HU13: Hess 2E 53
     (off Redcliff Rd.)

E

Eagle Ter. HU8: Hull 6D 28
Ealdane HU6: Hull 4D 16
Ealing Cl. HU8: Hull 1A 30
Earle's Rd. HU9: Hull 1G 45
Earlscourt HU6: Hull 5D 16
Earsham Cl. HU8: Hull 6D 20
Easby Ct. HU5: Hull 4B 26
Easedale Rd. HU9: Hull 3E 31
Easenby Av. HU10: Kir E 2D 40
Easenby HU14: Swan 3H 39
Easethorpe HU6: Hull 4F 17
East Acridge DN18: Bart H 3G 55
East Acridge Ho. DN18: Bart H 4G 55
Eastbourne St. HU3: Hull 3F 43
EAST CARR 6A 20
E. Carr Rd. HU8: Hull 5A 20
East Cl. HU17: Bev 2C 6
East Dale Rd. HU14: Welt 6A 38
EAST ELLA 2D 42
E. Ella Dr. HU4: Hull 2B 42
EAST END 3G 33
East End HU17: Walk 5B 8
East End HU12: Prest 4F 33
Eastern Vs. HU9: Hull (off Brazil St.) 6F 29
    HU9: Hull (off Holland St.) 6G 29
Eastfield HU15: N'th C 2A 34
Eastfield Cl. HU17: Bev 2F 7
Eastfield Rd. DN18: Bart H 5F 55
    HU8: Hull 2C 42
Eastgate HU13: Hess 1F 53
    HU17: Bev 5E 7
East Grove DN18: Bart H 3G 55
East Gro. HU4: Hull 4G 42
East Hann La. DN19: Bar H 3H 57
East Hull Pools 1F 45

East La. HU17: Bev 3C 6
E. Lodge Ride HU15: S'th C 2D 34
East Mt. HU14: N'th F 2E 51
East Mount Av. HU8: Hull 1C 30
Eastmount Recreation Cen. 6C 20
Easton Av. HU8: Hull 4D 28
     (off Woodhall St.)
East Park Av. HU8: Hull 3H 29
East Riding Bus. Cen. HU17: Bev 5H 7
East St. HU9: Hull 1E 45 (2H 5)
Eastwood Rd. HU17: Walk 2B 8
Ebberston Gro. HU5: Hull 3D 26
Ebor Cl. HU8: Hull 6D 20
Ecclesfield Av. HU9: Hull 5E 31
Eddlethorpe HU8: Hull 5E 29
Eden Cl. HU17: Bev 3C 6
Edendale HU7: Brans 6C 18
Eden Dr. HU8: Hull 3F 29
Eden Gro. HU3: Hull 3F 43
Eden Ri. HU10: Will 4D 24
Eden Rd. HU17: Bev 3C 6
Edgar St. HU3: Hull 4A 44 (6A 4)
Edgecumbe St. HU5: Hull 4H 27
Edgeware Av. HU9: Hull 5H 29
Edinburgh St. HU3: Hull 3F 43
Edison Gro. HU9: Hull 4H 29
Edith Cavell Ct. HU5: Hull 2E 27
Edmonton Vs. HU9: Hull 1C 46
Edom Vs. HU3: Hull 6H 27
     (off Mayfield St.)
Edward Collins Sq. HU9: Hull 1F 45
Edward St. HU13: Hess 1G 53
    HU17: Bev 4E 7
Egginton HU10: Kir E 1D 40
Egginton St. HU2: Hull 1C 44 (2D 4)
Eglington Av. HU8: Hull 2A 30
Egton Cl. HU8: Hull 6D 28 (1G 5)
Egton Vs. HU8: Hull 6E 29 (1H 5)
Egypt St. HU9: Hull 1C 46
Eildon Hills Cl. HU7: Brans 3G 19
Elder Av. HU9: Hull (off Abbey St.) 6F 29
Elderberry Dr. HU4: Hull 4B 42
Elderwood Ct. HU3: Hull 3A 44
Eldon Dr. HU12: Prest 5E 33
Eldon Gro. HU3: Hull 3E 43
     (off Athol St.)
    HU3: Hull 2F 43
     (Granville St.)
    HU5: Hull 4H 27
     (off Goddard Av.)
    HU5: Hull 4A 28
     (Beverley Rd.)
Eleanor Ct. HU9: Hull 4C 30
Elgar Rd. HU4: Anla 4A 42
Ella Gro. HU8: Hull 1G 5
Ella Pk. HU10: Anla 1E 41
Ella St. HU5: Hull 4G 27
Ellens Vs. HU9: Hull 6F 29
     (off Holland St.)
Ellerbeck Ct. HU9: Hull 5G 19
     (off More Hall Dr.)
Ellerburn Av. HU6: Hull 4F 17
Ellerby Gro. HU9: Hull 4A 30
ELLERKER 6D 34
Ellerker La. HU15: S'th C 5C 34
Ellerker Ri. HU10: Will 4D 24
Ellerker Rd. HU17: Bev 5C 6
Ellerker Wold La. HU15: Elle 5F 35
Ellesmere Av. HU8: Hull 2B 30
Ellingham Cl. HU8: Hull 6C 20
Ellis Cl. HU12: Prest 4F 33
Ellis St. HU9: Hull 6F 29
ELLOUGHTON 3E 37
Elloughton Dale HU15: Ello 3E 37
Elloughton Gro. HU6: Hull 1E 27
    HU16: Cott 6F 15
Elloughton Rd. HU15: Ello 6D 36
Elloughtonthorpe Way HU15: Brou 6F 37
Elm Av. HU8: Hull 4F 29
    HU15: Ello 5E 37
Elmbridge Pde. HU9: Hull 5F 31
Elm Cl. HU17: Bev 3C 6
Elm Cft. HU17: Walk 2A 8
Elmdale DN18: Bart H 5E 55
Elmfield HU6: Hull 6G 17
Elmfield Dr. HU16: Cott 6H 15
Elm Gro. HU3: Hull 1E 43
Elm La. DN19: Gox 3D 58
Elmsall Dr. HU17: Bev 2B 6
Elms Dr. HU10: Kir E 6D 24
Elms, The HU3: Hull 3F 43
Elm St. HU5: Hull 4A 28
Elmswood HU13: Hess 6D 40
Elm Ter. HU5: Hull 4A 28
Elm Tree Av. HU12: Thorn 6G 49
Elmtree Av. HU14: N'th F 2D 50
Elm Tree Cl. HU12: Thorn 6G 49
Elm Tree Ct. HU16: Cott 6H 15
Elm Vs. HU9: Hull (off Brazil St.) 6F 29
Elsham Ri. HU13: Hess 1E 53
Elsiemere Wlk. HU4: Hull 2A 42
Elsie Vs. HU9: Hull (off Holland St.) 6F 29
Elsternwick Av. HU8: Hull (off Durham St.) . 4F 29
Elston Cl. HU6: Hull 6A 18

Elswick Gdns. DN18: Bart H 2F 55
Elsworth Ct. HU5: Hull 5B 26
Elvaston Pk. HU7: King 2A 18
Eleveley Dr. HU10: Kir E 5A 24
Elvidge Cl. HU17: Bev 1E 9
Elvington Cl. HU6: Hull 6F 17
Elwell Av. HU17: Bev 5D 6
Emberton Pk. HU7: King 1C 18
Emerald Gro. HU3: Hull 4F 43
Emily St. HU9: Hull 1F 45
Emmott Rd. HU6: Hull 5H 17
Empringham St. HU9: Hull 1G 45
Empson Ter. HU17: Bev 5D 6
Ena's Cres. HU3: Hull 3G 43
Ena's St. HU3: Hull 2G 43
Endeavour Cres. HU9: Hull 6C 30
Endike La. HU6: Hull 6C 16
    HU16: Cott. 6C 16
Endsleigh St. HU3: Hull 1F 43
Endsleigh Vs. HU5: Hull 4G 27
     (off Reynoldson St.)
Endymion St. HU8: Hull 5E 29
Enfield Ct. HU7: Hull 6H 19
Enfield M. HU17: Bev 4E 7
England Rd. HU11: Bil 5G 21
English Cl. HU3: Hull 4B 44 (6B 4)
English St. HU3: Hull 4A 44 (6A 4)
English St. Unit Factory Est.
    HU3: Hull 3B 44 (6B 4)
Ennerdale HU7: Brans, Hull. 4B 18
Ennerdale Leisure Cen. 6B 18
Enstone Gth. HU7: Brans. 2E 19
Enterprise Pk. Ind. Est. HU3: Hull 4G 43
Epping Cl. HU8: Hull 6H 19
EPPLEWORTH 2B 24
Eppleworth Rd. HU16: Cott. 5D 14
Epworth St. HU9: Hull 5A 28
Ermiston Vs. HU9: Hull 6G 29
     (off Rosmead St.)
Ernest Hill Ct. HU5: Hull 4F 27
Ernest Kirkwood Cl. HU5: Hull 5C 26
Ernest's Av. HU9: Hull 6G 29
     (off Holland St.)
Esk Cres. HU5: Hull 3A 28
Eskdale Av. HU5: Hull 5H 29
Esmond St. HU6: Hull 1A 28
Essex St. HU4: Hull 5D 42
Estcourt St. HU9: Hull 6G 29
Estcourt Vs. HU9: Hull 6G 29
     (off Estcourt St.)
Esther's Av. HU3: Hull 4F 43
     (off Eastbourne St.)
Etherington Ct. HU17: Bev 5G 7
Etherington Dr. HU6: Hull 1A 28
Etherington Rd. HU6: Hull 1H 27
Eton St. HU3: Hull (not continuous). 4G 43
Etton Cl. HU16: Cott. 1F 25
Etton Gro. HU6: Hull 1E 27
Euston Ct. HU3: Hull 3H 43
Eva's Av. HU3: Hull 1E 43
     (off De La Pole Av.)
Evelyn Gdns. HU14: N'th F 2E 51
Evergreen Dr. HU6: Hull 3G 17
Everingham Wlk. HU5: Hull 5B 26
Eversfield Cl. HU7: King 2B 18
Everthorpe Cl. HU3: Hull 3H 43
    HU15: Brou 6F 37
Everthorpe La. HU15: N'th C 2B 34
Exchange All. HU1: Hull 3F 5
     (off Bowlalley La.)
Exchange Ct. HU1: Hull (off Lowgate) 3F 5
Exchange St. HU5: Hull 4B 28
Exeter Gro. HU9: Hull 5B 30
Exeter St. HU16: Cott 5B 16
Exmouth St. HU5: Hull 3H 27
Exton Cl. HU7: Brans 2C 18

F

Faceby Wlk. HU5: Hull (off Lythe Av.) 3D 26
Fairbourne Cl. HU7: Brans 5D 12
Faircourt HU6: Hull 5D 16
Fairfax Av. HU5: Hull 2E 27
Fairfax Dr. HU12: Hed 1E 49
Fairfield Av. HU10: Kir E 5D 24
Fairfield Dr. DN18: Bart H 5G 55
Fairfield Rd. HU5: Hull 3D 26
Fairfields Pit (Nature Reserve) 1A 58
Fairfield Vw. HU15: Brou 6G 37
Fairholme La. HU7: Waw 4B 12
Fairlawn HU17: Bev 2B 6
Fairmount Av. HU3: Hull 1E 43
Fairways, The HU8: Hull 6B 20
Fairway, The HU10: Kir E 6A 24
Falcon Cl. HU4: Hull 6C 42
Falkirk Cl. HU7: Brans 5D 12
Falkland Rd. HU9: Hull 5F 31
Falkland Way DN18: Bart H 2G 55
Falmouth St. HU5: Hull (not continuous). . . 3H 27
Falsgrave Gro. HU5: Hull 1C 42
Faraday St. HU9: Hull 4H 29
Far Bell Pl. HU9: Hull 4D 30

Farbridge La. HU12: Hed . . . 3E 49
Far Ings La. DN18: Bart . . . 2A 54
Far Ings Nature Reserve . . . 1A 54
Far Ings Rd. DN18: Bart H . . . 2C 54
Far Ings Vis. Cen. . . . 1B 54
Farlington Cl. HU9: Hull . . . 1D 30
Farndale Av. HU9: Hull . . . 5H 29
Farnella Cl. HU3: Hull . . . 3F 43
Farnley Sq. HU5: Hull (off Ella St.) . . . 4H 27
Faroes Cl. HU9: Hull . . . 3B 30
Farrand Rd. HU12: Hed . . . 2D 48
Farringdon St. HU5: Hull . . . 4B 28
Farrows Pond DN19: Gox . . . 3D 58
Farthing Dr. HU7: King . . . 2A 18
Faversham Av. HU4: Hull . . . 2A 42
Fawcett Cl. HU3: Hull . . . 5A 28
Fawley Cl. HU5: Hull . . . 3B 28
Feather La. DN19: Bar H . . . 6E 57
Felbridge Cl. HU9: Hull . . . 4F 31
Feldane HU6: Hull . . . 4D 16
Fenby Ct. HU13: Hess . . . 6G 41
Fenchurch St. HU5: Hull . . . 5B 28
Ferens Art Gallery . . . 2C 44 (4D 4)
Ferens Av. HU6: Hull . . . 2G 27
Ferens Ct. HU1: Hull . . . 2B 44 (4C 4)
  HU9: Hull . . . 5G 29
Ferens Gdn. HU16: Cott . . . 4G 15
Ferens Hall HU16: Cott . . . 5G 15
Ferens Haven HU8: Hull . . . 3H 29
Ferens Recreation Cen. . . . 4F 27
Ferens Vs. HU9: Hull . . . 6H 29
  (off Rosmead St.)
Ferens Way HU1: Hull . . . 1B 44 (3C 4)
  HU2: Hull . . . 1B 44 (2B 4)
Ferguson Rd. HU17: Walk . . . 6B 8
Fern Av. HU9: Hull . . . 6G 29
  (off Middleburg St.)
Fern Cl. HU2: Hull . . . 6C 28
Fern Cl. HU13: Hess . . . 1H 53
Fern Dale HU5: Hull . . . 4H 27
  (off Goddard Av.)
Ferndale HU5: Hull . . . 4H 27
  (off Lambert St.)
  HU8: Hull . . . 6E 29
Fern Dale HU9: Hull . . . 5G 29
  (off Sherburn St.)
Ferndale Av. HU5: Hull . . . 3H 27
  (off Edgecumbe St.)
  HU5: Hull . . . 3H 27
  (off Exmouth St.)
  HU10: Will . . . 5E 25
Fern Gro. HU5: Hull . . . 4B 28
  (off Folkstone St.)
  HU5: Hull . . . 6F 27
  (off Perth St.)
Fernhill Rd. HU5: Hull . . . 3C 26
Fernland Cl. HU15: Brou . . . 6E 37
Fernleigh Vs. HU8: Hull . . . 4G 29
  (off Lee St.)
Ferriby Gro. HU6: Hull . . . 1E 27
Ferriby High Rd.
  HU14: N'th F . . . 1E 51
Ferriby Rd. DN18: Bart H . . . 5A 54
  HU13: Hess . . . 1C 52
Ferriby Station (Rail) . . . 2E 51
Ferries St. HU9: Hull . . . 1G 45
Ferry Ct. HU15: Brou . . . 6C 36
Ferry La. HU7: Hull . . . 3D 28
  HU17: Wood . . . 3D 10
Ferry Mdws. Pk. HU7: King . . . 2B 18
Ferry Rd. DN19: Bar H . . . 1D 56
  DN19: Gox . . . 5C 58
  HU7: Waw . . . 3G 11
  HU13: Hess . . . 1F 53
  HU15: S'th C . . . 4A 34
Ferry Rd. E. DN19: Bar H . . . 4E 57
Ferry Vw. HU12: Thorn . . . 5F 49
Fewson Gth. HU12: Hed . . . 2F 49
Feyzin Dr. DN18: Bart H . . . 4D 54
Field Rd. DN19: Gox . . . 2G 59
Fieldside Cl. HU12: Thorn . . . 6F 49
Fieldside Gth. HU6: Hull . . . 3G 17
Field St. HU9: Hull . . . 1E 45
Figham Rd. HU17: Bev . . . 5G 7
Figham Springs Way
  HU17: Bev . . . 6E 7
Filey Gro. HU3: Hull . . . 3E 43
  (off Rhodes St.)
Fimber Av. HU16: Cott . . . 1H 25
Finch Cft. HU8: Hull . . . 5G 19
Finchley Cl. DN18: Bart H . . . 2E 55
  HU8: Hull . . . 1A 30
Finch Pk. HU17: Bev . . . 2C 6
Findon Cl. HU7: King . . . 1B 18
Fingall M. HU5: Hull . . . 3C 26
Finkle La. DN18: Bart H . . . 3F 55
Finkle St. HU1: Hull . . . 3C 44 (5E 5)
  HU15: N'th C . . . 2A 34
  HU16: Cott . . . 6H 15
Finningley Gth. HU7: Brans. . . . 3E 19
Finsbury Gro. HU2: Hull . . . 6B 28
Fire Sta. Ho's. HU5: Hull . . . 3A 44
Firethorn Cl. HU3: Hull . . . 3A 44 (5A 4)
Firglades Ct. HU3: Hull . . . 3H 43

First La. HU10: Anla, Hess . . . 2H 41
  (not continuous)
  HU13: Hess . . . 5H 41
  HU15: S'th C . . . 3D 34
Fir Trees HU10: Anla . . . 2E 41
Fisher Cl. HU10: Will . . . 4E 25
Fishermore Av. HU13: Hess . . . 6G 41
Fishermans Wlk. HU3: Hull . . . 4H 43
Fisher Sq. HU17: Bev . . . 5D 6
Fish St. HU1: Hull . . . 3C 44 (5E 5)
Fishwick Av. HU13: Hess . . . 1F 53
Fitness First Health Club . . . 3B 28
Fitzroy St. HU5: Hull . . . 4A 28
Flag Wlk. HU6: Hull . . . 4H 17
Flaxdale Ct. HU5: Hull . . . 5D 26
Flaxton Rd. HU5: Hull . . . 5C 26
Fleet Bus. Pk. HU13: Hess . . . 1G 53
Fleet Ct. HU5: Hull . . . 4B 28
Fleet Gth. HU12: Hed . . . 2F 49
Fleetgate DN18: Bart H . . . 3E 55
Flemingate HU17: Bev . . . 5E 7
Flemingdale HU7: Brans . . . 5C 18
Fleming Wlk. HU4: Hull . . . 6C 42
Fleming Wlk HU16: Cott . . . 2H 25
  (off Parkway, The)
Fletcher Cl. HU13: Hess . . . 6F 41
Fletcher Ga. HU12: Hed . . . 2E 49
Flinton Gro. HU9: Hull . . . 5B 30
Flinton St. HU3: Hull (not continuous) . . . 4G 43
Floral Av. HU3: Hull . . . 3E 43
  (off Seymour St.)
  HU9: Hull . . . 5G 29
  (off Rensburg St.)
Florence Av. HU3: Hull . . . 3G 43
  HU13: Hess . . . 1G 53
Florence Ct. HU5: Hull . . . 4H 27
Florence Gro. HU8: Hull . . . 3D 28
  (off Lorraine St.)
Florence Nightingale Ct.
  HU5: Hull . . . 2E 27
Florin Dr. HU7: King . . . 2A 18
Folkstone Av. HU5: Hull . . . 4B 28
  (off Folkstone St.)
Folkstone St. HU5: Hull . . . 4B 28
Folkton Av. HU16: Cott . . . 2H 25
Folland Way HU9: Hull . . . 1F 45
Forber Av. HU9: Hull . . . 4D 30
Forbes Av. HU6: Hull . . . 4H 17
Ford Cl. HU17: Bev . . . 1E 7
Foredyke Av. HU7: Hull . . . 2D 28
Forester Way HU4: Hull . . . 5C 42
Forge Cl. HU12: Thorn . . . 6G 49
Forge Pl. HU16: Skid . . . 5C 14
Forkedale DN18: Bart H . . . 4D 54
Formby Cl. HU16: Cott . . . 6D 16
Fortune Cl. HU8: Hull . . . 2A 30
Forty Acre HU10: Anla . . . 1G 41
Forty Steps HU10: Anla . . . 1G 41
Fossdale Cl. HU8: Hull . . . 6H 19
Foss Gro. HU8: Hull . . . 6C 20
Foster St. HU5: Hull . . . 4D 28
Foston Gro. HU8: Hull . . . 5B 30
Fotherbie Gth. HU12: Hed . . . 2D 48
Fotherby Wlk. HU17: Bev . . . 3F 7
Fountain Cl. HU13: Hess . . . 5D 40
Fountain Rd. HU2: Hull (not continuous) . . . 5B 28
Fountain St. HU3: Hull . . . 2A 44 (3A 4)
Fountains Way HU17: N'th C . . . 2B 34
Four Acre HU10: Kir E . . . 2D 40
Foxglove Cl. HU7: King . . . 2C 18
Foxhill Cl. HU9: Hull . . . 4F 31
Foxholme Rd. HU7: Brans . . . 5G 19
Foynes Grn. HU8: Hull . . . 1D 30
Fraisthorpe HU6: Hull . . . 4F 17
Frampton Cl. HU7: Brans . . . 6E 19
Frances Av. HU4: Hull . . . 4H 43
Francis St. HU2: Hull . . . 1B 44 (1C 4)
Franklin Av. HU9: Hull . . . 1F 45
  (off Franklin St.)
Franklin St. HU9: Hull . . . 6F 29
Franklin Vs. HU8: Hull . . . 1G 5
Frederick Reckitt Havens
  HU8: Hull . . . 4G 29
Freehold St. HU3: Hull . . . 1A 44 (1A 4)
Freeman Av. HU15: Ello. . . . 6E 37
Freemantle Av. HU9: Hull . . . 4D 30
Freetown Ct. HU6: Hull . . . 6G 17
Freetown Way HU2: Hull . . . 1B 44 (1B 4)
Freightliner Rd. HU3: Hull . . . 6E 43
Frensham Cl. HU7: King . . . 1C 18
Fresh Fields HU15: Brou . . . 6E 37
Friars La. HU17: Bev . . . 5E 7
Friary Wlk. HU17: Bev . . . 5E 7
  (off Eastgate)
Frodsham St. HU9: Hull . . . 1C 46
Frome Rd. HU8: Hull . . . 5D 20
Froscoles Cl. HU15: N'th C . . . 1A 34
Fryston Cl. HU15: Ello. . . . 5E 37
Fuchsia Dr. HU4: Hull . . . 6A 42
Fulford Cres.
  DN19: New H. . . . 2A 58
  HU10: Will. . . . 6H 25
Fulford Gro. HU9: Hull . . . 4F 31
Fulmar Cl. HU7: Brans . . . 4G 19

Furness Cl. HU7: Brans. . . . 5D 12
Furniss Ct. DN18: Bart H. . . . 4D 54

G

Gainford Gro. HU9: Hull. . . . 4F 31
Galfrid Rd. HU11: Bil . . . 5G 21
Gallands Cl. HU14: Swan . . . 3F 39
Gallands Rd. HU11: Sproat . . . 2F 23
Galleon Ct. HU3: Hull . . . 2F 45
Galliard Cl. HU3: Hull . . . 4F 43
Gallows La. HU17: Bev . . . 3B 6
GANSTEAD . . . 3E 21
Ganstead Gro. HU9: Hull . . . 4A 30
Ganstead La. HU11: Bil . . . 6E 21
Ganton Av. HU16: Cott . . . 2H 25
Ganton Cl. HU8: Hull . . . 1C 30
Ganton Way HU10: Will. . . . 6G 25
Garbutt Cl. HU12: Prest . . . 4F 33
Gardens, The HU3: Hull . . . 3H 43
  HU4: Hull . . . 1G 29
GARDEN VILLAGE . . . 4F 29
Gardham Cl. HU17: Walk . . . 6A 8
Garfield Cl. HU9: Hull . . . 5E 31
Garholme Vs. HU3: Hull . . . 5G 29
  (off Rensburg St.)
Garland Cl. HU9: Hull . . . 2D 30
Garnet Gro. HU3: Hull . . . 4H 43
Garrick Cl. HU8: Hull . . . 2A 30
Garrison Rd. HU1: Hull. . . . 3D 44 (5F 5)
  HU9: Hull . . . 3D 44 (5G 5)
GARRISON SIDE . . . 2D 44 (4G 5)
Garrison Side HU1: Hull . . . 3D 44 (4G 5)
Garrowby Wlk. HU5: Hull . . . 4B 26
Garth Av. HU11: Bil . . . 5H 21
Garth, The HU9: Hull . . . 4H 41
  HU16: Cott . . . 1H 25
Garton Gro. HU5: Hull . . . 1B 42
Garvey Way HU12: Hed . . . 3G 49
Gatehouse Rd. DN19: Gox . . . 6C 58
Gatwick Gth. HU7: Brans . . . 3E 19
Gatwick Ho. HU7: Brans . . . 3E 19
Gayles M. HU5: Hull . . . 3C 26
Gee St. HU3: Hull . . . 3H 43
Gemsbok Cl. HU4: Hull . . . 6C 42
Geneva Way HU7: Hull . . . 1E 29
George La. HU17: Walk . . . 2C 8
George Odey Ct. HU17: Bev . . . 5E 7
George's Pl. HU1: Hull . . . 2C 44 (3E 5)
Georges St. HU3: Hull . . . 3F 43
  (off Springburn St.)
George St. DN18: Bart H . . . 3E 55
  HU1: Hull. . . . 2C 44 (3D 4)
  HU12: Hed . . . 2E 49
  HU16: Cott . . . 5H 15
  HU17: Bev . . . 4E 7
George Yd. HU1: Hull . . . 2D 44 (3F 5)
Georgina Cl. DN18: Bart H . . . 5D 54
German Nook La. HU17: Wood . . . 3E 11
Gershwin Av. HU4: Anla . . . 4A 42
Gibraltar Way HU7: King . . . 3A 18
Gibson La. HU14: Welt . . . 4A 50
Gibson St. HU2: Hull . . . 6C 28
Gifford Cl. HU7: Brans . . . 6D 12
Gilbert Av. HU3: Hull . . . 3E 43
Gildane HU6: Hull . . . 4D 16
Gillamoor Cl. HU8: Hull . . . 5H 19
Gillett St. HU3: Hull . . . 4G 43
Gilling M. HU3: Hull . . . 3C 26
Gillshill Rd. HU8: Hull . . . 3G 29
Gillyon Cl. HU17: Bev. . . . 5G 7
  (off Bielby Dr.)
GIPSYVILLE . . . 5D 42
Gisburn Rd. HU13: Hess . . . 6G 41
Glade, The HU17: Bev. . . . 5G 7
Gladstone St. HU3: Hull . . . 2H 43
  HU13: Hess . . . 1F 53
Gladstone Vs. HU9: Hull . . . 5F 29
  (off Holland St.)
Gladys Vs. HU5: Hull . . . 5E 29
  (off Brecon St.)
Glaisdale HU3: Hull . . . 2E 43
  HU5: Hull. . . . 4H 27
  (off Goddard Av.)
Glaisdale Gro. HU9: Hull . . . 6A 30
Glamis Rd. HU13: Hess . . . 6G 41
Glanford Gro. DN19: Bar H . . . 5F 57
Glasgow St. HU3: Hull . . . 3F 43
Glasshouse Row HU8: Hull . . . 5D 28
Glebe Cl. HU7: Waw . . . 4A 12
Glebe Dr. HU11: Bil . . . 6H 21
Glebe Rd. HU7: Hull . . . 2D 28
  HU7: Waw . . . 4H 11
Glebe Way DN18: Bart H. . . . 6E 55
Glencoe Av. HU3: Hull (off Clyde St.) . . . 3E 43
Glencoe St. HU3: Hull . . . 2E 43
Glencoe Vs. HU3: Hull . . . 6G 29
  (off New Bridge Rd.)
Glencourt HU6: Hull . . . 6D 16
Glendale Cl. HU10: Kir E . . . 5D 24
Gleneagles Cres. DN19: New H . . . 2A 58

Gleneagles Pk. HU8: Hull 5A 20
Glenfell Cl. HU7: Hull 1G 29
Glenfield Dr. HU10: Kir E 5C 24
Glenhall Ri. DN19: Bar H 5E 57
Glenham Dr. HU10: Will 6G 25
Glenrock Pk. HU15: Brou 5C 36
Glen, The HU10: Kir E 5C 24
   HU17: Bev 6G 7
Glenwood Cl. HU4: Hull 3F 29
Glenwood Dr. HU4: Anla 2A 42
Globe M. *HU17: Bev* 4D 6
            (off Sow Hill Rd.)
Gloucester Rd. HU10: Will 4F 25
Gloucester St. HU4: Hull 5D 42
Goathland Cl. HU4: Hull 2F 43
Goble Cl. DN18: Bart H 5G 55
Godbold Cl. HU17: Bev 4F 7
Goddard Av. HU5: Hull 4F 27
Goddard Cl. DN18: Bart H 5D 54
Godman's La. HU10: Kir E 1C 40
Goldcrest Cl. HU7: Brans 4G 19
Golden Ct. HU9: Hull 3B 30
Golden Gro. HU11: Bil 6E 21
Golf Links Dr. HU15: Brou 5C 36
Golf Links Rd. HU6: Hull 1D 26
Goodfell Rd. HU17: Bev 2F 7
Goodhand Cl. DN18: Bart H 5H 55
Goodhart Rd. HU7: Brans 4E 19
Goodmanham Way HU16: Cott 6F 15
Goodrich Cl. HU2: Hull 5B 28
Goodwin Pde. HU3: Hull 3A 44 (5A 4)
Goodwood Cl. HU17: Bev 2D 6
Gordan Pk. HU16: Cott 6B 16
Gordon Av. HU3: Hull 4F 43
   HU9: Hull (off Rensburg St.) 5G 29
Gordon St. HU3: Hull 3G 43
Gorsedale HU7: Brans 5B 18
Gorthorpe HU6: Hull 4F 17
Gorton Rd. HU10: Anla, Will 1F 41
Gosport Wlk. HU4: Hull 4H 41
Gothenburg Way HU7: Hull 6B 18
Goths La. HU17: Bev 3E 7
Gouldesborough Ct. HU5: Hull 3H 27
Goulding Ct. HU17: Bev 4D 6
Goulton St. HU3: Hull 5H 43
Gower Rd. HU4: Hull 5A 42
GOXHILL 5C 58
Goxhill Rd. DN19: Bar H 5G 57
Goxhill Station (Rail) 5C 58
Grafton St. HU5: Hull 4H 27
Graham Av. *HU3: Hull (off Airlie St.)* 3G 43
   HU4: Hull 6A 42
Grammar School Rd. HU5: Hull 4D 26
Grammar School Yd. HU1: Hull . . . 3C 44 (4E 5)
Grampian Way HU7: Brans 6D 12
Granary Cl. HU15: Ello 3E 37
Grandale HU7: Brans. 5B 18
Grange Av. DN18: Bart H 4E 55
Grange Cl. HU2: Hull 6C 28
Grange Cres. HU10: Anla. 2F 41
Grange Dr. HU16: Cott 5H 15
Grange La. HU14: N'th F 2E 51
   HU17: Mole 1E 7
Grange Pk. HU14: Swan 5F 39
   HU15: Brou 5D 36
Grange Pk. La. HU10: Will 4C 24
Grange Rd. HU9: Hull 3E 31
   HU12: Thorn 6H 49
Grangeside Av. HU6: Hull 1E 27
Grange Way HU17: Bev 1B 6
Grantchester Cl. HU5: Hull 5B 26
Grantham Av. HU7: King 1C 18
Grantley Gro. HU9: Hull 4D 30
Granville Av. *HU3: Hull* 3E 43
            (off Clyde St.)
   HU5: Hull 4G 27
          (off Reynoldson St.)
Granville Gro. *HU3: Hull* 3F 43
            (off Greek St.)
   HU5: Hull 4B 28
          (off Folkstone St.)
Granville St. HU3: Hull 2F 43
Granville Vs. *HU5: Hull* 4B 28
          (off Sculcoats La.)
Grape La. *HU12: Hed.* 2F 49
           (off Baxter Ga.)
Grasby Rd. HU8: Hull 2B 30
Grassam Cl. HU12: Prest. 5F 33
Grassdale Pk. HU15: Brou 6C 36
Grassington Cl. HU7: Brans 1C 18
Gravel Pit Rd. DN18: Bart H 4B 54
Grayburn Ct. HU17: Bev 4D 6
Grayburn La. HU17: Bev 5D 6
Great Field La. HU9: Hull 6D 30
Gt. Gutter La. HU5: Hull 5A 24
Gt. Gutter La. (East) HU10: Will 4D 24
Gt. Gutter La. (West) HU10: Will 5B 24
Gt. Hornton St. HU3: Hull 3H 43
Gt. Passage St. HU1: Hull 3B 44 (6B 4)
Gt. Thornton St. HU3: Hull 2A 44 (4A 4)
Gt. Union St. HU9: Hull 1D 44 (2G 5)
Greek St. HU3: Hull 3E 43
Green Acres HU10: Kir E 2D 40

Greenacres HU14: Swan 3H 39
Green Cl. HU6: Hull 6E 17
Greendale Ct. HU16: Cott 1F 25
Greenfield HU5: Hull 4B 26
Greenfield Gth. HU6: Hull 3G 17
Greenfields DN19: Gox 5D 58
Greengate La. DN19: Gox 5D 58
Greenhow Cl. HU8: Hull 5H 19
Green Island HU11: Bil 1F 31
Green La. DN18: Bart H 4G 55
   DN19: Bar H. 5F 57
   HU2: Hull. 6C 28
   HU10: Will 2C 24
   HU13: Hess 1H 53
   HU14: Welt 1A 50
   HU16: Cott. 6F 15
   HU16: Skid, Will 1C 24
Green Marsh Rd. HU12: Thorn 6G 49
Green Rd. HU12: Hed 3D 48
Greens La. HU7: Waw 4A 12
Greenstiles La. HU14: Swan. 3H 39
Green, The HU9: Hull 6H 29
   HU11: Sproat. 2F 23
   HU14: Swan. 3F 39
Greenway DN18: Bart H 3G 55
   HU4: Hull. 4D 42
Green Way HU13: Hess 2F 53
Greenways HU14: N'th F 6E 39
Greenway, The HU4: Hull 2B 42
Greenwich Av. HU9: Hull 2D 30
Greenwood Av. HU6: Hull 1D 26
   HU17: Bev 4F 7
Greenwood Gdns. HU17: Bev 1E 7
Greville Rd. HU12: Hed 2G 49
Greyfriars Cres. HU17: Bev. 5C 6
Greygarth Cl. HU7: Brans 6C 12
Greylees Av. HU6: Hull 4G 17
Greystone Av. HU5: Hull 1D 42
Grey St. HU2: Hull 1A 44 (1A 4)
Griffin Rd. HU9: Hull 3D 30
Grimscott Cl. HU7: Brans 3B 18
Grimston Rd. HU10: Anla 2H 41
Grimston St. HU1: Hull 1C 44 (2E 5)
Grindell St. HU9: Hull 6G 29
Grinton Av. HU5: Hull 6G 27
Grizedale HU7: Brans 5C 18
Grosmont Cl. HU8: Hull 5H 19
Grosvenor Pl. HU17: Bev 5C 6
Grosvenor St. HU3: Hull 6A 28 (1A 4)
GROVEHILL 5H 7
Grove Cl. HU17: Bev 3E 7
Grove Hill HU13: Hess 1F 53
Grovehill Ind. Est. HU17: Bev. 5H 7
Grovehill Rd. HU17: Bev 4E 7
Grove Ho. HU10: Anla 2G 41
Grove Ho. Vw. HU5: Hull 3A 28
Grove Pk. HU17: Bev. 3D 6
Grove St. HU5: Hull 5A 28
Grove, The DN19: Bar H 5E 57
   HU8: Hull 3F 29
Grundale HU10: Kir E 2D 40
Guildford Av. HU8: Hull 2G 29
Guildford Cl. HU17: Bev 1F 9
Guildhall Rd. HU1: Hull 2C 44 (3E 5)
Guillemot Cl. HU4: Hull 6C 42
Gullane Dr. HU6: Hull 3G 17
Guy Gth. HU12: Hed 2G 49
Guy's Cres. HU8: Hull 1B 30

H

Hackforth Wlk. HU5: Hull 2C 26
Hackness Gro. HU5: Hull. 6C 26
Haddon St. HU3: Hull 4E 43
Hadleigh Cl. HU7: Hull 5B 28
Haggs La. HU10: Will 3E 25
Haldane Ct. HU4: Hull 6C 42
Haldenby Ct. HU14: Swan 4F 39
Hales Cres. HU12: Hed 3D 48
Hales Entry HU9: Hull 2F 45
Haller St. HU9: Hull 6H 29
Hallgarth Way HU17: Bev 5E 7
Hallgate HU16: Cott 6H 15
Halliwell Cl. HU9: Hull 6F 31
Hall Pk. HU14: Swan. 3H 39
Hall Rd. HU6: Hull. 4D 16
   HU11: Sproat. 2F 23
Halls Ct. DN18: Bart H 5H 55
Hall St. HU2: Hull 1A 44 (1A 4)
Hall Wlk. HU15: Welt 4G 37
   HU16: Cott. 6B 16
   HU17: Walk 5A 8
Haltemprice Crematorium HU10: Will . . . 3D 24
Haltemprice Leisure Cen. 1F 41
Haltemprice St. HU3: Hull 3E 43
Halyard Cft. HU1: Hull 3C 44 (6D 4)
Hambledon Cl. HU7: Brans 6E 19
Hambling Dr. HU17: Bev 1D 6
Hamburg Rd. HU7: Hull 1D 28
Hamilton Dr. HU8: Hull 6A 20
Hamling Way HU4: Hull 6C 42

Hamlyn Av. HU4: Hull 1D 42
Hamlyn Dr. HU4: Hull 2D 42
Hammersmith Rd. HU8: Hull 1A 30
Hammond Rd. HU17: Bev 3F 7
Hampshire St. HU4: Hull. 5D 42
Hampstead Ct. HU3: Hull 5A 28
Hampton Cl. HU6: Hull. 5F 17
Hamshaw Ct. HU3: Hull 4H 43
Hands-on History Mus. 2C 44 (4E 5)
Hanley Rd. HU9: Hull 3C 26
Hanover Ct. HU4: Hull 2B 44 (4B 4)
   HU15: N'th C 2B 34
   HU17: Bev 4F 7
Hanover Sq. HU1: Hull 2C 44 (3E 5)
Ha'penny Bri. Way HU9: Hull 3E 45 (5H 5)
Harbour Way HU9: Hull 2F 45
Harcourt Dr. HU9: Hull 6F 29
Hardane HU6: Hull 4D 16
Hardington Cl. HU8: Hull. 5C 20
Hardwick Av. HU5: Hull 6G 27
Hardwick St. HU5: Hull. 6G 27
Hardys Rd. HU12: Hed 3D 48
Hardy St. HU5: Hull 3H 27
Harewood HU17: Mole 2A 6
Harewood Av. HU9: Hull 3B 30
Hargreave Cl. HU17: Bev 2D 6
Harland Rd. HU15: Ello 4E 37
Harland Way HU16: Cott 4D 14
Harlech Cl. HU7: Brans 5C 12
Harleigh Av. HU7: Hull 1E 29
Harlequin Dr. HU7: King. 2C 18
Harlestone Ct. HU8: Hull 1C 30
Harley Av. *HU9: Hull* 6F 29
           (off Brazil St.)
Harley St. HU2: Hull 6B 28
Harlow Cl. HU8: Hull 6D 20
Harome Gro. HU5: Hull 1B 42
Harpham Gro. HU9: Hull 5B 30
Harpings Rd. HU5: Hull 5E 27
Harrier Rd. DN18: Bart H 2G 55
Harrington Ct. HU12: Hed 3G 49
Harrison Cl. HU11: Sproat 2F 23
Harris St. HU3: Hull 3E 43
Harrowdyke DN18: Bart H 4E 55
Harrow St. HU3: Hull (not continuous) 4G 43
Harry's Av. *HU3: Hull* 3E 29
           (off Lorraine St.)
Hartford Wlk. HU8: Hull 5D 20
Harthill Dr. HU3: Hull 3H 43
Hartland Cl. HU7: Brans 4C 18
Hartley Bri. HU9: Hull 2E 45
Hartoft Rd. HU5: Hull 4D 26
Hartsholme Pk. HU7: King 2B 18
Harvest Av. DN18: Bart H 5E 55
Harvest Ct. HU17: Bev 4D 6
Harvest Ri. DN19: Bar H 5E 57
Harwood Cl. HU12: Hed. 3F 49
Harwood Dr. HU4: Anla 2A 42
Hase Wlk. *HU13: Hess* 1F 53
          (off Station Rd.)
Haslemere Av. *HU5: Hull.* 4A 28
          (off Melwood Gro.)
Hastings Av. *HU5: Hull* 4B 28
          (off Folkstone St.)
Hastings Gro. HU5: Hull 1D 42
Hastings Rd. HU12: Thorn 6G 49
Hatfield Hi-Tech Pk. HU3: Hull 5H 43
Hatfield Wlk. HU8: Hull 5F 29
Hathersage Rd. HU8: Hull 2F 29
Hauxwell Gro. HU8: Hull 1A 30
Havelock St. HU3: Hull 4F 43
Haven Av. HU5: Brou. 6C 36
Haven Basin Rd. HU12: Hed 4E 49
Haven Gth. HU12: Hed 2G 49
   HU15: Brou 6C 36
Haven Mdw. DN18: Bart H 1E 55
Haven Rd. DN18: Bart H 3E 55
Haven Side HU12: Hed 4E 49
Haven Staithes HU12: Hed 3E 49
Haven, The HU3: Hull 2E 45 (4H 5)
   HU17: Walk 2C 8
Haverflats Cl. HU5: Hull 5E 27
Hawes Wlk. HU5: Hull 3C 26
Hawkesbury St. Hull 3H 29
Hawkshead Grn. HU4: Hull 1B 42
Haworth St. HU6: Hull. 2H 27
Hawthorn Av. HU3: Hull 2E 43
   HU18: Bart H 2E 43
Hawthorne Av HU10: Will 5F 25
Hawthorne St. HU5: Hull 5E 25
Hawthorne Gdns. DN19: Gox 4D 58
Hawthorne Ho. HU17: Bev 1E 7
Hawthorn Ri. HU13: Hess 5C 40
Hawthorn Ga. DN18: Bart H 5G 55
Hawthorn Ri. DN19: Bar H 5E 57
Hawthorns, The HU8: Hull 5H 19
Hawthorn Unit Factory Est.
   HU3: Hull. 4E 43
Hayburn Av. HU5: Hull 4D 26
Haydock Gth. HU7: Brans 2D 18
Haydon Cl. HU10: Will. 6E 25
Haye's Av. *HU5: Hull (off Ella St.)* 4G 27
Haymarket Cl. HU8: Hull 2A 30
Haymer Dr. HU12: Hed 3G 49

Hayton Gro. HU4: Hull 4C 42
Hayward Cl. HU17: Walk. 2C 8
Hazelbarrow Dr. HU10: Will . . . 1G 41
Hazel Gro. HU3: Hull 3A 44 (4A 4)
Headlands Cl. HU13: Hess 6D 40
Heads La. HU13: Hess 6D 40
Hearfield Ter. HU13: Hess 1G 53
Heathcote St. HU6: Hull 2A 28
Heather Cl. HU5: Hull 5C 26
Hebden Av. HU8: Hull 1C 30
Hebrides Cl. HU3: Hull 3B 30
Hedgerow Cl. DN19: Bar H . . . 5E 57
Hedgerow Cl. HU6: Hull 4G 17
Hedley Cl. HU15: S'th C 4B 34
HEDON 2E 49
Hedon Mus. 2E 49
Hedon Rd. HU9: Hull 2E 45 (3H 5)
Hellyers Ct. HU4: Hull 6C 42
Helm Dr. HU9: Hull 2F 45
Helms Av. HU12: Prest 5E 33
Helmsdale HU5: Hull 5G 29
Helmsley Gro. HU5: Hull 1B 42
Helperby Wlk. HU5: Hull. 3D 26
Helsinki Rd. HU7: Hull 1C 28
Helvellyn Cl. HU7: Brans 1D 18
Hemble Way HU7: King. 2B 18
Hemmingway Wlk. HU13: Hess . . 5E 41
Hemswell Av. HU9: Hull 6E 31
Hengate HU17: Bev 4D 6
Henley Dr. HU9: Hull 5H 29
Henley Vs. HU5: Hull 4A 28
                    (off Adderbury Gro.)
Henry Vernone Ct. HU1: Hull. 6E 5
                    (off Pier St.)
Henson Vs. HU5: Hull 5A 28
Hepscott Wlk. HU8: Hull 6E 21
                    (off Wansbeck Rd.)
Hepworth's Arc. HU1: Hull. 4E 5
Herbert Pollard Ho. HU9: Hull . . 5F 31
Hereford Cl. HU17: Bev 1F 9
Hereford St. HU4: Hull 5D 42
Hermes Cl. HU9: Hull 2D 30
HERON 3E 55
Heron Cl. HU12: Hed 3D 48
Heron St. HU3: Hull 3G 43
Hertfordshire Cl. HU5: Hull . . . 5C 26
Heslerton Av. HU16: Cott 2H 25
HESSLE 1F 53
HESSLE CLIFF 3E 53
Hessle Rd. HU1: Hull 3A 44 (6A 4)
    HU3: Hull (not continuous) . . 4E 43 (6A 4)
    HU4: Hull. 6A 42
Hessle Station (Rail) 2E 53
Hessle Vw. DN18: Bart H 4D 54
Hewson's La. DN18: Bart H . . . 2E 55
Hickling Cl. HU10: Anla 2H 41
Higham Cl. HU8: Hull 5H 19
Higham Way HU15: Ello. 6F 37
Highcourt HU6: Hull 5D 16
Highdales HU10: Kir E 6D 24
High Farm Ct. HU11: Bil 5G 21
Highfield HU7: Hull 6G 19
Highfield Cl. HU7: Hull 6G 19
Highfield Cres. DN18: Bart H . . 4G 55
    HU11: Bil. 5G 21
Highfield Ri. HU12: Prest 4F 33
Highfield Rd. HU17: Bev 2E 7
Highfields DN19: Bar H 5E 57
    HU15: S'th C 3E 35
Highfield Way HU14: N'th F . . . 2D 50
Highgate HU17: Bev 5E 7
Highgate Cl. HU17: Bev 1B 30
Highgate Ct. HU17: Bev 5E 7
                    (off Highgate)
Highgrove Way HU7: King 1B 18
High Mdws. HU10: Kir E 6D 24
High Rd. HU15: Ello 3F 37
High St. DN18: Bart H 3E 55
    DN19: Bar H. 5F 57
    HU1: Hull 2D 44 (2F 5)
    HU14: N'th F 1D 50
Hightrees Mt. HU8: Hull 6H 19
Hilary Gro. HU4: Hull 6A 42
Hilda's Av. HU5: Hull (off Perth St. W.) . . 6F 27
Hildyard Cl. HU10: Anla 2G 41
    HU12: Hed 3F 49
Hill Brow HU10: Kir E 2C 40
Hillcrest HU17: Bev 2B 6
Hillcrest Av. HU13: Hess 6E 41
Hillcrest Dr. HU17: Bev 2C 6
Hilldale Cotts. HU15: S'th C . . . 5C 34
Hillman Rd. HU13: Hess 5G 41
Hill Ri. HU15: Ello 4D 36
Hillside Dr. DN18: Bart H 4D 54
Hill St. HU8: Hull. 4D 28
Hillsway Cl. HU8: Hull 2G 29
Hill Top Vw. HU11: Coni 1G 21
Hilston Gro. HU8: Hull 5B 30
Hinderwell St. HU5: Hull 5H 27
Hinkleton Cl. HU8: Hull 5F 29
Hirncroft Cl. HU8: Hull 5H 19
HMP Hull HU9: Hull 1H 45
Hobart St. HU3: Hull. 3A 44 (5A 4)
Hobson Ct. HU17: Bev (off Sample Av.) . . 3E 7

Hobson Rd. HU15: Ello 4E 37
Hodder Gro. HU8: Hull 6D 20
Hodge Cl. HU7: Hull 1F 45
Hodgson Av. HU17: Bev 3E 7
Hodgson St. HU8: Hull 1D 44 (1F 5)
Hogg La. HU10: Kir E 6C 24
Holborn St. HU8: Hull. . . . 1E 45 (1H 5)
Holbrook Cl. HU7: Hull 2E 29
Holcombe Cl. HU8: Hull 5C 20
Holcroft Gth. HU12: Hed 2F 49
Holderness Cotts. HU12: Paul. . . 6A 48
    HU12: Thorn 5G 49
Holderness Cres. HU17: Bev . . . 3E 7
Holderness Rd. HU8: Hull . . . 1E 45 (1H 5)
    HU9: Hull 1E 45 (1H 5)
Holderness Vs. HU3: Hull 3F 43
                    (off Rhodes St.)
    HU9: Hull 1D 46
Holgate Cl. HU17: Bev 5G 7
Holgate Cl. DN18: Bart H 5G 55
Holgate Pl. HU14: Swan 3G 39
Holland St. HU9: Hull 6F 29
Hollies, The HU5: Hull 3H 27
                    (off Sidmouth St.)
    HU10: Will 4F 25
    HU17: Bev 1E 7
Hollis Ct. HU9: Hull 1F 45
Holly Dr. HU16: Cott 1F 25
Holly Gro. HU8: Hull 4F 29
Holly Hill HU15: Welt 5H 37
Holly Oak Adventure Pk. 1A 16
Hollytree Av. HU5: Hull 1A 42
Hollywell Cl. HU9: Hull 3F 31
Holme Chu. La. HU17: Bev 5F 7
Holme Cres. HU16: Cott 6F 15
Holme Farm HU17: Walk. 5A 8
Holmes La. HU11: Bil 4H 21
Holm Gth. Dr. HU8: Hull 2C 30
Holmpton Gro. HU9: Hull 5C 30
Holtby Cl. HU9: Hull 1D 30
Holwell Rd. HU7: Brans, Hull . . 2D 18
Holwick M. HU5: Hull 2C 26
Holydyke DN18: Bart H 3E 55
Holyrood Av. HU3: Hull 1E 43
                    (off Spring Bank W.)
    HU9: Hull 6F 29
                    (off Brazil St.)
Holyrood Vs. HU9: Hull 5G 29
                    (New Bri. Rd.)
    HU9: Hull 1F 45
                    (off Franklin St.)
Home Cl. HU4: Hull 3B 42
Home Grn. HU16: Cott 1H 25
Homestead Rd. HU12: Thorn . . . 6H 49
Homethorpe HU6: Hull 4F 17
Honeysuckle Pl. HU15: Brou . . . 6E 37
Honiton Rd. HU7: Brans 4D 18
Hood St. HU8: Hull 6D 28
Hooks La. HU12: Thorn. 6G 49
Hopewell Rd. HU8: Hull 3C 30
Hop Gro. HU5: Hull (off Chesnut Av.) . . 4H 27
Hopkins St. HU9: Hull 3C 30
Hopper Cl. DN18: Bart H 5G 55
Hoppers, The DN18: Bart H . . . 3F 55
Hopwood Cl. HU3: Hull 6A 28
Horbury Av. HU9: Hull 4C 30
Horkstow Rd. DN18: Bart H . . . 6C 54
Hornbeam Ct. HU16: Cott 1A 26
Hornbeams Ct. HU7: Hull 6G 19
Hornbeam Wlk. HU16: Cott. . . . 1A 26
Hornby Gro. HU9: Hull 3D 30
Hornsea Vs. HU5: Hull 4B 28
                    (off Folkstone St.)
Horsegate DN19: Gox 4E 59
Hotham Dr. HU5: Hull 6A 26
Hotham Rd. HU15: N'th C 1A 34
Hotham Rd. Nth. HU5: Hull . . . 3D 26
Hotham Rd. Sth. HU5: Hull . . . 6A 26
Hotham Sq. HU17: Bev 4G 7
Hotham St. HU9: Hull 1G 45
Hotton Cl. HU9: Hull 5D 30
Houghton Wlk. HU5: Hull 4B 26
Hourne Ct. HU13: Hess 6F 41
Hourne, The HU13: Hess 6F 41
Housemartin Dr. HU8: Hull . . . 4G 19
Houston Dr. HU5: Hull 3A 28
Hove Rd. HU5: Hull 5B 26
Hovingham Cl. HU8: Hull 5H 19
Howdale Rd. HU8: Hull 5G 19
Howden Croft Hill HU15: Elle . . 6D 34
Howe La. DN19: Gox. 5C 58
Howsham Cl. HU8: Hull 1E 31
Hoylake Cl. HU16: Cott 1D 26
Hucknall Gth. HU7: Brans 3E 19
Hudson Cl. HU13: Hess 1E 53
Hudson Gdns. HU5: Hull 5A 28
Hudson St. HU8: Hull 6A 28
HULL & EAST RIDING BUPA HOSPITAL . . 3F 41
Hull & East Riding Mus. 2D 44 (4F 5)
Hull Arena. 3B 44 (6C 4)
HULL BRIDGE 1H 7
Hull Bri. Rd. HU17: Bev, Tick . . 2E 7
Hull Bus. Cen. HU1: Hull . . . 2C 44 (3E 5)

Hull Bus. Pk. HU8: Hull. 5D 28
Hull City F.C. (Kingston Communication Stadium)
                    . . . . . 1G 43
Hull Indoor Sports Cen. 5E 27
Hull Kingston Rovers R.L.F.C. (Craven Pak. Stadium)
                    . . . . . 6D 30
Hull Maritime Mus. 2C 44 (3D 4)
HULL MATERNITY HOSPITAL . . . 6B 30
Hull New Theatre 1C 44 (2D 4)
HULL NUFFIELD HOSPITAL 6E 15
Hull Rd. HU4: Anla 2A 42
    HU5: Hull. 1C 26
    HU6: Hull. 1C 26
    HU10: Anla 2G 41
    HU11: Coni 2F 21
    HU12: Hed, Salt. 2G 47
    HU13: Hess 1G 53
    HU16: Cott. 1C 26
    HU17: Bev, Wood 4G 7
HULL ROYAL INFIRMARY 2A 44
Hull R.L.F.C. (Kingston Communication Stadium)
                    . . . . . 1G 43
Hull Screen 1B 44 (2F 5)
Hull Station (Rail) 2B 44 (3B 4)
Hull Truck Theatre 1A 44 (2A 4)
Hull Vikings Speedway (Craven Pk. Stadium)
                    . . . . . 6D 30
Humber Bri. HU13: Hess. 4D 52
Humber Bridge Country Pk. . . . 2C 52
Humber Bri. Ind. Est. DN18: Bart H . . 2H 55
Humber Bridge Water Ski Club . . 1C 56
Humber Cres. HU15: Ello 6E 37
Humberdale Cl. HU14: Swan . . . 4G 39
Humberdale Dr. HU14: N'th F . . 1H 51
Humber Dock St. HU1: Hull . . 3C 44 (5E 5)
Humber Ind. Est. HU14: Welt . . 2A 50
Humber Pl. HU1: Hull. . . . 3C 44 (6E 5)
Humber Rd. DN18: Bart H 2E 55
    HU14: N'th F 3E 51
Humber St. HU1: Hull 3C 44 (5E 5)
Humber Ter. DN18: Bart H 1E 55
Humber Vw. DN18: Bart H 4D 54
    HU1: Hull. 3D 44 (5G 5)
    HU14: Swan 4G 39
Humber Way HU13: Hess 6E 41
Humbleton Rd. HU12: Prest . . . 1H 33
Hungate DN18: Bart H 3E 55
Hungate Ho. DN18: Bart H 3E 55
                    (off Hungate)
Hungerhills Dr. HU11: Bil 5H 21
Hunsley Av. HU5: Hull 5A 26
Hunsley Rd. HU17: Walk. 6A 8
Hunter Cl. HU12: Prest 5F 33
Hunter Gro. HU3: Hull 4F 43
Hunter Rd. HU15: Ello. 5D 36
Huntingdon St. HU4: Hull 5D 42
Huntley Dr. HU5: Hull 5F 27
Hurley Cl. HU8: Hull 3A 30
Hurn Cl. HU8: Hull. 6H 19
Hurn Vw. HU17: Bev 3C 6
Hursthwaite Rd.
    HU15: Brou 6F 37
Hutton Cl. HU5: Hull 4D 26
Hutt St. HU3: Hull 6A 28 (1A 4)
Huzard Cl. HU17: Walk 2C 8
Hykeham Cl. HU17: King. 1C 18
Hymers Av. HU3: Hull 1G 43
Hyperion St. HU9: Hull 1D 44 (2G 5)

I

Icehouse Rd. HU3: Hull 2A 44 (4A 4)
Icelandic Cl. HU3: Hull 3H 43
                    (off Linnaeus St.)
Idas Cl. HU9: Hull 3D 44 (5G 5)
Ilchester Cl. HU7: Brans 6E 19
Ilford Rd. HU5: Hull 5B 26
Ilkley Vs. HU9: Hull (off Estcourt St.) . . 6G 29
Ilthorpe HU6: Hull 4F 17
Impala Way HU4: Hull 5C 42
Imperial Cl. HU4: Hull 3B 30
Ingland Cl. HU9: Hull 5C 30
Ingleby Cl. HU8: Hull 5A 20
Inglefield Cl. HU17: Bev 2D 8
INGLEMIRE 1E 27
Inglemire Av. HU6: Hull 2H 27
Inglemire La. HU6: Hull 1C 26
    HU16: Cott, Hull 1C 26
Ingleton HU15: Ello 5E 37
Ingleton Av. HU4: Hull 2B 42
Inglewood Dr. HU4: Anla 2A 42
Ingmires HU15: Welt 5G 37
Ingram Av. HU11: Bil. 6G 21
Ings La. HU6: Wood. 1F 17
    HU14: N'th F 3E 51
    HU15: Brou 6D 36
    HU15: Elle 6C 34
Ings Rd. HU7: Hull 1G 29
    HU7: King 1H 17
    HU8: Hull. 1G 29
    HU17: Mole. 1C 6
Ings Shop. Cen. HU8: Hull . . . 2A 30

Inmans Rd. HU12: Hed 2F 49
Innescourt Rd. Hull. 5D 16
Innsworth Gth. HU7: Brans 3E 19
Inverewe Way HU16: Cott. 1G 25
Iona Cl. HU8: Hull 5H 19
Ireland Wlk. HU4: Anla 4A 42
Irene Av. HU8: Hull. 5F 29
Irene Gro. HU3: Hull .3G 43
Irenes Av. HU5: Hull (off Perth St. W.) 6F 27
Irene's Av. HU8: Hull (off Lorraine St.) 3E 29
Iridium Ct. HU13: Hess. 1H 53
Isis Ct. HU9: Hull 3E 45 (5H 5)
Island, The DN19: Bar H (off Cross St.) 4F 57
Isledane HU6: Hull. 4E 17
Itlings La. HU13: Hess 1G 53
Ivanhoe Vs. HU7: Hull (off Estcourt St.) 6H 29
Iveson Cl. HU12: Hed 2E 49
Iveson Lodge HU12: Hed (off Fletcher Ga.) . . .2E 49
Ivybridge Wlk. HU9: Hull. 5F 31
Ivy Dene Vs. HU9: Hull (off Estcourt St.) 6G 29
Ivy Gro. HU5: Hull (off Perth St.) 6F 27
Ivyleigh Av. HU3: Hull (off Pretoria St.) 2F 43
Ivy Ter. HU8: Hull (off Barnsley St.) 5E 29
Ivy Vs. HU9: Hull (off Middleburg St.) 6G 29
  HU9: Hull (off Rosmead St.) 6G 29

J

Jack Harrison Ct. HU3: Hull 5A 28
Jackson St. HU3: Hull 4A 44
Jack Taylor La. HU17: Bev 4G 7
Jade Gro. HU3: Hull. .4F 43
Jalland Lodge HU9: Hull 3C 30
Jalland St. HU8: Hull. 5F 29
James Ingle M. HU17: Bev 5F 7
James Niven Ct. HU9: Hull 5G 29
Jameson St. HU1: Hull. 2B 44 (3C 4)
  (not continuous)
James Reckitt Av. HU8: Hull 5E 29
Jarrat St. HU1: Hull 1C 44 (2D 4)
Jasmine Cl. DN19: Gox. 4D 58
Jasmine Gro. HU7: King 2C 18
Jason Gth. HU7: Brans 3F 19
Jefferson Cl. HU17: Bev 2D 6
Jefferson Ct. HU9: Hull 6F 29
Jefferson Dr. HU15: Brou 5D 36
Jendale HU7: Brans. .4C 18
Jenning St. HU8: Hull 6D 28
Jenny Brough La. HU13: Hess 4B 40
Jenny Brough Mdws. HU13: Hess. 5C 40
Jenthorpe HU6: Hull. 4F 17
Jervis Rd. HU9: Hull .1E 31
Jesmond Dene HU9: Hull 5G 29
  (off Rustenburg St.)
Jesmond Gdns. HU9: Hull. 5G 29
Jesmond Rd. HU16: Cott. 6B 16
Jetcourt HU6: Hull. 5D 16
Jill Gro. HU13: Hess .1G 53
Jipdane HU6: Hull 4E 17
Jobsons Cl. HU15: S'th C 4B 34
John Gray Ct. HU10: Will. 5E 25
John Harrison's Cl. DN19: Bar H. 4F 57
John Newton Way HU7: Brans 3A 18
Johnson Ct. HU12: Hed. 3D 48
Johnston Ct. HU17: Bev 1C 6
John St. HU2: Hull 1C 44 (2D 4)
Joscelyn Av. HU7: Hull 3A 18
Jubilee Sq. HU2: Hull 1C 44 (1E 5)
Julian Cl. HU5: Hull .1H 41
Julian's Wlk. HU10: Anla 2G 41
Junction Sq. DN18: Bart H 3E 55
Junella Cl. HU3: Hull .4F 43
Juniper Chase HU17: Bev 4C 6

K

Karelia Ct. HU4: Anla 3A 42
Kathleen Rd. HU8: Hull 4D 28
Katrine Cl. HU7: Hull. 1G 29
Keble Gro. HU8: Hull 5B 30
Kedrum Rd. HU9: Hull. 5A 30
Keel Ct. HU17: Bev 5G 7
Keel Rd. HU6: Hull 4H 17
Kelberdale Cl. HU7: King 1C 18
Keldgate HU17: Bev 5D 6
Keldgate Cl. HU17: Bev 5D 6
Keldgate Rd. HU16: Cott 5E 15
  HU17: Bev 6B 6
Keldgate Shopping Cen. HU17: Bev 1F 9
Keldmarsh Nature Reserve 6D 6
Kelgate Cl. HU8: Hull. 5H 19
Kelston Dr. HU13: Hess. 5G 41
Kelvin St. HU9: Hull .4H 29
Kemp Rd. HU14: Swan 5F 39
Kempton Cl. HU17: Bev 2D 6
Kempton Rd. HU3: Hull. 2D 42
Kendal Ho. HU3: Hull 2H 43
Kendal Way HU4: Hull. 1B 42
Kenilworth Av. HU5: Hull 2E 27
Kenmore Dr. HU6: Hull 3G 17

Kennet Rd. HU8: Hull 6D 20
Kennington Wlk. HU16: Cott. 6C 16
Kensington Gro. HU3: Hull 2F 43
  (off Granville St.)
Kent Cl. HU9: Hull 1F 45
Kentmere Cl. HU7: Brans 5D 12
Kent Rd. HU16: Cott .1H 25
Kenwardly Rd. HU10: Will 6F 25
Kerdane HU6: Hull 4E 17
Kerry Dr. HU10: Kir E .2C 40
Kerry Pit Way HU10: Kir E 2D 40
Kesteven Way HU7: King. 1B 18
Kestrel Av. HU7: Brans, Hull 4G 19
Keswick Gdns. HU6: Hull. 6D 16
Kettlethorpe Dr. HU15: Brou 5D 36
Kettlewell Ct. HU7: Brans 6C 12
Ketwell La. HU12: Hed 2E 49
Keynes Pk. HU7: King. 2B 18
Kidd La. HU15: Welt .4G 37
Kilburn Av. HU2: Hull. 6B 28
Kilcoy Dr. HU7: King .1B 18
Kildale Cl. HU8: Hull. 6H 19
Kiln Beck Bus. Pk. HU17: Bev 5H 7
Kiln Gro. HU10: N'th C 1A 34
Kiln Row HU10: N'th C 2A 34
Kilnsea Gro. HU9: Hull. 4A 30
Kilnwick Av. HU5: Hull. 4B 26
Kilton Ct. HU8: Hull. .5G 19
Kilvin Dr. HU17: Bev 2F 7
Kimberley Av. HU3: Hull (off Seymour St.) 3E 43
Kimberley St. HU3: Hull 1H 43
Kimmeridge Cl. HU7: Brans 6E 19
Kinderscout Cl. HU7: Brans 1C 18
King Charles Cl. HU10: Will 1F 41
King Edwards Ter. HU15: Brou 6C 36
King Edward St. HU1: Hull 2B 44 (3C 4)
  HU2: Hull 2B 44 (3C 4)
Kingfisher Cl. HU7: Brans. 4G 19
Kingfisher Ri. HU7: Hull. 6H 19
King's Bench St. HU3: Hull 3H 43
Kingsbury Way HU7: King 1B 18
Kingscott Cl. HU7: Brans. 3C 18
Kings Cross Cl. HU3: Hull 2H 43
Kings Gdns. HU5: Hull 4G 27
  (off Goddard Av.)
Kingsgarth DN18: Bart H 4F 55
  (off Whitecross st.)
Kings Leigh HU3: Hull. 2H 43
Kingsley Av. HU8: Hull 4H 29
Kingsley Cl. HU15: Brou 6D 36
Kingsley Dr. HU10: Will. 5E 25
Kings Mead HU17: Wood 1C 10
Kings Pl. HU12: Hed .2E 49
Kingsport HU3: Hull .1F 43
Kings Sq. HU17: Bev .4E 7
Kingston Av. HU13: Hess 1G 53
Kingston Communications Stadium 1G 43
Kingston Ind. Est. HU3: Hull 4A 44
Kingston Pk. HU1: Hull. 3B 44 (5C 4)
Kingston Pk. Tennis Cen., The 4B 44 (6B 4)
Kingston Ri. HU10: Kir E 5D 24
Kingston Rd. HU10: Will. 5E 25
Kingston Shop. Cen. HU9: Hull. 6F 29
Kingston Sq. HU1: Hull 1C 44 (2D 4)
  HU2: Hull 1C 44 (2D 4)
Kingston St. HU1: Hull. 3B 44 (6C 4)
Kingston Vw. DN18: Bart H 2C 44 (4D 4)
KINGSTON UPON HULL 5G 55
Kingston Vw. DN18: Bart H 5G 55
Kingston Vs. HU9: Hull (off Estcourt St.) 6G 29
Kingston Way HU7: Hull 1C 28
Kingston Wharf HU1: Hull 3B 44 (6C 4)
King St. DN18: Bart H 4F 55
  DN19: Gox. 5D 58
  HU1: Hull. 2C 44 (4E 5)
  HU16: Cott. 6A 16
  HU17: Wood 1C 10
Kingsway HU16: Cott .1A 26
Kingswood Retail Pk. HU7: King 3A 18
Kingtree Av. HU16: Cott 6A 16
King William Ho. HU1: Hull 2D 44 (4F 5)
Kinloss Gth. HU7: Brans 3F 19
Kinthorpe HU6: Hull .4F 17
Kiplington Cl. HU3: Hull 1F 43
Kipling Wlk. HU4: Hull 6C 42
Kirby Dr. HU16: Cott .6A 16
Kirkby St. HU2: Hull. .6C 28
Kirk Cl. HU7: Hull 6G 19
Kirk Cft. HU17: Bev 6H 15
Kirkdale Gdns. HU5: Hull (off Exmouth St.) . . .3H 27
Kirkebie Cl. HU12: Hed 3G 49
KIRK ELLA 2D 40
Kirkham Cl. HU13: Hess 6G 41
Kirkham Dr. HU5: Hull 4G 27
Kirkholme Way HU17: Bev 4G 7
Kirklands Rd. HU5: Hull 6D 26
Kirk Ho. HU10: Anla .2G 41
Kirk La. HU17: Walk 5B 8
Kirk Ri. HU10: Kir E 1D 40
Kirk Rd. HU12: Prest .4E 33
Kirkstead Av. HU8: Hull (off Kirkstead St.) 4D 28
Kirkstead St. HU8: Hull 4D 28
Kirkstone Rd. HU5: Hull 4C 26
Kirkway HU10: Kir E .1C 40
Kitchen La. HU17: Bev 6D 6

Knapton Av. HU5: Hull. 3D 26
Knightley Way HU7: King 2A 18
Knightsbridge Ct. HU3: Hull 5A 28
Knightscourt HU6: Hull 5D 16
Knights Way HU17: Bev. 4E 7
Knole Pk. HU7: King .2B 18
Knowles Av. HU6: Hull 4H 17
Knowsley Av. HU16: Cott 5H 15
Kottingham Av. HU5: Hull. 5A 28
  (off Beverley Rd.)
Kyle Cl. HU8: Hull 6D 20

L

Laburnum Av. HU5: Hull (off Hardy St.) 3H 27
  HU8: Hull 3F 29
Laburnum Cl. HU13: Hess 1F 53
Laburnum Dr. HU5: Hull 1A 42
  HU17: Bev 1E 7
Laburnum Gro. HU8: Hull 3D 28
  (off Lorraine St.)
Ladbower Cl. HU8: Hull. 5H 19
Ladygate HU17: Bev 4D 6
Ladyside Cl. HU7: Brans. 1D 18
Ladysmith Rd. HU9: Hull. 5F 25
Ladywell Ct. HU15: Welt (off Church St.) 5G 37
Ladywell Ga. HU15: Welt 5G 37
Lagoon Dr. HU7: Brans 4G 19
Lairgate HU17: Bev 4D 6
Lake Dr. HU8: Hull 3H 29
Lakeside Gro. HU4: Hull 4C 42
Lake Vw. HU8: Hull 3H 29
Lambert Av. HU15: Ello 5E 37
Lambert Pk. Rd. HU12: Hed 3E 49
Lambert St. HU5: Hull 4H 27
Lambton St. HU5: Hull 3H 27
Lambwath Rd. HU8: Hull 3F 29
Lamorna Av. HU8: Hull 3E 29
Lanark St. HU5: Hull .6G 27
Lancaster Dr. HU8: Hull 2F 29
Lancelot Ct. HU9: Hull. 2F 29
Land of Green Ginger HU1: Hull. 2C 44 (4E 5)
Landress La. HU17: Bev (not continuous). 5D 6
Langdale Av. HU5: Hull 4D 26
  HU17: Bev 4E 7
Langdale Cres. HU16: Cott 1H 25
Langford Way HU4: Hull 1A 42
Langham Rd. HU12: Thorn 6G 49
Langholm Cl. HU17: Bev. 3C 6
Langley Pk. HU7: King 2C 18
Langsett Rd. HU8: Hull. 5G 19
Langtoft Gro. HU6: Hull 6E 17
Langtree Cl. HU7: Brans 4C 18
Lansdowne St. HU3: Hull 2H 43
Lanyon Cl. HU7: Brans 5F 19
Lapwing Cl. HU7: Brans 4G 19
Larard Av. HU6: Hull .4H 17
Larch Cl. HU5: Hull 4A 28
Larch Dr. HU12: Thorn. 6F 49
Larchmont Cl. HU15: Ello 5D 36
Larne Rd. HU9: Hull .2C 30
Lashbrook Gth. HU4: Hull 4A 42
Lastingham HU15: Ello 5E 37
Lastingham Cl. HU6: Hull 6E 17
Laughton Rd. HU17: Bev 2E 7
Laurel Av. HU5: Hull (off Perth St.) 6G 27
Laurel Cl. HU5: Hull .1A 42
Laurel Cl. HU17: Bev .4C 6
Laurel Gro. HU3: Hull (off Perry St.) 2G 43
Laurels, The HU5: Hull (off Raglan St.) 3H 27
Laurel Vs. HU9: Hull (off Estcourt St.) 6G 29
Lavender Cl. HU7: King. 2C 18
Lavender Wlk. HU7: King 1B 42
  HU17: Bev 6D 6
Lawns Gth. HU16: Cott 5H 15
Lawns, The HU7: Hull 6G 19
  HU10: Anla 1E 41
  HU17: Bev 2B 6
Lawnswood HU13: Hess 6E 41
Lawnswood Cl. HU7: Hull 1G 29
Lawrence Av. HU8: Hull 2A 30
Lawson Av. HU16: Cott 5A 16
Lawson Cl. HU17: Walk. 6B 8
Lawsons Cl. HU6: Hull 1C 28
Laxthorpe HU6: Hull. 4F 17
Laxton Gth. HU10: Kir E 5C 24
LB Av. HU3: Hull (off Clyde St.) 3E 43
Lea Cres. HU16: Cott 1H 25
Leadhills Way HU7: Brans 3G 19
Leads Bungalows HU7: Hull 1F 29
Leads Rd. HU7: Hull .2D 28
Lealholme Ct. HU8: Hull 5H 19
Leame Cl. HU3: Hull .1F 43
Leander Rd. HU9: Hull 3C 30
Leases, The HU17: Bev 5D 6
Lea, The HU15: S'th C .2F 9
Leathley Cl. HU17: Bev 1F 9
Leconfield Cl. HU9: Hull 5E 31
Ledbury Rd. HU5: Hull 4C 26
Leeming Gth. HU7: Brans 3F 19
Lee Smith St. HU9: Hull 1H 45
Lee's Rest Ho's. HU4: Hull 2C 42

Lee St. HU8: Hull 3F 29
Lees Wlk. HU1: Hull .1F 43
Lee Vs. HU8: Hull (off Lee St.) 4G 29
Legard Dr. HU10: Anla 2G 41
Legarde Av. HU4: Hull 2B 42
Legion Cl. HU15: Brou 6D 36
Leicester St. HU3: Hull 6A 28
Leitholm Cl. HU7: Brans 6D 12
LELLEY 1H 33
Lelley Balk HU12: Prest 6H 23
Lelley Rd. HU12: Prest 3D 32
Lenham La. HU1: Hull 2B 44 (4C 4)
Leningrad Rd. HU7: Hull 3F 13
Leonard's Av. HU3: Hull 3F 43
                                  (off Rhodes St.)
Leonards Av. HU5: Hull 3A 28
Leonard St. HU3: Hull 6A 28
Leslie Av. HU8: Hull .3D 28
                                  (off Lorraine St.)
Leura Gro. HU3: Hull 4G 43
Leven Gro. HU9: Hull 4B 30
Levisham Cl. HU6: Hull 6E 17
Levita Av. HU9: Hull .4D 30
Lexington Dr. HU4: Hull 3B 42
Leyburn Av. HU6: Hull 2D 26
Leyland Av. HU3: Hull 5G 29
Liberty La. HU1: Hull 2D 44 (4F 5)
Lichfield Cl. HU2: Hull 6B 28
     HU17: Bev 1F 9
Liddell St. HU2: Hull 1B 44 (1C 4)
Lilac Av. HU5: Hull 3H 27
     HU8: Hull 4E 29
     HU10: Will 5E 25
     HU17: Bev 1E 7
Lilac Rd. HU15: Brou 6E 37
Lily Gro. HU3: Hull (off Greek St.) 3E 43
Lime Av. HU10: Will .5F 25
     HU15: Brou 6E 37
Limedane HU6: Hull .4E 17
Lime Gro. DN19: Gox 4E 59
Limerick Cl. HU8: Hull (not continuous) 6C 20
Limes, The HU5: Hull (off Ella St.) 4G 27
     HU15: S'th C 4B 34
Lime St. HU8: Hull 1D 44 (1F 5)
Lime Tree Av. HU7: Hull 6G 19
     HU8: Hull 4F 29
     HU13: Hess 1G 53
     HU17: Bev 2E 7
Lime Tree La. HU11: Bil 6G 21
Lime Tree Vs. HU7: Hull 6G 19
Lincoln Castle Way
     DN19: New H . . . . .1G 57 & 2A 58
Lincoln Dr. DN18: Bart H 5G 55
Lincoln Grn. HU4: Hull 1B 42
Lincoln St. HU2: Hull 6C 28
Lincoln Way HU17: Bev 2E 9
Linden Av. HU16: Cott 5B 16
Lindengate Av. HU7: Hull 2E 29
Lindengate Way
     HU7: Hull 1E 29
Linden Gro. HU3: Hull (off Greek St.) 3F 43
     HU5: Hull (off Folkstone St.) 4B 28
Lindsey Pl. HU4: Hull 2C 42
Lingcourt HU6: Hull .5E 17
Lingdale Rd. HU9: Hull 4F 31
Linkfield Rd. HU5: Hull 2D 26
Link Rd. HU16: Cott .1H 25
Link, The HU4: Hull .3B 42
Linnaeus St. HU3: Hull 2H 43
Linnet Dr. HU8: Hull .5G 19
Linthorpe Gro. HU10: Will 6F 25
Linton HU15: Ello 5E 37
Linton Cl. HU17: Bev 6D 6
Lisle Ct. HU1: Hull 2C 44 (4D 4)
Lismore Av. HU4: Hull 3B 30
Lissett Gro. HU6: Hull 5H 17
Lister Ct. HU1: Hull 2D 44 (3G 5)
Lister St. HU1: Hull 3B 44 (6A 4)
Littlebeck Cl. HU3: Hull 1F 43
Lit. Clover HU17: Bev 2E 7
Littlefair Rd. HU9: Hull 1B 46
Lit. George St. HU8: Hull 6D 28
Littleham Cl. HU7: Brans 4E 19
Lit. Mason St. HU2: Hull 1D 44 (2F 5)
Littlemoor Cl. HU15: N'th C 2B 34
Lit. Queen St. HU1: Hull 2B 44 (3C 4)
Lit. Reed St. HU2: Hull 1C 44 (2D 4)
Lit. Weighton Rd.
     HU16: Skid 4A 14
     HU17: Walk 6A 8
Lit. Wold La. HU15: S'th C 3E 35
Littondale HU17: Brans 5B 18
     HU15: Ello 5F 37
Liverpool St. HU3: Hull (not continuous) 4F 43
Livingstone Rd. HU13: Hess 2F 53
Lizzie's Av. HU3: Hull 3E 43
                                  (off Rhodes St.)
Loatley Grn. HU16: Cott 1B 26
Lock Keepers Cl. HU9: Hull 2F 45
Lockton Gro. HU5: Hull 6C 26
Lockwood Dr. HU17: Bev 1D 6
Lockwood Rd. HU17: Bev 1C 6
Lockwood St. HU2: Hull 6C 28
Lodge Av. DN18: Bart H 5G 55

Lodge Cl. HU13: Hess 1G 53
     HU15: Ello 3E 37
Lodge St. HU9: Hull .4H 29
Loftus Gro. HU9: Hull 3F 31
Loganberry Dr. HU4: Hull 4B 42
Logan Cl. HU7: Brans 5F 19
Lois Cres. HU3: Hull .3G 43
Lombard St. HU3: Hull 2B 44 (3B 4)
Lomond Rd. HU5: Hull 6D 26
Londesborough Barracks HU3: Hull 2A 44
                                  (off Londesborough St.)
Londesborough St. HU3: Hull 1H 43 (2A 4)
Londesborough St. Bus. Cen.
     HU3: Hull 2H 43
Longcroft Pk. HU17: Mole 3B 6
Longdales La. HU11: Coni 2F 21
Longden St. HU3: Hull 1F 43
Long Dr. HU10: Kir E .6A 24
Longford Gro. HU9: Hull 4F 31
Long La. HU17: Bev .6E 7
Longmans La. HU16: Cott 6A 16
Lonsdale St. HU3: Hull 2F 43
Lord Roberts Rd. HU17: Bev 5E 7
Lords La. DN19: Bar H 5F 57
Lorenzo Way HU9: Hull 4A 30
Lorne Cl. HU3: Hull 6C 28
Lorraine St. HU8: Hull 3D 28
Lothian Way HU7: Brans 6D 12
Louis Dr. HU5: Hull 6A 26
Louis Pearlman Cen. HU3: Hull 4H 43
Louis St. HU3: Hull 6H 27
Lovat Cl. HU1: Hull 3A 44 (6A 4)
Love La. HU12: Hed .3E 49
     HU15: S'th C 2D 34
Loveridge Av. HU5: Hull 4F 27
Lowdale Cl. HU5: Hull 5D 26
Lowerdale HU15: Ello 5E 37
Lower Mdws. DN18: Bart H 3G 55
Low Farm Rd. HU11: Bil 3E 21
Lowfield Cl. HU10: Anla 2G 41
Lowfield Ho. HU10: Anla 2G 41
                                  (off Lowfield Rd.)
Low Field La. HU14: Welt . . . . . .2A 50 & 6H 37
                                  (not continuous)
Lowfield Rd. HU10: Anla 3F 41
     HU17: Bev 1E 7
Lowgate HU1: Hull 2D 44 (3F 5)
     HU7: Hull 6G 19
Lowgate Cl. HU7: Hull 6G 19
Lowland Cl. HU7: Brans 4G 19
Low Mill La. HU15: N'th C 2A 34
Low St. HU14: N'th F 1E 51
Lowther St. HU3: Hull 2F 43
Loxley Grn. HU4: Hull 1A 42
Loxley Way HU15: Brou 6F 37
Loyds Cl. HU15: S'th C 4B 34
Loyd St. HU10: Anla .2G 41
Lucian Wlk. HU4: Hull 6H 41
Luck La. HU12: Prest 4D 32
Lulworth Av. HU4: Hull 5H 41
LUND 5G 7
Lund Av. HU16: Cott .6F 15
Lunds, The HU10: Kir E 2D 40
Lunedale Cl. HU8: Hull 5H 19
Lunn's Cres. DN18: Bart H 5E 55
Lurk La. HU17: Bev (off Hallgarth Way) 5E 7
Luthers Ri. HU10: Will 4D 24
Luton Rd. HU5: Hull .6E 27
Lymington Gth. HU4: Hull 5H 41
Lyndhurst Av. HU16: Cott 6C 16
Lyndhurst Cl. HU17: Bev 4G 7
Lynmouth Cl. HU7: Brans 3D 18
Lynngarth Av. HU16: Cott 6B 16
Lynton Av. HU4: Hull 5A 42
     HU5: Hull (Chanterlands Av.) 6F 27
     HU5: Hull (Perth St. W.) 6F 27
Lynwood Av. HU10: Anla 2F 41
Lynwood Gro. HU5: Hull (off Goddard Av.) . . .4H 27
Lyric Cl. HU3: Hull 1H 43
Lytham Dr. HU16: Cott 1C 26
Lythe Av. HU5: Hull 2C 26

M

Mable's Vs. HU9: Hull (off Holland St.) 6G 29
Mace Vw. HU17: Bev 6E 7
Machell St. HU2: Hull 1C 44 (1E 5)
McKinley Av. HU3: Hull 3G 43
                                  (off Albermarle St.)
Macon St. HU5: Hull (off Minton St.) 3A 28
Madeley St. HU3: Hull 4H 43
Madison Gdns. HU5: Hull 5F 27
Madoline Gro. HU9: Hull 6G 29
                                  (off Estcourt St.)
Madron St. HU7: Brans 4E 19
Mafeking Gro. HU3: Hull 3E 43
                                  (off Seymour St.)
Magdalen Ct. HU12: Hed 2G 49
Magdalen Ga. HU12: Hed 2E 49
Magdalen La. HU12: Hed 2F 49
Magnolia Ct. HU3: Hull 3H 43

Maiden Ct. HU7: Brans 3G 19
Main Rd. HU1: Bil, Sproat 6E 21
     HU12: Hed, Paul, Thorn . . . . . .4E 49 & 5F 49
     HU14: Welt 1A 50
Main St. HU2: Hull 5C 28
     HU7: Waw 4A 12
     HU10: Will (not continuous) 3D 24
     HU11: Coni 1G 21
     HU12: Paul 6A 48
     HU12: Prest 4E 33
     HU14: Swan 3G 39
     HU15: Elle 6D 34
     HU15: Ello 4D 36
     HU16: Skid 4B 14
Maisons De Dieu HU17: Bev 4D 6
Majestic Ct. HU3: Hull 3B 30
Maldon Dr. HU9: Hull 2F 45
Malham Av. HU4: Hull 2B 42
Mallard Cl. HU17: Bev 2D 6
Mallard Rd. HU9: Hull 2C 30
Mallards Reach HU16: Cott 4B 16
Mallin Lodge HU9: Hull 3B 30
Mallyan Cl. HU8: Hull 5H 19
Malmo Rd. HU7: Hull 1B 28
Malm St. HU3: Hull 2G 43
Malpas Cl. HU7: Brans 3C 18
Maltby La. DN18: Bart H 3E 55
Maltings, The HU17: Bev 4F 7
Maltkiln Rd. DN18: Bart H 2E 55
Malton Rd. HU17: Mole 2A 6
Malton St. HU9: Hull 1D 44 (1G 5)
Malvern Av. HU3: Hull 3F 43
     HU5: Hull (off Ella St.) 4H 27
Malvern Cres. HU5: Hull 4C 26
Malvern Rd. HU5: Hull 4C 26
Manchester Sq. DN19: New H 2A 58
Manchester St. HU3: Hull 4F 43
                                  (not continuous)
Mancklin Av. HU8: Hull 1G 29
Manderville Cl. HU12: Hed 3F 49
Manet Rd. HU8: Hull .5F 29
Manilla Cl. DN18: Bart H 1E 55
Manor Cl. HU11: Sproat 2F 23
     HU17: Bev 3D 6
Manor Ct. HU10: Kir E 1A 40
Manor Dr. HU15: Ello 4E 37
Manorfields HU10: Kir E 1A 40
Manor Gth. HU16: Skid 4A 14
Manorhouse La. HU17: Walk 5A 8
Manor Ho. St. HU1: Hull 3B 44 (6C 4)
Manor La. DN19: Bar H 4F 57
     DN19: Gox 4C 58
Manor Pk. HU12: Prest 4F 33
     HU17: Bev 3D 6
Manor Rd. HU5: Hull .6A 26
     HU12: Prest 4E 33
     HU12: Thorn 6H 49
     HU14: Swan 4F 39
     HU15: N'th C 1A 34
     HU17: Bev 4D 6
Manor St. HU1: Hull 2C 44 (3E 5)
Mansfield Pk. HU5: Hull 3G 27
Manston Gth. HU7: Brans 3F 19
Manvers St. HU5: Hull 3H 27
Maple Av. HU10: Will .6G 25
Maple Cl. HU5: Hull 1B 42
     HU17: Bev 2E 7
Maple Gro. HU8: Hull 4F 29
     HU13: Hess 5C 40
Maple Leaf Ct. HU16: Cott 1G 25
Maple Pk. HU12: Hed 1F 49
Maple Wlk. HU5: Hull 4A 28
Maplewood Av. HU5: Hull 1H 41
Mapleton Gro. HU9: Hull 4B 30
Marbury Pk. HU7: King 2B 18
Marchant Cl. HU17: Bev 1C 6
Mardale Av. HU7: Hull 3E 31
Mareham Av. HU3: Hull (off Ena St.) 2G 43
MARFLEET 1C 46
Marfleet Av. HU9: Hull 1C 46
Marfleet La. HU9: Hull 2B 30
                                  (not continuous)
Margaret Gro. HU13: Hess 1G 53
Margaret St. HU3: Hull 6A 28
Marina Ct. HU1: Hull 3C 44 (5E 5)
Marina Recreation Cen. 3B 44 (6C 4)
Marin Ct. HU17: Bev .5G 7
Marine Av. HU14: N'th F 3D 50
Mariners Cl. HU9: Hull 2F 45
Mariners Ct. HU17: Bev 5F 7
Marine Wharf HU1: Hull 3C 44 (6C 4)
Maritime Ho. HU3: Hull 5H 43
Market Cl. HU15: S'th C 3D 34
Market Grn. HU16: Cott. 6A 16
                                  (off King St.)
Market Hill HU12: Hed 2E 49
Market La. DN18: Bart H 4F 55
Market Pl. DN18: Bart H 4F 55
     DN19: Bar H 5F 57
     HU1: Hull (Sth. Church Side) 4E 5
     HU1: Hull (Garrison Rd.) 3D 44 (5F 5)
     HU12: Hed 2E 49
     HU15: S'th C 3D 34

Marlborough Av. HU4: Hull 5D 42
(off Hampshire St.)
HU5: Hull 6F 27
HU13: Hess 6E 41
Marlborough Ter. HU2: Hull 1B 44 (1B 4)
Marlowe St. HU8: Hull 4F 29
Marmaduke St. HU3: Hull 4H 43
Marne St. HU5: Hull 6F 27
Marsdale HU7: Brans 5C 18
Marsden Landing HU6: Hull 4A 18
Marshall Av. HU10: Will. 6F 25
HU12: Prest. 6E 33
Marshall St. HU5: Hull 4H 27
Marsh Dr. HU17: Bev. 6D 6
Marshington Cl. HU3: Hull 1F 43
Marsh La. DN18: Bart H 2F 55
DN19: Bar H, New H . . . . .1D 56 & 3A 58
(not continuous)
Marske Wlk. HU5: Hull 3D 26
Martin Cl. HU9: Hull 3C 30
Martin's Cl. DN19: Bar H 4F 57
Martin St. HU17: Bev 5G 7
Marton Gro. HU6: Hull. 1E 27
Marvel St. HU9: Hull 1E 45 (2H 5)
Marydene Dr. HU6: Hull 1H 27
Masons Ct. DN18: Bart H 5D 54
Mason St. HU2: Hull 1C 44 (2E 5)
Maspin Ct. HU7: King 2B 18
Massey St. HU3: Hull 3G 43
Massey St. HU3: Hull 4F 43
Mast Dr. HU9: Hull .2G 45
Matlock Vs. HU9: Hull. 6G 29
(off Estcourt St.)
Mattocks La. HU12: Hed 1F 49
Maulson Dr. HU11: Bil. 6H 21
Maurice Av. HU8: Hull 4D 28
Maxim Ct. HU3: Hull 3H 43
Maxwell St. HU8: Hull 4D 28
Maybury Rd. HU9: Hull 3A 30
Maye Gro. HU5: Hull 4B 28
(off Folkestone St.)
HU5: Hull 6F 27
(off Perth St. W.)
HU8: Hull 5E 29
(off Dansom La. Nth.)
Maye Gro. HU8: Hull. 1G 5
Mayfair Ct. HU5: Hull 4A 28
Mayfield Av. HU3: Hull 6H 27
(off Mayfield St.)
Mayfield St. HU3: Hull 6H 27
Mayfield Vs. HU3: Hull 6H 29
(off Rosmead St.)
Mayfield Wlk. HU3: Hull 6H 27
May Gdns. HU7: Hull 2D 28
May Gro. HU13: Hess 6E 41
Mayland Av. HU5: Hull 6H 25
Mayland Dr. HU16: Cott. 6F 15
May St. HU5: Hull .3A 28
May Ter. HU5: Hull .3A 28
Maythorpe Cl. HU3: Hull 1F 43
May Tree Av. HU8: Hull 4F 29
Mayville Av. HU8: Hull 3D 28
Meadley Ct. HU17: Bev 4H 7
Meadow Bank HU17: Bev 1E 7
Meadowbank Rd. HU3: Hull 1D 42
Meadow Cl. DN19: Gox. 3D 58
Meadow Dr. DN18: Bart H. 5G 55
Meadow Gth. HU6: Hull 3G 17
Meadows, The HU6: Wood 2F 17
HU7: Brans 5B 18
HU10: Kir E 6A 24
HU15: S'th C 5B 34
HU17: Bev. 6G 7
Meadow Vale HU9: Hull 6G 29
(off Estcourt St.)
Meadow Wlk. HU14: Swan 3G 39
Meadow Way HU16: Cott 1G 25
HU17: Walk 5C 8
Mead St. HU8: Hull 1G 29
Mead Wlk. HU4: Hull 2B 42
Meaux Rd. HU7: Waw 1C 12
HU17: Waw 1C 12
Mechanic La. HU3: Hull 3A 44 (6A 4)
Meden Av. HU15: Brou 6F 37
Medina Rd. HU8: Hull 1D 30
Medlar Dr. HU15: Brou 6F 37
Megabowl Bowling Alley 5G 43
Megson Av. HU17: Walk 2B 8
Melbourne Ho. HU1: Hull 5B 4
Melbourne St. HU5: Hull 3H 27
Melrose Av. HU3: Hull 3E 43
(off Rhodes St.)
Melrose Cres. HU3: Hull 3F 43
(off Greek St.)
Melrose Pk. HU17: Bev 5E 7
Melrose St. HU3: Hull 2E 43
Melrose Vs. HU5: Hull 4H 27
(off Chesnut Av.)
MELTON 6B 38
Melton Bottom HU14: Welt 6A 38
Meltonby Av. HU5: Hull 4B 26
Melton Flds. HU14: N'th F. 1B 50
Melton Old Rd. HU14: Welt. 6A 38
Melton Rd. HU14: N'th F. 1D 50

Melville St. HU1: Hull 3B 44 (5B 4)
Melwood Gro. HU5: Hull 4A 28
Mendip Cl. HU3: Hull 3H 43
Mere Flats HU14: Swan 4G 39
Mere Way HU14: Swan 3G 39
Merlin Cl. HU8: Hull 5G 19
Merlin St. HU9: Hull 1E 45
Merrick St. HU9: Hull 1E 45
Merryman Gth. HU12: Hed 3E 49
Mersey St. HU8: Hull 5F 29
Mersey Vs. HU9: Hull 6H 29
(off Rosmead St.)
Merton Gro. HU9: Hull. 5A 30
Mews, The HU3: Hull 3H 43
Mickley Gro. HU9: Hull 4D 30
Middleburg St. HU9: Hull 6G 29
Middledyke La. HU16: Cott. 4C 16
Middle Gth. Dr. HU15: S'th C 3D 34
Middlegate Cl. DN19: Bar H 5E 57
Middleham Cl. HU9: Hull 6H 29
Middlehowe Grn. HU17: Walk 5A 8
Middlehowe Rd. HU17: Walk 5A 8
Middle La. HU12: Hed 3E 49
HU12: Prest. 4C 32
HU17: Bev (off Morton La.) 4E 7
Middlemarsh HU7: Hull 2E 29
Middle Rd. HU9: Hull 2D 30
Middlesex Rd. HU8: Hull. 1A 30
Middleton Av. HU9: Hull 5G 29
(off Rensburg St.)
Middleton Cl. HU17: Bev. 3F 7
Middleton Cl. HU3: Hull 6H 27
Middleton St. HU3: Hull 6H 27
Middleton Vs. HU3: Hull (off Clyde St.) 3E 43
Midgley Cl. HU3: Hull 3H 43
Midland St. HU1: Hull 2B 44 (4B 4)
Midmere Av. HU7: Brans 5E 19
Midway Gro. HU4: Hull 4D 42
MILE HOUSE 4G 29
Milestone Ct. DN18: Bart H 4F 55
HU15: N'th C 2A 34
Milford Gro. HU9: Hull. 5F 31
Millbeck Bank HU15: S'th C 6A 34
Mill Beck Ct. HU16: Cott 5A 16
Mill Beck La. HU16: Cott 4A 16
Millbrook Way DN18: Bart H 5G 55
Milldane HU6: Hull .4D 16
Miller's Wlk. HU5: Hull 4E 27
Millfields DN18: Bart H 5E 55
Millfields Way DN19: Bar H 5E 57
MILL HILL (West End) 4D 34
(Elloughton)
Mill Hill HU15: Elle .6D 34
Millhouse Woods La. HU16: Cott 4A 16
Mill La. DN19: Bar H 3D 58
DN19: Gox. 3D 58
DN10: Kir E 1D 40
HU15: Ello. 4D 36
HU15: N'th C 1A 34
HU15: N'th C 1A 34
HU16: Cott 5G 15
HU17: Bev 3E 7
Mill La. Bus. Pk. HU17: Bev 4E 7
Mill La. Ct. HU17: Bev (off Mill La.). 4E 7
Mill La. W. HU15: Brou, Ello. 5C 36
Millport Dr. HU4: Hull 6A 42
Mill Ri. HU14: Swan 4E 39
HU16: Skid 4C 14
Mill Rd. HU11: Sproat 2F 23
HU14: Swan 4D 38
HU16: Cott, Skid 5D 14
Mill St. HU2: Hull 2B 44 (3B 4)
Mill Vw. Ct. HU17: Bev 5G 7
Mill Vw. Rd. HU17: Bev 5F 7
Mill Wlk. HU16: Cott 1B 26
Millway HU15: N'th C 1A 34
Milson Cl. DN18: Bart H 4E 55
Minehead Rd. HU7: Brans 3D 18
Minerva Ter. HU1: Hull 3C 44 (6E 5)
Minnie's Gro. HU3: Hull 6H 27
(off Mayfield St.)
HU3: Hull 1F 43
(off Walton St.)
HU3: Hull 3E 43
(off Beilby St.)
Minster Av. HU17: Bev. 5E 7
Minster Cl. HU8: Hull 1H 29
Minster Ct. HU17: Bev 5D 6
(off Minster Moorgate)
Minster Moorgate HU17: Bev 5D 6
Minster Moorgate W. HU17: Bev 5D 6
Minster Wharf HU17: Bev. 5G 7
Minster Yd. Nth. HU17: Bev 5E 7
Minster Yd. Sth. HU17: Bev 5E 7
Mintfields Rd. HU17: Bev 4F 7
Minton St. HU5: Hull 3A 28
Mint Wlk. HU17: Bev .6E 7
Mirfield Gro. HU9: Hull 4D 30
Mitcham Rd. HU8: Hull 1B 30
Mizzen Rd. HU6: Hull 4H 17
Moat Hill HU10: Anla 2G 41
Moffat Cl. HU8: Hull 2F 29
MOLESCROFT 2C 6
Molescroft Av. HU17: Bev 2C 6
Molescroft Dr. HU17: Bev 2C 6

Molescroft M. HU17: Bev 2B 6
Molescroft Pk. HU17: Bev. 2B 6
Molescroft Rd. HU17: Bev. 2B 6
Mollison Rd. HU4: Hull. 5H 41
Mollison Rd. W. HU4: Hull 5H 41
Monic Av. HU13: Hess. 5G 41
Monkton HU15: Ello .5F 37
Monkton Cl. HU16: Cott 1G 25
Monkton Wlk. HU6: Hull 6D 20
Monmouth St. HU4: Hull. 5D 42
Mons St. HU5: Hull .6F 27
Montcalm Wlk. HU16: Cott. 1G 25
Montreal Av. HU3: Hull 3G 43
(off Albermarle St.)
Montreal Cres. HU16: Cott 1F 25
Montrose Av. HU3: Hull 3E 43
(off Seymour St.)
HU8: Hull 5E 29
Montrose St. HU8: Hull 5E 29
Moorbeck Cl. HU6: Hull. 2E 27
Moorfoot Cl. HU7: Brans 1D 18
Moor Grn. HU4: Hull 1A 42
Moorhouse Rd. HU5: Hull 6A 26
Moorings, The HU14: N'th F 3E 51
Moorlands, The HU15: S'th C 4A 34
Moor La. HU17: Walk 4A 8
Moors La. HU15: S'th C 4A 34
More Hall Dr. HU8: Hull 5G 19
Moreton Bay HU11: Bil 1F 31
Morgan Way DN19: New H 1G 57
Morley's La. HU17: Bev 4D 6
(off Walkergate)
Morley St. HU3: Hull 4D 28
Morley's Vs. HU9: Hull 5F 29
(off Sherburn St.)
Morpeth St. HU3: Hull 1A 44 (1A 4)
Morrill St. HU9: Hull 5G 29
Morris Rd. HU5: Hull 2D 42
Mortimer Av. HU10: Anla 2G 41
Mortlake Cl. HU8: Hull 1H 29
Morton La. HU17: Bev. 4D 6
Morton St. HU3: Hull 1H 43
Moseley Hill HU11: Bil 6F 21
Motherwell Cl. HU3: Hull 2F 29
Mt. Airy La. HU15: S'th C 4D 34
Mount Av. DN18: Bart H. 4E 55
HU13: Hess 6E 41
Mount Pleasant DN19: New H. 3A 58
HU8: Hull 5D 28
HU9: Hull 6F 29
Mount Retail Pk., The HU9: Hull. 6F 29
Mt. Vernon HU11: Bil. 6F 21
Mount Vw. HU14: N'th F 6E 39
Moy Ct. HU6: Hull 6F 17
Muirfield Pk. HU5: Hull 5F 27
Mulberry Ct. HU9: Hull 5C 30
Mulcourt HU6: Hull. 5E 17
Mulgrave St. HU8: Hull 6D 28
Mullion Cl. HU7: Brans 5F 19
Multi-sport Indoor Cen. 1F 43
Munroe Cl. HU8: Hull 2F 29
Murray Cres. HU16: Cott. 1G 25
Murrayfield Rd. HU5: Hull 5E 27
Mus. of Army Transport 5F 7
Muston Av. HU16: Cott 1H 25
Muswell Cl. HU8: Hull 1B 30
Mylor Cl. HU7: Brans 3D 18
Myrtle Av. HU3: Hull 4H 43
HU9: Hull 1E 45
(off Williamson St.)
Myrtle Gro. HU3: Hull 3F 43
(off Springburn St.)
HU8: Hull 3D 28
(off Lorraine St.)
Myrtle Vs. HU3: Hull 6H 27
(off Spring Bank.)
Myrtle Way HU15: Brou 6E 37
Mytongate HU1: Hull 3B 44 (5C 4)
Myton St. HU1: Hull 2B 44 (4C 4)

N

Naburn St. HU3: Hull 4F 43
Nairn Cl. HU6: Hull .4G 17
Nalton Ct. HU16: Cott 1H 25
Nandike Cl. HU10: Anla 2G 41
Napier Cl. HU17: Bev 3D 6
Narrow La. HU14: N'th F 1E 51
Narvick Rd. HU7: Hull. 1B 28
Nashcourt HU6: Hull 5E 17
National Av. HU5: Hull. 4E 27
Navenby Gro. HU7: King 1C 18
Navigation Way HU9: Hull 2F 45
Naylors Row HU9: Hull 1E 45 (2H 5)
Neasden Cl. HU8: Hull 1H 29
NEAT MARSH 4H 31
Neat Marsh Rd. HU12: Prest 5H 31
Neatshead Gth. HU7: Brans. 3F 19
Nectan Cl. HU4: Hull 4F 43
Needham Cl. HU17: Bev (off Bielby Dr.) 4G 7
Nelson Cl. HU1: Hull 3C 44 (6E 5)
Nelson Rd. HU5: Hull 1A 42

Nelson St. HU1: Hull 3C 44 (6E 5)
Nelson Vs. HU8: Hull 1G 5
Nepean Gro. *HU3: Hull (off Tyne St.)* 4G 43
Neptune St. HU3: Hull 4A 44
Nesfield Av. *HU5: Hull* 6F 27
(off Perth St. W.)
Ness Cl. HU12: Prest 4E 33
Ness La. HU12: Prest 4E 33
Nestlings, The HU8: Hull 2G 29
Nestor Gro. HU9: Hull 1D 30
Netherton Rd. HU4: Hull 4A 42
Neville Av. HU17: Bev 3F 7
Neville Cl. HU3: Hull 3A 44 (6A 4)
Neville Gth. HU12: Hed 2F 49
Newbald Gro. HU6: Hull 6E 17
Newbald Rd. HU17: Bev, Walk . . . . . . 6A 6 & 1A 8
Newbald Way HU16: Cott 6F 15
Newbegin HU17: Bev 4D 6
New Bridge Rd. HU9: Hull 6F 29
Newby Cl. HU7: King 1B 18
New Cleveland St. HU8: Hull 6D 28 (1G 5)
Newcomen St. HU9: Hull 5G 29
New Cross St. HU1: Hull 2C 44 (3D 4)
NEW FIELD 3B 48
Newfield La. HU15: S'th C 4A 34
Newfinkle Ct. HU16: Cott 6H 15
New Garden St. HU1: Hull 1C 44 (2D 4)
New George St. HU2: Hull 1C 44 (1E 5)
NEW HOLLAND 2A 58
New Holland Rd. DN19: Bar H 5G 57
New Holland Station (Rail) 1A 58
Newholme Cl. HU6: Hull 1E 27
Newington Av. HU4: Hull 3C 42
Newington St. HU3: Hull 4E 43
NEWLAND 3A 28
Newland Av. HU5: Hull 4H 27
Newland Cl. HU5: Hull 3H 27
Newland Gro. HU5: Hull 3H 27
Newland Homes, The HU6: Hull 2H 27
NEWLAND PARK 3H 27
Newland Pk. HU5: Hull 3F 27
Newland Pk. Av. HU6: Hull 2G 27
Newlands Science Pk. HU6: Hull 1G 27
Newlands HU5: Hull 3H 27
Newlyn Cl. HU7: Brans 5F 19
HU13: Hess 6H 41
New Michael St. HU1: Hull 3B 44 (5B 4)
New Nth. Bri. Ho. HU1: Hull 1D 44 (2F 5)
Newport HU3: Hull 3E 55
Newport Cl. HU3: Hull 3A 44
Newport Rd. HU15: N'th C 2A 34
New Princes Av. HU12: Hed 2D 48
New Rd. HU12: Hed 2D 48
HU15: Brant 1D 36
Newsham Gth. HU4: Anla 3A 42
Newstead Av. *HU5: Hull* 6F 27
(off Newstead St.)
Newstead St. HU5: Hull 6F 27
New St. HU3: Hull 3E 43
Newtondale HU7: Brans 5C 18
Newton Dr. HU17: Bev 6D 6
Newton St. HU3: Hull 4G 43
Newton Thorpe Cotts. HU14: Swan 3F 39
Newton Vs. *HU9: Hull* 6G 29
(off Estcourt St.)
Newtown Ct. HU9: Hull 6H 29
Newtown Sq. HU9: Hull 1H 45
NEW VILLAGE 6C 16
New Village Rd. HU16: Cott 5B 16
New Wlk. HU14: N'th F 2E 51
New Walk HU17: Bev 3C 6
New Walkergate HU17: Bev 4D 6
Nicholas Cl. DN18: Bart H 5D 54
Nicholson Cl. HU17: Bev 4G 7
Nicholson Ct. HU16: Cott 6H 15
Nicholson Dr. DN18: Bart H 5G 55
Nicholson St. HU5: Hull 4B 28
Nidderdale HU7: Brans 5B 18
Nightingale Cl. HU17: Walk 2C 8
Nithdale Gdns. HU5: Hull 4B 28
Nith Gro. HU8: Hull 5D 20
Noddle Hill Way
HU7: Brans 2D 18
Nolloth Cres. HU17: Bev 4E 7
Nolloth Vs. *HU17: Bev* 4E 7
(off Nolloth Cres.)
Nordale Cl. HU8: Hull 5H 19
Nordham HU15: N'th C 1A 34
Norfolk Bank La. HU15: Elle 6A 34
Norfolk St. HU2: Hull 1B 44 (1B 4)
HU17: Bev 3C 6
Norland Av. HU4: Hull 1B 42
Norland Ct. *HU13: Hess* 1H 53
(off Hull Rd.)
Norman Cl. DN18: Bart H 4G 55
Normandy Av. HU17: Bev 2D 8
Normanton Ri. HU4: Hull 1B 42
Nornabell Dr. HU17: Bev 1D 6
Nornabell St. HU8: Hull 5F 29
Norrison Av. HU6: Hull 4H 17
Nth. Bar Within HU17: Bev 4D 6
Nth. Bar Without HU17: Bev 3C 6
NORTH CARR 2E 19

NORTH CAVE 2A 34
Nth. Church Side HU1: Hull 2C 44 (4E 5)
Nth. Country Ct. HU9: Hull 5H 29
Northcroft Dr. HU8: Hull 5H 19
Northdale Pk. HU14: Swan 3G 39
North Dr. HU10: Anla 2F 41
HU14: Swan 3G 39
NORTH END 2E 59
North End DN19: Gox 4D 58
Northern Gateway HU9: Hull 1B 46
NORTH FERRIBY 1E 51
NORTHFIELD 6G 41
Northfield HU14: Swan 3G 39
Northfield Av. HU13: Hess 5F 41
Northfield Cl. HU15: S'th C 4B 34
Northfield Rd. HU3: Hull 2E 43
HU11: Coni 1G 21
HU17: Bev 2B 6
Northfield Vs. *HU9: Hull* 6G 29
(off Rosmead St.)
Northgate HU13: Hess 6F 41
HU16: Cott 5H 15
HU17: Walk 5B 8
Northgate Ho. HU16: Cott 5A 16
Northgate Pl. HU13: Hess 6F 41
North Lincolnshire & Humberside Sailing Club
. . . . 1A 56
NORTH MOOR 3C 16
North Moor La. HU16: Cott 1C 16
Northmoor La. HU16: Cott 5B 16
Northolme Circ. HU13: Hess 6F 41
Northolme Cres. HU13: Hess 6F 41
Northolme Rd. HU13: Hess 6F 41
Northolt Cl. HU8: Hull 6H 19
Northorpe Cl. HU9: Hull 5D 30
North Point Shop. Cen.
HU7: Brans 4E 19
North Rd. HU4: Hull 2D 42
Northstead Cl. HU10: Will 4F 25
North St. DN19: Bar H 4F 57
HU2: Hull 1B 44 (2B 4)
HU10: Anla 2F 41
Northumberland Av. HU2: Hull 5C 28
Northumberland Ct. HU2: Hull 5C 28
North Walls HU1: Hull 2D 44 (3F 5)
Northwood Cl. HU8: Hull 6D 20
Northwood Dr. HU13: Hess 5D 40
Norton Gro. HU4: Hull 4C 42
Norton St. HU17: Bev 5D 6
Norwich Ct. HU17: Bev 1F 9
Norwood HU17: Bev 4D 6
Norwood Cl. HU10: Anla 1F 41
Norwood Ct. HU17: Bev 3E 7
Norwood Dale HU17: Bev 4D 6
Norwood Far Gro. HU17: Bev 2E 7
Norwood Gro. HU17: Bev 2D 6
Norwood St. HU3: Hull 1H 43
Noseley Way HU7: King 1C 18
Novello Gth. HU4: Anla 4A 42
Nunburnholme Av. HU14: N'th F 2D 50
Nunburnholme Pk. HU5: Hull 1A 42
Nun La. HU12: Prest 4E 33
Nunnery Cotts. HU12: Prest 6H 23
Nunnery Wlk. HU15: S'th C 4B 34
Nunnington Cl. HU5: Hull 4G 27
Nurseries, The HU17: Bev 2C 6
Nursery Cl. DN18: Bart H 3G 55
HU12: Thorn 5F 49
Nursery Cl. HU15: Brou 6E 37
Nursery Gdns. HU17: Bev 6D 6
Nursery Wlk. HU16: Cott 6C 16
Nuttles La. HU12: Prest 2H 33

O

Oak Av. HU3: Hull 1E 43
HU10: Will 5E 25
HU15: Ello 5E 37
Oak Cl. HU11: Sproat. 2F 23
HU17: Bev 2F 7
Oakdale Av. HU10: Will 6F 25
Oakdene HU16: Cott 6A 16
Oak Dr. HU5: Hull 1A 42
Oakfield Ct. HU6: Hull 2E 27
Oak Gro. DN19: Bar H 6E 57
HU12: Hed 2D 48
Oak Hill HU10: Will 4D 24
Oakington Gth. HU7: Brans 4F 19
Oaklands HU10: Will 5D 24
HU13: Hess 5E 41
Oakland Vs. *HU5: Hull* 4G 27
(off Reynoldson St.)
Oak Rd. HU6: Hull 6H 17
Oaksley Carr HU17: Wood. 1B 10
Oak Sq. HU7: Waw 3A 12
Oak Tree Cl. HU17: Bev 2C 6
Oaktree Dr. HU8: Hull 5G 19
Oak Tree Dr. HU17: Bev 2C 6
Oak Tree Est. HU12: Prest 5E 33
Oakwell Gro. HU8: Hull 5E 29
Oakwood Cl. HU5: Hull 1H 41

Oban Av. *HU3: Hull* 1E 43
(off De La Pole Av.)
Occupation La. HU14: Swan 1G 39
Ocean Blvd. HU9: Hull 2E 45 (4H 5)
Octagon, The HU10: Will 6E 25
Odeon Cinema (HU1) 4B 44 (6C 4)
(HU3) 6F 43
Old Annandale Rd. HU10: Kir E 6D 24
Oldbeck Rd. HU17: Bev 4H 7
Old Ct. HU17: Bev 3C 6
Old Dairy DN19: Bar H 5G 57
Oldfield Av. HU6: Hull 6H 17
Oldgate HU16: Skid 3B 14
Old Gt. HU17: Skid 1B 14
Old La., The HU17: N'th F 2E 51
Old Manor Lawns HU17: Bev 5E 7
Old Pond Pl. HU14: N'th F 3E 51
Old Stables, The HU17: Bev 4C 6
Oldstead Av. HU6: Hull 6E 17
Old Waste HU17: Bev 4D 6
Olivier Ct. HU4: Hull 5D 42
On Hill HU14: Swan 3G 39
Onyx Gro. HU3: Hull 4F 43
Orchard Cen., The HU13: Hess 1F 53
Orchard Cl. DN18: Bart H 5G 55
DN19: Bar H 6E 57
HU10: Anla 1G 41
HU17: Bev 3C 6
Orchard Ct. HU15: S'th C 3D 34
Orchard Cft. HU16: Cott 4A 16
Orchard Dr. HU13: Hess. 1F 53
Orchard Dr. HU17: Bev 2C 6
Orchard Pk. & North Hull Enterprises
HU6: Hull 3D 16
Orchard Pk. Rd. HU6: Hull 4D 16
(Hall Rd.)
HU6: Hull 4C 16
(Middledyke La.)
Orchard Rd. HU4: Anla 3A 42
HU16: Skid 4B 14
Orchard, The HU10: Will 2C 30
Orchard Vw. *HU15: N'th C* 1A 34
(off Church St.)
Oribi Cl. HU4: Hull 6B 42
Oriel Cl. HU17: Walk 2C 8
Oriel Gro. HU9: Hull 5B 30
Orion Cl. HU3: Hull 3G 43
Orkney Cl. HU8: Hull 5H 19
Ormerod Cres. HU5: Hull 4C 26
Ormerod Rd. HU5: Hull 4C 26
Ormesby Wlk. *HU5: Hull* 3C 26
(off Sedburgh Av.)
Ormington Vs. *HU9: Hull* 1F 45
(off Field St.)
Ormonde Av. HU6: Hull 2A 28
Orniscourt HU6: Hull 5E 17
Orpington Vs. *HU9: Hull* 5G 29
(off Rensburg St.)
Osborne St. HU1: Hull 2B 44 (4B 4)
Oslo Rd. HU7: Hull 6B 18
Osprey Cl. HU4: Hull 4G 17
Ossett Cl. HU8: Hull 5F 29
Oswald Ct. HU5: Hull 4C 26
Otley Cl. HU9: Hull 4D 30
Ottawa Cl. HU16: Cott 1G 25
Otterburn St. HU3: Hull 3F 43
Outer Trinities HU17: Bev 5E 7
Outgang, The HU15: Brant 2B 36
Outlands Rd. HU16: Cott 1C 26
Outram Cl. HU2: Hull 6B 28
Oval, The HU8: Hull 4F 29
HU10: Will 6F 25
HU15: Ello 5E 37
Overland Rd. HU16: Cott. 1B 26
Overstrand Dr. HU7: Hull. 6G 19
Overton Av. HU10: Will 5F 25
Overton Ct. DN18: Bart H. 5D 54
Owbridge Ct. HU1: Hull 2B 44 (4B 4)
Owen Av. HU13: Hess 1H 53
Owthorne Vs. *HU9: Hull (off Rosmead St.)* . . 6G 29
Oxenhope Rd. HU6: Hull 5A 18
Oxford Cl. HU17: Bev 1F 9
Oxford St. HU2: Hull 5D 28
Oxmarsh La. DN19: New H 2A 58

P

Pacific Ct. HU1: Hull 4F 5
Packman La. HU10: Kir E 6C 24
Paddock Ri. DN19: Bar H 5E 57
Paddocks, The HU10: Kir E 1C 40
Paddock, The HU4: Anla 3A 42
HU14: N'th F 6E 39
HU14: Swan 3H 39
HU15: S'th C 3D 34
HU16: Cott. 6B 16
HU17: Bev 2C 6
Paddock Vw. HU11: Bil 6B 22
Padstow Cl. HU7: Brans 3C 18
Padstow Ho. HU7: Brans 3C 18
Paisley St. HU3: Hull 2F 43

Palmcourt HU6: Hull 5E 17
Palmer Av. HU10: Will. 6E 25
Palmer La. DN19: Bar H 5F 57
Parade, The HU5: Hull 5A 28
Paragon Arc. HU1: Hull 2B 44 (3C 4)
Paragon Ind. Est. HU1: Hull 2A 44 (4A 4)
Paragon Sq. HU1: Hull 2B 44 (3C 4)
Paragon St. HU1: Hull 2B 44 (3C 4)
Parcevall Dr. HU7: King 2B 18
Park & Ride
    Priory Pk. 1H 53
    Walton St. 1F 43
Park Av. DN18: Bart H 4E 55
    HU3: Hull 2F 43
    (off Perry St.)
    HU4: Hull. 5D 42
    (off Gloucester St.)
    HU5: Hull 5F 27
    HU13: Hess 5F 41
    HU16: Cott 5H 15
    HU17: Bev 3D 6
Parkdale DN18: Bart H 5E 55
Parkfield Av. HU14: N'th F 2D 50
Parkfield Dr. HU3: Hull 1E 43
Park Gro. HU5: Hull 5H 27
    HU9: Hull 5G 29
Parkhurst Cl. HU8: Hull 6D 20
Parklands Cres. HU14: N'th F 1D 50
Parklands Dr. HU14: N'th F 1D 50
Parklands, The HU15: S'th C 3D 34
Park La. HU5: Hull (not continuous) 5A 28
    HU16: Cott 4G 15
    HU17: Walk 2A 14
Park La. E. HU4: Hull (not continuous) 3B 42
Park La. W. HU4: Hull 3B 42
Park Rd. HU5: Hull 5A 28
    HU11: Sproat 2E 23
    HU15: Welt 6G 37
Park Row HU2: Hull 1A 44 (1A 4)
    HU11: Sproat 2E 23
    HU13: Hess 6F 41
Parkside Cl. HU5: Hull 5G 27
    HU16: Cott 6G 15
Parkstone Rd. HU6: Hull 5H 17
Park St. HU2: Hull 1A 44 (2A 4)
    HU3: Hull 2A 44 (3A 4)
Park, The HU14: Swan 4F 39
Park Vw. DN18: Bart H 5F 55
    HU4: Hull 4D 42
    HU7: Hull 5G 19
Park Vw. Cl. DN19: Bar H 6E 57
Park Wlk. HU4: Anla 3A 42
Parkway, The HU10: Will 6F 25
    HU16: Cott 1H 25
Parliament St. HU1: Hull 2C 44 (4E 5)
    HU15: Welt 5G 37
Parnham Dr. HU7: King 1B 18
Parthian Rd. HU9: Hull 3D 30
Pasture Ho. M. HU17: Bev 4C 6
Pasture La. HU11: Burt C 1F 23
    HU17: Bev 4C 6
Pasture Rd. DN18: Bart H 3G 55
Pasture Rd. Nth. DN18: Bart H 2G 55
Pasture Rd. Sth. DN18: Bart H 3G 55
    (not continuous)
Pasture Ter. HU17: Bev 4C 6
Paterson Ho. HU5: Hull 5F 27
Pathway, The HU1: Hull 2C 44 (3E 5)
Patrington Gth. HU7: Brans 4F 19
Patterdale Rd. HU5: Hull 1D 42
PAULL 6A 48
Paull Rd. HU12: Salt 2A 48
Pavilion Cl. HU8: Hull 4E 29
Pavilion Cres. HU5: Hull 3A 28
    (off Worthing St.)
Paxdale HU7: Brans 4B 18
Peacehaven Cl. HU7: Brans 5E 19
Peace Wlk. HU12: Prest 5F 33
Peach Tree Cl. HU3: Hull 3A 44
Pearson Av. HU5: Hull 4A 28
Pearson Pk. HU5: Hull 5H 27
Pearson Ct. HU2: Hull 1B 44 (2B 4)
Pearson Way HU6: Hull 3C 28
Pease Ct. HU1: Hull 2D 44 (3G 5)
Peaseholme HU13: Hess 6D 40
Pease St. HU3: Hull 2B 44 (4B 4)
Peckforten Cl. HU7: Brans 3G 19
Peckham Cl. HU8: Hull 1H 29
Peel Pl. HU3: Hull 6A 28
    HU17: Bev 4C 6
Peel St. HU3: Hull 6A 28
Peggy Farrow La. HU15: Ello 2E 37
Pelham Cl. DN18: Bart H 5D 54
    HU17: Bev 2F 9
Pelham Dr. HU9: Hull 1F 45
Pemberton Gdns. HU5: Hull 4B 28
    (off Folkstone St.)
Pemberton St. HU5: Hull 1E 45 (1H 5)
Pembroke Gro. HU9: Hull 5A 30
Pembroke Vs. HU9: Hull 6G 29
    (off Rosmead St.)
Pendeen Gro. HU8: Hull 3E 29

Pendle Cl. HU7: Brans 1D 18
Pendrill St. HU3: Hull 5B 28
Penistone Ct. HU9: Hull 1G 45
Pennine Way HU7: Brans 6C 12
Pennington St. HU8: Hull 1E 45 (1H 5)
Pennyholme Cl. HU7: King 1B 18
Pennyman Rd. HU7: Bev 3F 7
Penrose Cl. HU7: Brans 3C 18
Penshurst Av. HU13: Hess 5G 41
Pentland Cl. HU8: Hull 5A 20
Penwith Dr. HU10: Anla 1G 41
Peploe Cres. DN19: New H 3A 58
Peploe La. DN19: New H 3A 58
Peppleton Cl. HU7: Hull 2F 29
Percy Cotts. HU5: Hull 6H 27
    (off Mayfield St.)
Percy St. HU2: Hull 1B 44 (2C 4)
Peregrine Cl. HU4: Hull 6C 42
Perivale Cl. HU8: Hull 1B 30
Perran Cl. HU7: Brans 5E 19
Perry St. HU3: Hull 2F 43
Perth St. HU5: Hull 6F 27
Perth St. W. HU5: Hull 6E 27
Perth Vs. HU5: Hull 6F 27
    (off Perth St. W.)
Petersfield Cl. HU7: Brans 6E 19
Petersham Cl. HU7: Brans 1B 30
Petuaria Cl. HU15: Brou 6C 36
Pevensey Cl. HU7: Brans 5E 19
Philip Larkin Cl. HU6: Hull 2H 27
Phoenix Bus. Pk. HU17: Bev 3E 7
Phoenix Cl. HU8: Hull 2A 30
Pickering Cres. HU4: Hull 5C 42
Pickering Homes HU4: Hull. 5C 42
Pickering Rd. HU4: Hull 2C 42
Pickerings, The HU14: N'th F 3E 51
Pickering Vw. HU4: Hull 5C 42
Pidgeoncote La. DN19: Gox 5D 58
Pier St. HU1: Hull 3C 44 (6E 5)
Pighill La. HU17: Bev 1C 6
Pilots Way HU9: Hull 3E 45 (5H 5)
Pinderfield Cl. HU8: Hull 1B 30
Pine Mdws. HU10: Kir E 1C 40
Pine Wlk. HU15: Ello 4E 37
Pinewood Gro. HU5: Hull 1B 42
Pinfold HU15: S'th C 4B 34
Pinfold Ct. HU12: Prest 5E 33
Pinfold M. HU7: Bev 4E 7
Pitman Av. DN18: Bart H 5D 54
Pitsford Cl. HU7: Brans 3D 18
Pitt St. HU3: Hull 1E 43
Plane St. HU3: Hull 2F 43
Plantation Cl. HU17: Bev 4G 7
Plantation Dr. HU14: N'th F 1C 50
    HU15: S'th C 4B 34
Plantation Dr. E. HU4: Hull 2B 42
Plantation Dr. W. HU4: Hull 2B 42
Plaxton Bri. Rd. HU17: Wood 4D 10
Plimsoll Way HU9: Hull 2E 45 (3H 5)
Plover Dr. HU15: Ello 4E 37
Plowden Rd. HU3: Hull 3D 42
Plum Tree Rd. HU11: Sproat 2F 23
Plumtree Rd. HU12: Thorn 6G 49
Plum Tree Wlk. HU15: S'th C 3E 35
Plym Gro. HU8: Hull 6D 20
Pollard Ct. HU5: Hull 4A 28
Polo Vs. HU5: Hull (off Perth St. W.) 6F 27
Ponds Way DN18: Bart H 3D 54
Pond Vw. Cotts. HU15: Brant 1D 36
Pool Bank La. HU15: Welt. 6H 37
Poorhouse La. HU9: Hull 6D 30
Poplar Av. HU4: Hull 4G 27
    (off Reynoldson St.)
Poplar Cl. HU4: Anla 3A 42
Poplar Ct. HU7: Hull 6F 19
Poplar Dr. HU17: Bev. 2E 7
Poplar Gro. HU8: Hull 3D 28
    (off Lorraine St.)
    HU12: Hed. 2D 48
Poplars, The DN19: Bar H 5F 57
    HU5: Hull (off Ella St.) 4G 27
    HU8: Hull (off Durham St.). 4F 29
    HU12: Thorn 6G 49
Poplars Way HU17: Bev. 1E 9
Popple St. HU9: Hull 2E 45 (3H 5)
Porlock Dr. HU7: Brans 3D 18
Port Av. HU6: Hull 4H 17
Porter St. HU1: Hull 3A 44 (6A 4)
Portland Pl. HU2: Hull 1B 44 (2B 4)
Portland St. HU2: Hull 1A 44 (2A 4)
Portmadoc Cl. HU7: Brans 5C 12
Portobello St. HU9: Hull 3A 30
Portsmouth Wlk. HU4: Hull. 4A 42
    (off Ashby Rd.)
Posterngate HU1: Hull 2C 44 (4D 4)
Potter Hill 5F 7
    (off Flemingate)
Potterill La. HU7: Hull. 6G 19
Potters Cl. DN19: Gox. 4D 58
Poultney Gth. HU12: Hed 2G 49
Premier Gro. HU5: Hull 3H 27
Prescott Av. HU15: Brou 6D 36
PRESTON 5E 33
Prestongate HU13: Hess 1F 53

Preston La. DN18: Bart H 4F 55
    HU11: Bil 6A 22
Preston Rd. HU9: Hull 5A 30
    HU12: Hed 6E 33
Pretoria Av. HU3: Hull 3E 43
    (off Seymour St.)
Pretoria St. HU3: Hull 3E 43
Pretoria Vs. HU5: Hull 4H 27
    (off De Grey St.)
Priestgate DN18: Bart H 4F 55
    HU11: Bil 6G 19
Primrose Dr. HU5: Hull 6B 26
Primrose Pk. HU17: Wood 1C 10
Primrose Vs. HU13: Hess 6F 41
Prince Charles Dr. DN18: Bart H. 5G 55
Prince Philip Dr. DN18: Bart H 5G 55
Princes Av. HU3: Hull (off Greek St.) 3E 43
    HU5: Hull 6H 27
    HU12: Hed. 2D 48
    HU13: Hess 1F 53
Princes Dock St. HU1: Hull 2C 44 (5D 4)
Princes Quay Shop. Cen. HU1: Hull 2C 44 (4D 4)
Prince's Rd. HU5: Hull 4H 27
Princess Dr. DN18: Bart H. 5G 55
Princess Gdns. HU5: Hull 4H 27
    (off Goddard Av.)
Princess Gro. HU3: Hull (off Ena St.) 2G 43
PRINCESS ROYAL HOSPITAL, THE 6B 20
Princess St. HU2: Hull 1C 44 (1E 5)
Princess Way HU17: Bev 2E 9
Prince St. HU1: Hull 2C 44 (4E 5)
Principal Trad. Pk. HU3: Hull 5F 43
Priory Av. HU14: N'th F 5F 51
Priory Cl. HU14: Swan 3G 39
Priory Cres. HU16: Cott. 1A 26
Priory Dr. HU5: Hull. 4C 26
Priory Farm Dr. HU4: Hull 6C 42
Priory Gro. HU4: Hull 4C 42
Priory La. DN19: Bar H 4F 57
Priory Rd. HU5: Hull 3B 26
    HU16: Cott, Hull 6A 16
    HU17: Bev 5F 7
Priory Tec Pk. HU13: Hess 1G 53
Priory Way HU4: Hull 1H 53
Prospect Cen., The HU2: Hull 1B 44 (2C 4)
Prospect Pl. HU2: Hull 1E 45 (2H 5)
Prospect St. HU2: Hull 1B 44 (2B 4)
Providence Cres. DN18: Bart H 4E 55
Providence Row DN19: Bar H 6E 57
    HU2: Hull. 6B 28
Prunus Av. HU10: Will. 5G 25
Pryme St. HU1: Hull 1B 44 (1B 4)
    HU10: Anla 2G 41
Pullcroft Rd. HU13: Hess 5E 41
Pulman St. HU3: Hull 1F 43
Purton Gro. HU7: Brans 5D 18
Putney Cl. HU8: Hull 1H 29
Pykestone Cl. HU7: Brans. 1D 18
Pyrus Dr. HU4: Hull 6A 42

Q

Quadrant, The HU6: Hull 1E 27
Quaker La. HU17: Bev. 4C 6
Quaker's La. HU15: N'th C (off Church St.) 1A 34
Quantock Cl. HU3: Hull 3A 44 (6A 4)
Quarrington Gro. HU7: King 1C 18
Quay St. HU1: Hull 2C 44 (3E 5)
Quebec Dr. HU16: Cott. 1F 25
Queen Elizabeth Way DN18: Bart H 5G 55
Queen's All. HU1: Hull 3D 44 (5F 5)
Queen's Av. DN18: Bart H 3F 55
Queensbury Way HU14: Swan. 4F 39
Queen's Cl. HU16: Cott. 5A 16
Queen's Dock Av. HU1: Hull 2C 44 (3D 4)
Queen's Gdns. HU1: Hull 4G 27
    (off Goddard Av.)
Queen's Ga. HU16: Cott 5A 16
Queensgate HU17: Bev 1E 9
Queen's Ga. St. HU3: Hull 3G 43
Queensmead HU17: Bev 2E 9
Queen's Rd. HU5: Hull 4H 27
Queens Rd. HU17: Bev 3F 7
Queen St. DN18: Bart H 1C 55
    HU1: Hull. 3C 44 (5E 5)
Queen's Way HU16: Cott. 4A 16
Queensway HU17: Wood. 2C 10
Queensway, The HU6: Hull 4G 17
Queen Victoria Sq. HU1: Hull 2C 44 (3D 4)
Quillcourt HU6: Hull 5D 16
Quilter Av. HU4: Anla 3A 42
Quilter Dr. HU11: Bil 5G 21
Quorum, The HU4: Hull 5D 42

R

Radstock Wlk. HU8: Hull. 5D 20
Raglan Av. HU5: Hull (off Raglan St.) 3H 27

Raglan St. HU5: Hull 3H 27
Raich Carter Way HU6: Hull 3G 17
   HU7: King 3G 17
Raikes Ct. HU15: Welt. 5H 37
Railway Ho's. HU3: Hull 1A 44
Railway St. HU1: Hull 3C 44 (5D 4)
   HU17: Bev 5E 7
Rainham Cl. HU8: Hull 4H 19
Rainhill Rd. HU5: Hull 4F 27
Rainswood Cl. HU7: King 1C 18
Raleigh Dr. HU9: Hull 2G 45
   HU11: Sproat 2F 23
Raleigh Lodge HU11: Bil 1E 31
Ramsden Av. DN18: Bart H 4E 55
Ramsden Pl. HU16: Cott. 1G 25
Ramsgate Cl. HU8: Hull 5H 19
Rands Est. HU12: Prest 5F 33
Randsfield Av. HU15: Brou 6C 36
Rangely Cl. HU7: Brans 1D 18
Rannoch Cl. HU7: Brans 6D 12
Ransome Way HU15: Ello 5D 36
Rauceby Cl. HU7: King 1C 18
Ravendale DN18: Bart H 5G 55
Ravenspurn Gro. HU9: Hull 4B 30
Ravenspur Rd. HU11: Bil 5H 21
Raven St. HU9: Hull 1G 45
Rawcliffe Gro. HU4: Hull 4C 42
Rawdale HU15: S'th C 3D 34
Rawling Way HU3: Hull 2H 43
Raywell Cl. HU10: Anla 1G 41
Raywell La. HU14: Swan 1F 39
Raywell St. HU2: Hull 1B 44 (1C 4)
Raywood Vs. HU3: Hull 3H 43
   (off Wellsted St.)
Reading Room Yd. HU14: N'th F. 2E 51
Rectory Cl. HU12: Prest 4E 33
Rectory La. HU12: Prest 4E 33
Redbourne St. HU3: Hull 3G 43
Redcar St. HU8: Hull 6D 28 (1H 5)
Redcliff Dr. HU14: N'th F 3E 51
Redcliff Rd. HU13: Hess 2E 53
Redfern Cl. HU3: Hull 3A 44 (6A 4)
Redgates HU17: Walk 6B 8
Red Ho. Farm HU12: Hed 2C 48
Redland Dr. HU10: Kir E 6D 24
Red Lion Ct. HU10: Anla 2F 41
Redmire Cl. HU7: Brans 1D 18
Red Ruth Cl. HU7: Brans 6F 19
Redwoods, The HU10: Will 4D 24
Reedham Gth. HU4: Hull. 5H 41
Reeds La. HU10: Anla 4A 30
Reed St. HU2: Hull 1B 44 (2C 4)
Reeth Wlk. HU5: Hull 3C 26
Reform St. HU2: Hull 1C 44 (1D 4)
Regency Ct. DN18: Bart H. 3D 54
Regent Cl. HU3: Hull 2H 43
   HU10: Will 5F 25
Regents Ct. HU16: Cott. 6H 15
Regent St. HU17: Bev 5E 7
Regent Ter. DN19: New H 2A 58
Regina Cres. HU5: Hull 5F 27
Regis Ct. HU9: Hull 3C 30
Register Sq. HU17: Bev 5D 6
Reigate Cl. HU3: Hull 2B 30
Reldene Dr. HU5: Hull 1A 42
Renfrew St. HU5: Hull 6G 27
Rensburg St. HU9: Hull 5G 29
Renton Ct. HU10: Anla 2G 41
Repton Dr. HU7: Hull 1G 29
Reservoir Rd. HU6: Hull 3C 28
Retford Gro. HU5: Hull 5F 31
Reynolds Cl. HU14: Welt. 6A 38
Reynoldson St. HU5: Hull 4G 27
Rhodes St. HU3: Hull 3E 43
Rhyl Cl. HU7: Brans 5C 12
Ribble Av. HU3: Hull 4G 43
Ribblesdale HU7: Brans 6D 18
Ribble St. HU3: Hull 4G 43
Ribycourt HU6: Hull. 5D 16
Riccall Cl. HU6: Hull 6F 17
Richardson Ct. HU2: Hull 5C 28
Richardson Rd. HU12: Hed 3D 48
Richmond Gdns. HU17: Bev 1E 9
Richmond Rd. HU13: Hess 6F 41
Richmond St. HU5: Hull 5G 27
Richmond Wlk. HU17: Bev 1E 9
Richmond Way HU17: Bev. 2E 9
Ridgestone Av. HU11: Bil. 6F 21
Ridgeway Rd. HU5: Hull 1A 42
Riding Flds. Sq. HU17: Bev. 4F 7
Riding M. HU17: Bev 4E 7
Ridings, The HU5: Hull 6H 25
   HU10: Anla. 3F 41
   HU14: N'th F 2E 51
   HU16: Cott 6G 15
   HU17: Bev 2B 6
Ridsdale HU7: Brans 5C 18
Rievaulx Ct. HU7: Hull 2D 28
Rigby Cl. HU17: Bev 1C 6
Rillington Av. HU16: Cott 1H 25
Rimswell Gro. HU9: Hull 4B 30
Ring Beck La. HU15: Elle 6E 35
Ringrose La. HU10: Anla 2F 41
Ringrose St. HU3: Hull 3E 43

Ringstead Gth. HU7: Brans 2D 18
Ripley Av. HU5: Hull 6F 27
   (off Perth St. W.)
Ripley Cl. HU6: Hull 5G 17
Riplingham Rd HU10: Kir E 5A 24
Riplingham Rd. HU14: Kir E 5A 24
   HU16: Skid 6A 14
Ripon Av. HU17: Bev 1F 9
Ripon Way HU9: Hull 6F 29
Risby Gro. HU6: Hull 1E 27
Risby Gth. HU16: Skid. 4A 14
Risby La. HU17: Walk 6B 8
Risby Pl. HU17: Bev 6D 6
Rise, The HU14: N'th F 1E 51
Rise Wlk. HU3: Hull 3H 43
Rishworth Cl. HU7: Brans 6D 12
Riston St. HU3: Hull 3H 43
Riverbank Ri. DN18: Bart H 4D 54
River Gro. HU4: Hull. 5D 42
Riversdale HU9: Hull (off Dene St.) 5G 29
Riversdale Rd. HU6: Hull 6H 17
Riverside Ct. HU13: Hess 3E 53
Riverside Works HU17: Tick 1H 7
River Vw. DN18: Bart H. 5G 55
   HU13: Hess 1G 53
Riverview Av. HU14: N'th F 3D 50
Riverview Gdns. HU7: Brans. 5B 18
Riverview Rd. HU17: Bev 4H 7
Rix Rd. HU7: Hull 2D 28
Robert Wood Av. HU17: Bev 5D 6
Robina Dr. HU4: Hull 6B 42
Robinson Row HU1: Hull 2C 44 (4E 5)
Robinswood Dr. HU7: Brans 4G 19
Roborough Cl. HU7: Brans 4E 19
Robson Av. HU6: Hull 4H 17
Robson Way HU8: Hull 5G 19
   HU12: Hed. 2D 48
Rochester Av. HU4: Hull 5A 42
Rockford Av. HU8: Hull 3E 29
Rockford Gro. HU8: Hull. 3E 29
Rockley Ct. HU10: Anla 2G 41
Rodney Cl. HU2: Hull 6B 28 (1C 4)
Roebank Arc. HU7: Brans 3C 18
Roger Gth. HU17: Will 5F 25
Rokeby Av. HU4: Anla 3A 42
Rokeby Cl. HU4: Anla 3A 42
   HU17: Bev. 2D 6
Rokeby Park HU4: Anla 3A 42
Rokel Ct. HU6: Hull 2H 27
Roland Av. HU3: Hull 3F 43
Rolston Cl. HU9: Hull 5D 30
Romford Gro. HU9: Hull 5F 31
Romney Gdns. HU4: Hull 4B 28
Ronaldsway Cl. HU9: Hull 3B 30
Ronson Cl. HU9: Hull 3E 31
Rookley Cl. HU8: Hull 1D 30
Roos Cl. HU17: Bev 1E 7
Roper St. HU1: Hull 2B 44 (4C 4)
Ropery Cl. HU17: Bev 4G 7
Ropery La. DN18: Bart H. 2E 55
Ropery Pk. (Ind. Est.) HU3: Hull 4A 44 (6A 4)
Ropery St. HU3: Hull 4A 44 (6A 4)
Rosamond St. HU3: Hull 4G 43
Rose Av. HU3: Hull (off Airlie St.) 3G 43
Rosebery Av. HU3: Hull 3H 27
Rosebery St. HU3: Hull 1E 43
Rosebery Vs. HU9: Hull 6G 29
   (off Rosmead St.)
Rosedale HU8: Hull 6E 29 (1H 5)
   HU9: Hull. 5H 29
Rosedale Av. HU9: Hull 5H 29
Rosedale Gro. HU5: Hull 6C 26
Rosedale Mans. HU3: Hull 2G 43
Rosedale Vs. HU9: Hull 6G 29
   (off Rosmead St.)
Rosedale Wlk. HU17: Bev 1F 9
Rosedene Row HU12: Thorn. 5G 49
Rosedene Vs. HU5: Hull 3H 27
   (off Raglan St.)
Rosemary Way HU17: Bev. 6F 7
Rosemount Cl. HU6: Hull 4G 17
Rosemount Grange HU13: Hess 5D 40
Rose Vs. HU9: Hull 6G 29
   (off Middleburg St.)
Rosewood Cl. HU4: Hull 1A 42
Rosey Row HU9: Hull. 1F 45
Roslyn Av. HU5: Hull 6G 27
Roslyn Cres. HU12: Hed 3E 49
Roslyn Rd. HU3: Hull 1D 42
Rosmead St. HU9: Hull 6G 29
Rosmead Vs. HU9: Hull (off Rosmead St.) . . . 6G 29
Rossett Ho. HU3: Hull 3A 44 (6A 4)
Rotenhering Staith HU1: Hull 5F 5
Rothesay Av. HU5: Hull 3H 27
Rothesay Cl. HU9: Hull 5H 29
Rotterdam Rd. HU7: Hull. 1D 28
Roundway, The HU4: Anla. 3A 42
Routh Av. HU17: Bev 4G 7
Rowan Av. HU17: Bev 1E 7
Rowan Cl. DN19: Bar H 5E 57
Rowan Ct. DN19: Gox 4D 58
Rowan Gth. HU16: Skid. 5A 14
Rowan Lodge HU8: Hull. 5F 29

Rowland Av. HU9: Hull. 1F 45
Rowlston Gro. HU9: Hull 4B 30
Roxburgh St. HU5: Hull 6G 27
Roxton Hall Dr. HU14: N'th F 1D 50
Royale Ct. HU9: Hull 3A 30
Royal Gth. HU17: Bev 6D 6
Royal Mail Cotts. HU12: Thorn. 6G 49
Royal Wlk. HU16: Cott 1C 26
Royston Gro. HU8: Hull. 5E 29
Ruard Rd. DN19: Gox 3F 59
Ruards La. DN19: Gox. 3E 59
Rudston Gro. HU9: Hull 4B 30
Rufforth Gth. HU7: Brans 4G 19
Rugby St. HU3: Hull 5G 43
Rugmere Cl. HU3: Hull 3A 44
Ruislip Cl. HU8: Hull 1B 30
Runcorn Gth. HU4: Hull 5A 42
Ruskin Av. HU3: Hull. 2G 43
   (off Ruskin St.)
Ruskin St. HU3: Hull 2G 43
Russells Row HU11: Sproat 2F 23
Russell St. HU3: Hull 1B 44 (1C 4)
Rustenburg St. HU9: Hull 5G 29
Ruston Way HU17: Bev 1E 9
Ruswarp Gro. HU9: Hull 6D 16
Rutherglen Dr. HU9: Hull 3A 30
Rutland Rd. HU5: Hull 6D 26
Rydale Cl. HU5: Hull 3B 28
Rydales, The HU5: Hull 3B 28
Rydal Gro. HU3: Hull 4H 27
   (off De Grey St.)
   HU16: Cott 6G 15
Ryde Av. HU5: Hull 3A 28
Ryde St. HU5: Hull 4A 28
Rye Cres. HU15: Brou 6F 37
Ryedale HU15: Ello 5F 37
Ryedale Gro. HU9: Hull 5A 30
Ryehill Gro. HU9: Hull 4B 30
Ryland Vs. HU9: Hull 5G 29
   (off Rustenburg St.)

S

Sabina Ct. HU8: Hull 5H 19
Sable Cl. HU4: Hull 6B 42
Sackville Cl. HU17: Bev 2D 8
Sacred Ga. HU12: Hed 4G 49
Saddle Cl. DN19: Gox 5E 59
Saddleworth Cl. HU7: Brans 1D 18
Saffrondale HU10: Anla 1F 41
Sage Cl. HU17: Bev 6E 7
Sailors Wharf HU9: Hull 2F 45
Sainsbury Way HU13: Hess 1H 53
St Abbs Cl. HU9: Hull 3D 44 (5G 5)
St Aidan Way HU9: Hull. 4A 30
St Albans Ct. HU17: Bev 1F 9
St Alban's Mt. HU6: Hull. 2H 27
St Andrew's Ho. HU1: Hull 3A 44 (5A 4)
St Andrew's Mt. HU10: Kir E 6D 24
St Andrews Retail Pk. HU3: Hull 4G 43
St Andrew St. HU17: Bev 5E 7
   (off Flemingate)
St Andrew's Vs. HU5: Hull 4H 27
   (off Prince's Rd.)
St Andrews Way HU8: Hull 3F 29
St Anne's Dr. HU16: Cott. 6C 16
St Anne's Wlk. HU15: Welt 5G 37
St Anthony's Cl. HU6: Hull 2H 27
St Anthony's Dr. HU12: Hed. 2F 49
St Anthony's Pk. HU12: Hed 2F 49
St Augustine's Av. HU5: Hull 4H 27
   (off Prince's Rd.)
St Augustine's Ct. HU12: Hed 2E 49
   (off Iveson Cl.)
St Augustine's Ga. HU12: Hed 2E 49
St Augustine's M. HU12: Hed 2E 49
St Austells Cl. HU9: Hull. 4A 30
St Barnabas St. HU3: Hull 4H 43
St Barnabas Dr. HU14: Swan 3H 39
St Bartholomew's Way HU8: Hull 1B 30
St Bede Cl. HU4: Hull 3D 42
St Benedict Cl. HU7: Brans 3E 19
St Catherines Cl. HU5: Hull. 4B 28
St Chad DN19: Bar H 4F 57
St Clements Pl. HU2: Hull. 5B 28
St David Cl. HU17: Bev 5E 7
   (off Hallgarth Way)
St David's Cl. HU16: Cott 6B 16
St Edmund's Cl. HU9: Hull 4C 26
St Ellens Ct. HU17: Bev. 5E 7
   (off Eastgate)
St Frances Cl. HU5: Hull. 4B 26
St George's Av. HU3: Hull 3F 43
St George's Gro. HU3: Hull 2F 43
St George's Rd. HU3: Hull 2F 43
St Georges Ter. HU3: Hull 4G 43
   (off Redbourne St.)
St George's Vs. HU3: Hull 1E 45
St George's Wlk. HU9: Hull 4C 30
St Giles Ct. HU9: Hull 5D 30
St Gile's Cft. HU17: Bev 5D 6

St Hedda's Ct. HU5: Hull 4C 26
St Helena Gdns. HU5: Hull 4B 28
     (off Tunis St.)
St Helen's Dr. HU15: Welt. 5G 37
St Hilda St. HU3: Hull 5B 28
St Ives Cl. HU7: Brans 5F 19
St James Cl. HU7: Brans 5G 19
   HU12: Hed .3E 49
   HU13: Hess .1H 53
St James Ct. HU7: Hull 6G 19
   HU9: Hull 2E 45
St James M. HU13: Hess 6H 41
     (off Newlyn Cl.)
St James Reckitt's Village Haven HU8: Hull. . . .5F 29
St James Rd. HU14: Welt 6B 38
St James Sq. HU3: Hull 3A 44 (6A 4)
St James St. HU3: Hull 3A 44 (6A 4)
St Johns Bus. Pk. HU9: Hull 5A 30
St John's Cl. DN19: Gox 5D 58
St Johns Cl. HU12: Hed 3E 49
   HU17: Bev 2F 9
St Johns Ct. HU6: Hull 2A 28
St John's Gro. HU8: Hull 5A 30
St John St. HU17: Bev 5E 7
St John's Wlk. HU13: Hess 6G 41
St Joseph Dr. HU4: Hull. 3B 42
St Jude's Cl. HU5: Hull 4C 26
St Julians Wells HU10: Kir E. 1E 41
St Katherines Rd. HU15: S'th C 4A 34
St Lawrence Av. HU16: Cott 1G 25
St Leonards Cl. HU12: Hed. 3D 48
     (off Draper's La.)
St Leonards Rd. HU5: Hull 4A 28
St Leonard's Rd. HU17: Bev 2B 6
St Luke's Ct. HU10: Will 6G 25
St Lukes St. HU3: Hull 2A 44 (4A 4)
St Margarets Av. HU16: Cott 6F 15
St Margarets Cl. HU16: Cott 6F 15
St Margarets St. HU3: Hull 6D 20
St Mark's Sq. HU3: Hull 4A 44 (6A 4)
St Mark's Ter. HU17: Bev 4C 6
St Mark St. HU8: Hull 6D 28
St Martins Av. HU4: Hull 2D 42
St Martin's Cl. HU17: Bev 5D 6
St Martin's Ct. HU4: Hull 2C 42
St Martins Ct. HU12: Thorn 5G 49
St Martin's Rd. HU12: Thorn 6G 49
St Mary's Av. HU5: Hull 2C 26
St Mary's Cl. HU12: Thorn 6G 49
St Marys Cl. HU13: Hess 3D 52
St Mary's Cl. HU15: Ello 3D 36
   HU17: Bev 3C 6
St Mary's Dr. HU12: Hed 3G 49
   HU12: Thorn .6G 49
St Mary's La. DN18: Bart H 4F 55
St Marys La. HU17: Bev 4D 6
St Marys Mt. HU16: Cott 6B 16
St Mary's Wlk. HU17: Bev 3C 6
St Matthews Ct. HU17: Bev 5E 7
St Matthew St. HU3: Hull 3G 43
St Michael's Cl. HU8: Hull 1C 30
   HU16: Skid 4E 14
St Michael's Ct. DN19: Gox 5D 58
St Michael's Ct. HU12: Hed 3G 49
St Michael's Mt. HU6: Hull 2H 27
   HU14: Swan 3G 39
St Monica's Cl. HU5: Hull 3H 27
St Nicholas Av. HU4: Hull 6B 42
St Nicholas Dr. HU17: Bev 5F 7
St Nicholas Gdns. HU4: Hull 6C 42
St Nicholas Ga. HU12: Hed 3F 49
St Nicholas Rd. HU17: Bev 4F 7
St Ninians Wlk. HU5: Hull 5F 27
St Pancras Cl. HU3: Hull 3H 43
St Paul St. HU2: Hull 6B 28
St Peter's Av. HU10: Anla 1F 41
St Peter's Ct. DN18: Bart H 3E 55
St Peter's Orchard DN18: Bart H 3F 55
St Peter St. HU9: Hull 2D 44 (3G 5)
St Peters Vw. HU11: Bil 6G 21
St Quintins Cl. HU9: Hull 1F 45
Saints Cl. HU9: Hull 4A 30
St Silas St. HU2: Hull 6C 28
St Stephen's Cl. HU10: Will 6H 25
St Stephens Sq. HU1: Hull 2A 44 (3A 4)
St Stephens St. HU1: Hull 2A 44 (3A 4)
St Thomas More Rd. HU4: Anla 4H 41
St Thomas's Grange HU5: Hull 4C 26
St Wilfred's Av. HU3: Hull 3F 43
     (off Greek St.)
Salcey Cl. HU7: King 1B 18
Salisbury Av. HU3: Hull 3F 43
   HU17: Bev 1F 9
Salisbury Gdns. HU5: Hull 4G 27
     (off Raglan St.)
Salisbury St. HU5: Hull 4G 27
   HU13: Hess .1F 53
Salisbury Vs. HU9: Hull 6G 29
     (off Holland St.)
Salmon Gro. HU6: Hull 2G 27
Saltash Rd. HU4: Hull 6H 41
Saltburn Av. HU5: Hull. 4B 28
     (off Folkstone St.)
Saltburn St. HU3: Hull 4F 43

SALT END 2A 48
Salt End La. HU12: Salt (not continuous) . . .3H 47
Saltford Av. HU9: Hull 6G 31
Saltgrounds Rd. HU15: Brou. 6C 36
Salthouse La. HU1: Hull 2D 44 (3F 5)
Salton Av. HU5: Hull 3D 26
Saltshouse Rd. HU8: Hull 6H 19
Saltwell Pk. HU7: King 1B 18
Salvesen Way HU3: Hull 5F 43
Samman Cl. HU10: Anla 2E 41
Samman Rd. HU17: Bev 3F 7
Sample Av. HU17: Bev. 3E 7
Sancton Cl. HU5: Hull 5A 28
   HU16: Cott 6F 15
Sandale Ct. HU5: Hull 5D 26
Sandfield Dr. HU15: Ello 6E 37
Sandford Cl. HU7: Brans 3C 18
SANDHOLM 1G 7
Sand La. HU15: S'th C 3A 34
Sandlemere Cl. HU3: Hull 3F 43
Sandmoor Cl. HU8: Hull 6C 20
Sandpiper Dr. HU4: Hull 6A 42
Sandringham Cl. HU16: Cott 6H 15
Sandringham Cotts. HU15: Brant 1D 36
     (off Outgang, The)
Sandringham St. HU3: Hull 2F 43
Sandringham Vs. HU3: Hull. 3F 43
     (off Wells St.)
Sands Ct. HU14: N'th F 2E 51
Sands La. HU15: Elle 6D 34
   HU15: Ello. 3D 36
Sandwith Ct. HU17: Bev 3E 7
     (off Goths La.)
Sandycroft Cl. HU5: Hull 5H 25
Sandy Point HU11: Bil 1F 31
Saner's Cl. HU16: Cott 1A 26
Saner St. HU3: Hull 2G 43
Santolina Way HU4: Hull 6B 42
Sapperton Cl. HU7: King 1C 18
Sapphire Gro. HU3: Hull 4F 43
Sargeant Cl. HU12: Hed 3D 48
Saturday Mkt. HU17: Bev 4D 6
     (off Ladygate)
Saunders Cft. HU17: Walk 5A 8
Saunders La. HU17: Walk 5A 8
Savannah Av. HU5: Hull 3A 28
     (off Minton St.)
Savery St. HU9: Hull 5G 29
Savile Cl. HU17: Bev 2D 6
Saville Cl. HU1: Hull 2C 44 (3D 4)
Saville Row HU1: Hull. 3D 4
     (off Saville Ct.)
Saville St. HU1: Hull 2C 44 (3D 4)
Savoy Rd. HU8: Hull 2A 30
Sawston Av. HU5: Hull 4B 26
Saxby Rd. HU8: Hull 1B 30
Saxcourt HU6: Hull 5D 16
Saxon Cl. DN18: Bart H 4G 55
Saxondale HU4: Hull 1A 42
Saxon Ri. HU17: Bev 1C 6
Saxon Vs. HU3: Hull 4F 43
Saxon Way HU13: Hess. 1G 53
Scaife Cl. HU17: Bev 5F 7
Scaife M. HU17: Bev 5G 7
Scalby Gro. HU5: Hull 6C 26
Scale Cl. HU1: Hull 2D 44 (4F 5)
Scale La. Staith HU1: Hull 2D 44 (4F 5)
Scampton Cl. HU7: Brans 4F 19
Scarborough St. HU3: Hull 5F 43
Scarrington Cres. HU4: Hull 2A 42
Scarrow Cl. HU3: Hull 1F 43
Schofield Av. HU17: Bev 4F 7
   HU17: Wood .2C 10
Schofield Cl. DN19: Bar H 5E 57
School La. DN19: Gox. 5D 58
   DN19: New H. 2A 58
   HU10: Kir E 6C 24
   HU14: N'th F .2E 51
   HU17: Bev (not continuous) 4D 6
School La. M. HU17: Bev 4E 7
School Rd. HU12: Prest. 5E 33
School St. HU1: Hull 1B 44 (3C 4)
Schooner Ct. HU4: Hull 5A 42
Schubert Cl. HU4: Hull 3B 30
Scotney Cl. HU2: Hull 5B 28
Scott St. HU2: Hull 1C 44 (1E 5)
Scrubwood La. HU17: Bev (not continuous) . . .2C 6
SCULCOATES 4B 28
Sculcoates La. HU5: Hull 4A 28
Seafield Av. HU8: Hull 3A 30
Seagran Av. HU13: Hess 5G 41
Seagull Cl. HU4: Hull 6C 42
Seamer Av. HU8: Hull 1G 5
Seaton Gro. HU4: Hull 3D 42
Seaton Rd. HU13: Hess 6G 41
Sedburgh Av. HU5: Hull. 3C 26
Sedbury Cl. HU7: King 1B 18
Sedgebrook Gro. HU7: King 1C 18
Sedge Cl. DN18: Bart H 3F 55
Sefton St. HU3: Hull 4G 43
Segrave Gro. HU5: Hull 6C 26
Selby St. HU3: Hull 3F 43
Selina's Cres. HU9: Hull 6G 29
     (off Rosmead St.)

Selkirk St. HU5: Hull 6F 27
Selsey Cl. HU5: Hull 4A 28
Selworthy Cl. HU7: Brans 2D 18
Selwyn Av. HU14: N'th F 2E 51
Sequana Cl. HU9: Hull 2E 45 (4H 5)
Setterwood Gth. HU10: Will. 6F 25
Setting Cres. HU5: Hull 4C 26
Setting Rd. HU5: Hull 4C 26
Seven Corners La. HU17: Bev. 4C 6
Severndale HU5: Hull. 4G 27
     (off Goddard Av.)
Severn St. HU8: Hull 5F 29
Severn Vs. HU9: Hull 5F 29
     (off Rosmead St.)
Sewer La. HU1: Hull. 3C 44 (5E 5)
Sextant Rd. HU9: Hull 4H 17
Shadwell Ri. DN18: Bart H 3D 54
Shaftesbury Av. HU8: Hull. 2A 30
Shakespear Cl. HU3: Hull 6A 28 (1A 4)
Shannon Rd. HU8: Hull 6D 20
Shardeloes HU11: Bil. 1F 31
Shardeloes Ct. HU16: Cott 6A 16
     (off Newgate St.)
Sharpe Cl. DN18: Bart H 5E 55
Sharps La. HU17: Walk 6A 8
Sharp St. HU5: Hull 4G 27
Shaw St. HU9: Hull. 1E 45 (1H 5)
Shead Grn. HU4: Hull 2B 42
Sheffield Ter. DN19: New H 2A 58
Sheffield Vs. DN19: New H. 2A 58
     (off School La.)
Sheldon Cl. HU7: Brans. 3E 19
Sheldrake Way HU17: Bev. 2E 7
Shelley Av. HU9: Hull 4D 30
Shepherd La. HU17: Bev 2E 9
Shepherds Cl. HU17: Bev 2E 9
     (off Shepherds Lea)
Shepherds Lea HU17: Bev 2E 9
Sherbrooke Av. HU5: Hull 2D 26
Sherburn St. HU9: Hull 5G 29
Sheriff Highway HU12: Hed 3E 49
Sherwood Av. HU5: Hull 6G 27
   HU9: Hull. 5H 29
Sherwood Cl. HU17: Walk. 5C 8
Sherwood Cl. HU11: Bil. 1E 31
Sherwood Dr. HU4: Hull 1H 41
Sherwood Gro. HU5: Hull 6F 27
     (off Perth St.)
Shetland Cl. HU8: Hull 5H 19
Shevington Wlk. HU8: Hull 6D 20
Shields Rd. HU12: Hed 2D 48
Shilling Cl. HU7: King 1C 18
Shipley Cl. HU9: Hull 5D 30
Shipton Cl. HU9: Hull 1E 31
Shirethorn Cen. HU2: Hull 1B 44 (2B 4)
Shire Vw. HU17: Walk 6A 8
Shirley Av. HU5: Hull 6F 27
     (off Perth St. W.)
Shopeth Way HU17: Wood 2C 10
Shoreditch Cl. HU8: Hull 1A 30
Shorthill Cft HU17: Bev 6D 6
Short St. HU1: Hull 2A 44 (3A 4)
   HU1: Hull 2B 44 (3B 4)
Shorwell Cl. HU8: Hull 6D 20
Shropshire Cl. HU3: Hull 5C 26
Sibelius Rd. HU4: Anla 4A 42
Sicey La. HU17: Wood. 6F 11
Sidings Ct. HU15: Brou. 6C 36
Sidmouth St. HU5: Hull 3H 27
Sigston Rd. HU17: Bev 2F 7
Silkstone Wlk. HU8: Hull 6F 29
Silsden Av. HU6: Hull 5H 17
Silverdale HU9: Hull 6F 27
     (off Rosmead St.)
Silverdale Rd. HU6: Hull. 6H 17
Silver St. DN19: Bar H 6E 57
   HU1: Hull 2D 44 (4E 5)
Silvester Sq. HU1: Hull 1C 44 (2D 4)
Silvester St. HU1: Hull 1C 44 (2D 4)
Simpson Cl. DN19: Bar H 5F 57
Simson Ct. HU17: Bev (off Goths La.) 3E 7
Sinclair Cres. HU8: Hull 6A 20
Sinderby Wlk. HU5: Hull. 2C 26
Sirius Cl. HU3: Hull 3G 43
Sissons Way HU5: Hull 3B 28
Sister's Cotts. HU12: Thorn 6G 49
     (off St Mary's Dr.)
Sittingbourne Cl. HU8: Hull 4H 19
Sitwell St. HU8: Hull 6D 28
Skelton Av. HU5: Hull 4D 26
Skern Gro. HU9: Hull 5B 30
SKIDBY 5B 14
Skidby Carr La. HU6: Wood 1C 16
Skidby Gro. HU6: Hull 1E 27
Skidby Windmill & East Riding Mus. of Rural Life
     . . . . .5C 14
Skilgate Cl. HU7: Brans 3D 18
Skillings La. HU15: Brou 6D 36
Skipworth Cl. HU6: Hull 6G 17
Skirbeck Rd. HU5: Hull 1G 29
Sleaford Av. HU9: Hull 4F 31
Sledmere Gro. HU4: Hull 3D 42
Sleightholme Cl. HU7: King 1B 18

Sleights Cl. HU3: Hull 1F 43
Slingsby Cl. HU5: Hull 3C 26
Sloe La. HU17: Bev 6C 6
Smedley Cl. HU17: Bev 5F 7
Smithall Rd. HU17: Bev 1D 6
Snainton Gro. HU5: Hull 6C 26
Snowdon Way HU7: Brans 5C 12
Snowhill Cl. HU7: Brans 6D 12
Snuff Mill La. HU16: Cott 6A 16
(not continuous)
Softham Cl. HU7: Brans 3C 18
Soff La. DN19: Gox 6F 59
Somerden Rd. HU9: Hull 1F 47
Somerscales St. HU2: Hull 6B 28
Somerset Av. HU9: Hull 1F 45
(off Franklin St.)
Somerset St. HU3: Hull 3F 43
Somerville Ct. HU12: Hed 3F 49
(off Thorn Rd.)
Sophia Cl. HU2: Hull 6B 28
Sorbus Cl. HU3: Hull 2A 44 (4A 4)
Sorbus Vw. HU5: Hull 1B 42
Sorrel Dr. HU5: Hull 5C 26
Sorrell Cl. HU17: Bev 1F 9
Souhwick Cl. HU17: Bev 1E 9
Soutergate DN18: Bart H 3F 55
South Bridge Rd. HU9: Hull 3D 44 (5G 5)
(not continuous)
Southburn Av. HU5: Hull 1D 42
SOUTH CAVE 3D 34
South Cave Sports Cen. 3D 34
Sth. Church Side HU1: Hull 2C 44 (4E 5)
South Cl. HU6: Hull 6H 17
Southcoates Av. HU9: Hull 4H 29
Southcoates La. HU9: Hull 5G 29
Southcote Cl. HU15: S'th C 3D 34
Southcroft Dr. HU8: Hull 5H 19
Sth. Ella Dr. HU10: Kir E 1E 41
Sth. Ella Way HU10: Kir E 1D 40
SOUTH END 6F 59
Southern Dr. HU4: Hull 3B 42
SOUTH FIELD 2E 53
. . . . 2G 21
Southfield HU13: Hess 2E 53
South Field Ct. HU16: Cott 1G 25
Southfield Dr. HU14: N'th F 3D 50
HU17: Bev 2F 7
Southfield Rd. HU5: Hull 4F 27
Southgate HU13: Hess 1F 53
Southgate Cl. HU10: Will 4F 25
South Holderness Sports Cen. 6F 33
Sth. Humberside Ind. Est. DN18: Bart H . . . 2G 55
South La. HU13: Hess 1F 53
Sth. Orbital Trad. Pk.
HU9: Hull 2F 45
South Ri. HU16: Skid 4C 14
South St. HU1: Hull 2B 44 (3C 4)
HU16: Cott 6H 15
South Vw. HU4: Hull 2A 42
HU9: Hull 5G 29
(off Sherburn St.)
South Vw. HU12: Hed 2F 49
Southwell Av. HU9: Hull 6F 31
Southwell Cl. HU17: Bev 1F 9
Southwood Av. HU16: Cott 6G 15
Southwood Dr. HU16: Cott 6H 15
Southwood Gdns. HU16: Cott 1G 25
Southwood Rd. HU16: Cott 1G 25
Souter Ga. HU12: Hed 2E 49
Sovereign Way HU7: King 2A 18
Sow Hill Rd. HU17: Bev 4D 6
Spacemade Pk. HU8: Hull 4D 28
Spark Mill La. HU17: Bev 5F 7
Spark Mill Ri. HU17: Bev 5F 7
Sparkmill Ter. HU17: Bev 5F 7
Speedwell La. HU17: Walk 2C 8
Speeton Gro. HU5: Hull 1C 42
Spencer Cl. HU12: Hed 3E 49
HU16: Cott 6G 15
Spencer Ct. HU3: Hull 2G 43
Spencer St. HU2: Hull 1B 44 (2B 4)
HU17: Bev 4D 6
Spencer Way HU16: Cott. 5A 16
Sperrin Cl. HU9: Hull 3B 30
Spicers Rd. HU12: Hed 3D 48
Spindlewood HU15: Ello 3D 36
Spinnaker Cl. HU9: Hull 2F 45
Spinney Cft. HU12: Hed 3G 49
Spinney Cft. Cl. HU14: N'th F 1D 50
Spinney, The DN19: Bar H 5F 57
HU14: Swan 3G 39
HU16: Cott 1H 25
Spinney Wlk. HU4: Hull 2B 42
Spinney Way HU17: Walk 6B 8
Spire Vw. HU13: Hess 1F 53
Spout Hill HU15: Brant 6H 35
Spring Bank HU3: Hull 6H 27 (1A 4)
Spring Bank W. HU3: Hull 1E 43
HU5: Hull 1A 42
Springbok Cl. HU4: Hull 6C 42
Springburn St. HU3: Hull 3F 43
Springdale Cl. HU9: Hull 6C 30
HU10: Will 6G 25
Springdale Way HU17: Bev 6D 6

Springfield Av. HU15: Ello 5E 37
Springfield Cl. HU15: Welt 5G 37
(off Cowgate)
Springfield Ct. HU10: Anla 2H 41
Springfield Dr. HU17: Bev 2F 7
Springfield Rd. HU3: Hull 2E 43
Springfield Vs. HU3: Hull 3E 43
(off Pretoria St.)
Springfield Way HU10: Anla 1F 41
Spring Gdns. HU4: Anla 2A 42
HU8: Hull 1G 29
Spring Gdns. E. HU4: Anla 2A 42
Spring Gdns. Sth. HU4: Anla 3A 42
Spring Gdns. W. HU4: Anla 2A 42
Spring Gro. HU3: Hull 1F 43
Springhead Av. HU5: Hull 1H 41
Springhead Gdns. HU5: Hull 1H 41
Springhead La. HU4: Anla 2H 41
HU5: Anla, Hull (not continuous) 1H 41
Springhead Pumping Station (Yorkshire Water Mus.)
. . . . 1H 41
Spring St. HU2: Hull 1A 44 (2A 4)
Spring Va. HU11: Bil 1E 31
Springville Av. HU13: Hess 6G 41
SPROATLEY 2F 23
Sproatley Rd. HU11: Sproat 6F 23
HU12: Prest, Sproat. 4E 33
Spruce Rd. HU1: Hull 3B 44 (6B 4)
Spurn Lightship 3C 44 (5D 4)
Spyvee St. HU8: Hull 1D 44 (1F 5)
Square, The DN19: Gox 5D 58
HU13: Hess 1F 53
Stable La. DN18: Bart H (not continuous) . . . 2D 54
Stafford St. HU2: Hull 6B 28
Staines Cl. HU8: Hull 2B 30
Staithes Rd. HU12: Hed, Prest 1A 48
Stalybridge Av. HU9: Hull 5F 31
Stamford Gro. HU9: Hull 5F 31
Stanbury Rd. HU6: Hull 5H 17
Standage Rd. HU12: Thorn 6G 49
Standidge Dr. HU8: Hull 1B 30
Stanhope Av. HU9: Hull 4H 29
Stanley St. HU3: Hull 1H 43
Stannington Dr. HU8: Hull 6E 21
Stansfield Cl. HU9: Hull 5E 31
Stapleford Cl. HU9: Hull 4F 31
Starboard Av. HU6: Hull 4H 17
Starella Gro. HU3: Hull 4F 43
Startforth Wlk. HU5: Hull (off Lythe Av.) 3D 26
Stathers Wlk. HU10: Anla 2G 41
Station Av. HU15: N'th C 5A 28
Station La. HU12: Hed. 1E 49
Station Rd. HU12: Prest 5E 33
HU13: Hess 2F 53
HU14: N'th F 2E 51
HU15: Brou 6C 36
HU15: N'th C 2A 34
Station Rd. HU15: S'th C 1C 34
HU16: Cott 5B 16
Station Sq. HU17: Bev (off Trinity La.) 4E 7
Station Vw. HU14: N'th F 2E 51
Station Wlk. HU16: Cott 6B 16
Staveley Rd. HU9: Hull 4C 30
Staxton Ct. HU9: Hull 6G 29
Steep Hill HU15: S'th C 2F 35
Steeton Av. HU6: Hull 5H 17
Stembridge Cl. HU9: Hull 5F 31
Stephen Cres. DN18: Bart H 4G 55
Stephenson Cl. HU12: Hed 3G 49
Stephenson Cl. HU5: Hull 5H 29
Stephenson's Wlk. HU16: Cott 6C 16
STEPNEY 5A 28
Stepney La. HU5: Hull 5B 28
Stevenson's Way DN18: Bart H 5E 55
Stewart Gth. HU16: Cott 6F 15
Steynburg St. HU9: Hull 5G 29
Stirling St. HU3: Hull 2E 43
Stirling Vs. HU3: Hull 2E 43
(off Stirling St.)
Stockbridge Pk. HU15: Ello 3D 36
Stockbridge Rd. HU15: Ello. 3C 36
Stockholm Pk. HU12: Hed 3F 49
Stockholm Rd. HU7: Hull 6B 18
HU12: Thorn 6G 49
Stockleigh Cl. HU7: Brans. 4C 18
Stocksbridge Av. HU9: Hull 5F 31
Stockwell Gro. HU9: Hull 6F 31
Stockwell La. HU12: Hed 2E 49
Stoke St. HU2: Hull 6B 28
Stonebridge Av. HU9: Hull 5E 31
Stonecarr Ct. HU7: Waw 4A 12
Stone Cl. DN19: Bar H 6F 57
STONEFERRY 2D 28
Stoneferry Pk. HU8: Hull 4D 28
Stoneferry Rd. HU7: Hull 2D 28
HU8: Hull 2D 28
Stonegate HU5: Hull 5G 19
Stonepit Rd. HU14: Welt 3A 38
HU15: Elle, S'th C 6C 34
HU15: S'th C 5D 34
HU15: Welt (not continuous) 4H 37
Stonesdale HU7: Brans 6C 18
Stones Mt. HU16: Cott 6H 15

Storkhill Rd. HU17: Bev 3F 7
Stornaway Sq. HU8: Hull 5A 20
Story St. HU1: Hull 1B 44 (2C 4)
Stothards La. DN19: Gox 4D 58
Strand Cl. HU2: Hull 6B 28
Stratford Wlk. HU9: Hull 5F 31
Strathcona Av. HU5: Hull 3D 26
Strathcona Vs. HU5: Hull 1C 46
Strathearn St. HU5: Hull 3A 28
Stratherne Av. HU6: Hull 6H 17
Stratton Cl. HU4: Hull 6C 20
Stratton Pk. HU4: Swan 4G 39
Strawberry Gdns. HU9: Hull 1F 45
Strawberry St. HU9: Hull 1E 45 (2H 5)
Strawberry St. Ind Est. HU9: Hull 1E 45
Stray, The HU15: S'th C 2D 34
Streetlife Transport Mus. 2D 44 (3G 5)
Strensall Rd. HU5: Hull 5B 26
Strickland St. HU3: Hull 4H 43
Strines Gro. HU8: Hull 5G 19
Stromness Way HU8: Hull 5A 20
Stroud Cres. E. HU7: Brans 4D 18
Stroud Cres. W. HU7: Brans 4D 18
Studley Ct. HU8: Hull 1F 45
Studley Rd. HU8: Hull 6E 29
Styles Cft. HU14: Swan 4H 39
Subway Rd. HU3: Hull 4G 43
Suddaby Cl. HU9: Hull 4A 30
Suffolk St. HU5: Hull 3A 28
Suffolk Ter. HU5: Hull 3A 28
Sullivan Bus. Pk. HU3: Hull 5G 43
Sullivan Rd. HU4: Anla 4A 42
Summercroft Av. DN19: New H 3A 58
Summerdale DN18: Bart H 5E 55
SUMMERGANGS 5G 29
Summergangs Dr. HU12: Thorn 6G 49
Summergangs Rd. HU8: Hull 3F 29
Summergroves Way HU4: Swan 6A 42
Summermeadows HU11: Bil 6E 21
Sunbeam Rd. HU4: Hull 3C 42
Sunningdale Rd. HU4: Hull 4E 43
HU13: Hess 6F 41
Sunnybank DN18: Bart H 4D 54
Sunny Bank HU3: Hull 1G 43
Sunny Dene HU3: Hull 1E 43
(off De La Pole Av.)
Sunnydene Vs. HU9: Hull 6G 29
(off Estcourt St.)
Sunny Gro. HU5: Hull (off Sharp St.) 4H 27
Surbiton Cl. HU8: Hull 1A 30
Surrey Gth. HU4: Hull 4A 42
Sussex Cl. HU5: Hull 5C 26
Sutherland Av. HU6: Hull 6G 17
Sutton Cl. HU7: Brans 4E 19
Sutton Ct. HU8: Hull 6H 19
Sutton Fields Ind. Est. HU7: Hull 6B 18
(not continuous)
Sutton Gdns. HU7: Brans. 5E 19
Sutton Ho. Rd. HU8: Hull 1G 29
SUTTON INGS 2A 30
SUTTON ON HULL 6G 19
Sutton Rd. HU6: Hull 6H 17
HU7: Hull 6B 18
Sutton Rd. HU7: Waw 4B 12
HU8: Hull 6B 18
Sutton St. HU3: Hull 1A 44
Sutton Vw. HU8: Hull 3E 29
Sutton Way HU9: Hull 4C 30
Swabys Yd. HU17: Bev 4D 6
(off Walkergate)
Swaddale Av. HU10: Will 4G 25
Swainby Cl. HU8: Hull 5G 19
Swaledale Cl. HU15: Ello 5F 37
Swaledale Av. HU9: Hull 5H 29
Swale Rd. HU15: Brou. 6F 37
Swallowfield Dr. HU4: Hull 6A 42
Swallow Grange HU4: Hull 5G 19
Swallows, The HU4: Hull 4B 16
Swanage Wlk. HU4: Hull 4A 42
Swanella Gro. HU3: Hull 4F 43
Swanfield Rd. HU9: Hull 3D 30
SWANLAND 4G 39
Swanland Butts Cl. HU10: Kir E 2D 40
Swanland Dale
HU14: Kir E, Swan, Welt . . . . . 1E 39 & 5A 24
Swanland Gth. HU14: N'th F 6E 39
Swanland Gro. HU6: Hull 1F 27
Swanland Hill HU14: N'th F 1E 51
Swanland Rd. HU13: Hess 6D 40
Swanland Way HU16: Cott. 6F 15
Swann St. HU2: Hull 6C 28
Sweet Dews Gro. HU8: Hull 6G 29
Swinburne Cl. HU12: Hed 3F 49
Swinburne St. HU8: Hull 4G 29
Swinderby Gth. HU7: Brans. 3E 19
Swine Bank HU5: Will 4A 26
Swinegate HU13: Hess 1F 53
Swine La. HU11: Bil, Swin 1D 20
HU11: Coni 1F 21
Swinemoor Ind. Est. HU17: Bev 3G 7
(not continuous)
Swinemoor La. HU17: Bev 2F 7
Swinescaif Rd. HU15: S'th C 1D 34
Swithin Cl. HU4: Hull 6H 41

Sycamore Cl. HU5: Hull 1B 42
    HU12: Prest 5E 33
    HU13: Hess 5D 40
Sycamore Ct. HU5: Hull 5A 28
Sycamore Dr. HU12: Thorn 6F 49
Sycamores, The HU17: Bev 5G 7
Sydney Gro. HU3: Hull 4G 43
Sydney Ho. HU1: Hull 3B 44 (5B 4)
Sykes Cl. HU10: Anla 2G 41
    HU14: Swan 3F 39
Sykes La. DN19: Gox 1D 58
Sykes St. HU2: Hull 1C 44 (1E 5)
Sylvester Ct. HU17: Bev 4D 6
                                    (off Sow Hill Rd.)
Sylvester La. HU17: Bev 4D 6
                                    (off Sow Hill Rd.)
Sylvia Cl. HU6: Hull 1E 27
Symmons Cl. HU17: Bev 2F 7
Symons Cl. HU2: Hull 6B 28

T

Tadman Cl. HU17: Bev 1D 6
Tadman St. HU3: Hull 4A 44
Tall Trees HU13: Hess 5D 40
Tamar Gro. HU8: Hull 6E 21
Tan Dyke Way HU17: Bev 5F 7
Tanfield Gro. HU9: Hull 4D 30
Tangarth Ct. DN18: Bart H 3F 55
Tardrew Cl. HU17: Bev 2D 6
Tarran Av. HU6: Hull 4H 17
Tattersall Dr. HU17: Bev 5G 7
Tattersall Castle DN19: New H 1G 57
Tattershall Cl. HU2: Hull 5B 28
Tatton Pk. HU7: King 2B 18
Taunton Rd. HU4: Hull 5H 41
Tavistock St. HU5: Hull 3H 27
Taylor Av. HU9: Hull 3D 30
Taylor Ct. HU6: Hull 2G 27
Taylors Ri. HU17: Walk 5B 8
Teal Cl. HU17: Walk 6B 8
Teddington Cl. HU8: Hull 6H 19
Tedworth Rd. HU9: Hull 1D 30
Teesdale Av. HU9: Hull 6H 29
Tees Gro. HU8: Hull 5D 20
Telford St. HU9: Hull 4H 29
Temperance Av. HU3: Hull (off Clyde St.) . . . 3E 43
Temple Cl. HU15: Welt 5H 37
Temple La. HU15: Welt 5H 37
Temple St. HU5: Hull 5B 28
Temple Wlk. HU15: Welt 5H 37
Temple Waters HU7: King 2B 18
Temsdale HU7: Brans 6D 18
Tennison Ct. HU16: Cott 5H 15
Tennyson Av. HU5: Hull 5F 27
Tenterden Cl. HU7: Brans 6D 18
Tern Gro. HU8: Hull 1D 30
Terry St. HU3: Hull 5A 28
Thanet Rd. HU9: Hull 1E 31
Thaxted Cl. HU8: Hull 6C 20
Theakston M. HU17: Bev 1E 9
THEARNE 4F 11
Thearne Cl. HU5: Hull 3H 27
Thearne La. HU17: Wood 5E 11
Thern Rd. HU8: Hull 6D 28
Thirlby Wlk. HU5: Hull (off Dent Rd.) 3C 26
Thirlmere Av. HU3: Hull 3H 43
Thirsk M. HU5: Hull 2C 26
THIRTLEBY 2B 22
Thirtleby La. HU11: Coni 1G 21
Thirty Acre La. HU12: Hed 2F 49
                                    (off Magdalen La.)
Thistleton Gdns. HU5: Hull 4B 28
Thomas Clarkson Way HU7: Hull, King 3A 18
Thomas St. HU1: Hull 1E 45 (1H 5)
Thompson Av. HU17: Bev 4F 7
Thompson La. HU15: Ello 4D 36
Thompson Rd. HU12: Hed 3D 48
Thoresby St. HU5: Hull 6G 27
Thorgill Gro. HU5: Hull 3D 26
Thorn Barn Cl. HU12: Thorn 6H 49
Thornbridge Cl. HU9: Hull 3C 30
Thorndale HU7: Brans 4B 18
Thorneycroft Rd. HU12: Thorn 6G 49
Thorngarth La. DN19: Bar H 5F 49
THORNGUMBALD 6G 49
Thornham Cl. HU15: S'th C 4C 34
Thornham's Way HU15: Ello 3E 37
Thornhill Av. HU8: Hull 2F 29
Thorn La. DN19: Gox 5D 58
Thorn Leigh HU3: Hull 2H 43
Thorn Rd. HU12: Hed 3F 49
Thornton HU15: Ello 5E 37
Thornton Av. HU5: Hull 6F 27
                                    (off Newstead St.)
Thornton Cl. HU13: Hess 1E 53
Thornton Ct. HU3: Hull 2H 43
Thornton Dale HU9: Hull 5G 29
Thornton Gro. HU12: Prest 4E 33
Thornton Rd. DN19: Bar H 6F 57
    DN19: Gox. 6C 58

Thornton St. DN19: Bar H 6F 57
Thornwick Av. HU10: Will 6F 25
Thornwick Cl. HU3: Hull 3H 43
Thornwood Av. HU5: Hull 1A 42
Thorpepark Rd. HU6: Hull 4E 17
Thorpe Rd. HU15: Ello. 6E 37
Thurlow Av. HU17: Bev 2D 6
Thurlstone Ct. HU7: Brans 6C 12
Thurstan Cl. HU9: Hull 4E 31
    HU17: Bev .6C 6
Thurstan Rd. HU17: Bev 6C 6
Thwaite Hall HU16: Cott 6B 16
Thwaite St. HU16: Cott 6B 16
Thyme Way HU17: Bev 2F 9
Tichbourne Cl. HU3: Hull 3H 43
Tickton Gro. HU6: Hull 2E 27
Tiger La. HU17: Bev 4C 6
Tilbury Rd. HU4: Hull 5A 42
Tilia Cl. HU4: Hull 6A 42
Tilworth Rd. HU8: Hull 2A 30
Tinkler Cl. HU12: Hed 3D 48
Tinley Cl. HU16: Cott. 5A 16
Tison Gth. HU10: Anla. 2G 41
Tithe Rd. HU12: Prest 4H 31
Tiverton Rd. HU7: Brans 3C 18
Todds Cl. HU14: Swan. 4H 39
Tofts Rd. DN18: Bart H 6E 55
Togo Cres. HU3: Hull 3F 43
                                    (off Eastbourne St.)
Tokenspire Pk. (Ind. Est.)
    HU17: Wood 6H 7
Toll Gavel HU17: Bev 4D 6
Tollymore Pk. HU7: King. 2B 18
Tom Pott's Row HU14: Welt 1C 38
    HU15: Welt 1A 38
Tom Thumb Ind. Est. HU3: Hull 4A 44 (6A 4)
Tonbridge Gro. HU9: Hull 4E 31
Toogood St. HU2: Hull. 6C 28
Topaz Gro. HU3: Hull 4F 43
Topcliffe Gth. HU7: Brans 4F 19
Torchil Cl. HU10: Anla. 2D 40
Torpoint Dr. HU4: Hull 5A 42
Torquay Vs. HU9: Hull 6G 29
                                    (off Rosmead St.)
Torridge Gro. HU3: Hull. 6D 20
Torrington St. HU5: Hull 3H 27
Torrington Vs. HU3: Hull 1F 45
                                    (off Franklin St.)
Total Fitness Leisure Cen. 2D 24
Tottenham Cl. HU8: Hull 1A 30
Tourist Info. Cen.
    Hessle 2D 52
    Hull 2C 44 (3D 4)
Towan Cl. HU7: Brans 3C 18
Tower Hill HU13: Hess. 6F 41
Tower Hill Dr. HU13: Hess 1F 53
Tower Hill M. HU13: Hess 6F 41
Tower Ho. La. HU12: Salt 1G 47
Tower St. HU1: Hull 3D 44 (5G 5)
    HU9: Hull 2D 44 (4G 5)
Tower Vw. HU10: Anla. 3D 40
Townend La. HU15: N'th C 2A 34
Townend Rd. HU17: Walk 5A 8
Townsend Dr. HU16: Cott 1G 25
Town St. DN19: Bar H 6E 57
Tradesman's Row
    HU11: Sproat. 2F 23
                                    (off Sproatley Rd.)
Trafalgar St. HU3: Hull 6A 28 (1A 4)
Trafford Rd. HU10: Will 6F 25
Train Av. HU6: Hull 4H 17
Tranby Av. HU13: Hess 6D 40
Tranby La. HU10: Will 4B 40
    HU14: Hess, Swan 4G 39
Tranby Lodge Gdns. HU13: Hess 1D 52
Tranby Pk. Mdws. HU13: Hess 5D 40
Tranby Ride HU10: Anla 3D 40
Tranmere Cl. HU3: Hull 3G 43
Travis Rd. HU16: Cott 1G 25
Trawden Cl. HU7: Brans 6C 12
Treece Gdns. DN18: Bart H 3G 55
Trees, The HU6: Hull 2H 27
Tremayne Av. HU15: Ello. 6D 36
Trenton Av. HU4: Hull 2A 42
Trent Pk. HU7: King 1B 18
Trent Wlk. HU15: Brou. 6F 37
Trevor St. HU2: Hull. 6C 28
Triangle HU14: N'th F 2D 50
Triangle, The HU14: N'th F 2D 50
Trinity Cl. DN19: Gox. 4E 59
Trinity Ct. HU1: Hull. 5E 5
Trinity Gth. HU16: Skid 4B 14
Trinity Gro. HU5: Hull 4H 27
                                    (off Ella St.)
    HU9: Hull. 5A 30
    HU13: Hess 6F 41
    HU17: Bev 4E 7
Trinity Ho. La. HU1: Hull 2C 44 (4E 5)
Trinity Ho. Rest Homes HU4: Hull. 2C 42
Trinity Ho. Yd. HU1: Hull 2C 44 (4E 5)
Trinity La. HU17: Bev (not continuous) 4E 7
Trinity St. HU3: Hull (not continuous) 1H 43
Trinity Wlk. DN18: Bart H 2E 55
Trippett St. HU2: Hull 1D 44 (2F 5)

Triton Rd. HU9: Hull. 3E 31
Troon Cl. HU5: Hull 6C 20
Troutsdale Gro. HU9: Hull 6A 30
Trundle St. HU1: Hull 2B 44 (4C 4)
Truro Cl. HU7: Brans 5F 19
Tudor Cl. HU10: Kir E 5D 24
Tudor Dr. HU6: Hull 4G 17
Tunis St. HU5: Hull 4B 28
Turmar Way HU11: Bil. 5H 21
Turner Ct. HU3: Hull 2B 44 (4B 4)
Turner Rd. HU17: Bev 3E 7
Turner's La. HU14: N'th F 1E 51
Turrets, The HU12: Thorn 6G 49
Tuxford Gro. HU9: Hull. 4F 31
Tweed Gro. HU8: Hull 1D 30
Tween Dykes Rd. HU7: Hull. 6F 19
Twickenham Cl. HU8: Hull. 1B 30
Twyers La. HU12: Hed (not continuous) . . . 2D 48
Twyford Cl. HU3: Hull. 4F 31
Tynedale HU7: Brans. 6D 18
Tyne St. HU3: Hull 4G 43
Tyson Cl. DN18: Bart H 3F 55
Tythe Gth. HU15: N'th C 1A 34

U

UCG Cinema 3A 18
Ullswater Cl. HU8: Hull 2G 29
Ulrome Cl. HU9: Hull 5C 30
Ulverston Rd. HU4: Hull 5H 41
Unicorn Trad. Pk. HU9: Hull 1F 47
Union St. HU2: Hull 1C 44 (2D 4)
Unit Factory Est. HU3: Hull. 1H 43
Unity Av. HU3: Hess 1G 53
University of Hull Sports & Fitness Cen.
        . . . . 1G 27
University of Hull, The 2G 27
        . . . . 4G 15
University of Lincoln
    Anlaby Rd. Campus 2B 44 (4B 4)
    George St. Bldg. 1C 44 (2E 5)
    Hooper Bldg. 2D 44 (3F 5)
    Salthouse Annexe 2D 44 (3F 5)
    School of Art & Design 2D 44 (3F 5)
University of Lincolnshire & Humberside . . . 1H 27
Upavon Gth. HU7: Brans 5F 19
Up. Union St. HU1: Hull 2B 44 (4B 4)
Uppleby Ct. DN18: Bart H 5G 55
                                    (off Kingston Vw.)
Upton St. HU8: Hull 5E 29
Uxbridge Gro. HU9: Hull 4F 31

V

Valentine Cl. HU4: Hull 6H 41
Vale, The HU10: Kir E 1C 40
Valerie St. HU9: Hull 5G 7
Valetta St. HU9: Hull 1E 47
Valiant Dr. HU9: Hull 2E 31
Valley Dr. HU10: Kir E 1C 40
Vane St. HU3: Hull 6A 28 (1A 4)
Varah Cl. DN18: Bart H 5D 54
Vaughan Rd. HU13: Hess 2F 53
Vauxhall Gro. HU3: Hull. 3A 44
Ventnor St. HU5: Hull 3H 27
Venture Bus. Pk. HU3: Hull 4G 43
Vera Gro. HU3: Hull 2E 43
                                    (off Stirling St.)
Vermont Cres. HU5: Hull 3A 28
                                    (off Worthing St.)
Vermont St. HU5: Hull 3A 28
Vermont Vs. HU5: Hull 3A 28
                                    (off Vermont St.)
Vernon Ho. HU6: Hull. 4F 17
Vernon St. HU1: Hull 2C 44 (3D 4)
Vestry La. DN18: Bart H 4F 55
Vicarage Ct. HU15: Ello 3D 36
Vicarage Gdns. HU15: Ello 3D 36
Vicarage La. HU13: Hess 6F 41
Vicarage M. HU15: Ello. 3D 36
                                    (off Vicarage Gdns.)
Vicarage Wlk. HU15: N'th C 2A 34
Vicar La. HU1: Hull. 3C 44 (5E 5)
    HU12: Hed 2E 49
                                    (off Church Ga.)
    HU17: Bev .4D 6
Viceroy Cl. HU2: Hull 6C 28
Victoria Av. HU3: Hull. 6H 27
                                    (off Mayfield St.)
    HU3: Hull. 3H 43
                                    (Boulevard)
    HU3: Hull. 3G 43
                                    (Wellsted St.)
    HU5: Hull 5F 27
                                    (Prince's Av.)
    HU5: Hull 5B 28
                                    (Stepney La.)
    HU9: Hull. 5G 29
                                    (off Rustenburg St.)
    HU10: Will. 4D 24

VICTORIA DOCK VILLAGE 3E 45 (5H 5)
Victoria Dr. DN18: Bart H 2E 55
Victoria Gdns. HU5: Hull 2E 55
Victoria Sq. HU5: Hull 5F 27
Victoria Ho. DN18: Bart H 3E 55
Victoria Rd. HU17: Bev 3E 9
Victoria Sq. HU5: Hull (off Ella St.) 4H 27
Victoria St. HU13: Hess 1H 53
Victoria's Way HU16: Cott. 6A 16
Victoria Vs. HU3: Hull 3E 43
(off Clyde St.)
Victor St. HU9: Hull (not continuous) 6F 29
Victory Way DN18: Bart H 2G 55
Viking Cl. HU10: Will 4D 24
Village Farm Rd. HU12: Prest. 5E 33
Village Rd. HU8: Hull 4F 29
Villiers Ct. HU12: Hed 3G 49
Vincent Cl. HU4: Hull 6H 41
Vine Cl. HU16: Cott. 5H 15
Virginia Cres. HU5: Hull 3A 28
(off Worthing St.)
Voases Cl. HU10: Anla 2F 41
Voases La. HU10: Anla 2F 41
Vulcan St. HU6: Hull 3C 28

W

Waddington Ct. HU5: Hull 3G 27
Wadebridge Gro. HU9: Hull 5F 31
Wadham Gro. HU5: Hull 5A 30
Wadhurst Cl. HU7: Brans 6D 18
Wadsworth Av. HU4: Hull 4H 17
Wainfleet Av. HU16: Cott. 6H 15
Wake Av. HU16: Cott. 1H 25
Wakefield Av. HU9: Hull 4D 30
Walcott St. HU3: Hull 4H 43
Waldegrave Av. HU8: Hull 2A 30
Walgrave St. HU5: Hull 3H 27
Walkergate HU17: Bev 4D 6
Walker St. HU3: Hull 3H 43 (6A 4)
(Rawling Way)
HU3: Hull 2F 43
(Anlaby Rd.)
WALKINGTON 5B 8
Walkington Rd. HU17: Bev 1C 8
Walmsley St. HU3: Hull 1A 44 (1A 4)
Walnut Cl. HU16: Cott. 1C 26
Walnut Tree Way HU4: Hull 5C 42
Walrus Arc. HU13: Hess 1F 53
(off Prestongate)
Walsall Gth. HU4: Hull 4A 42
Walter's Ter. HU5: Hull 3H 27
Waltham Cl. HU17: Bev 3E 7
Waltham La. HU17: Bev 4D 6
Waltham St. HU1: Hull 2C 44 (3D 4)
Walton St. HU3: Hull 1F 43
Walworth Cl. HU8: Hull 6H 19
Wandell's Vw. HU15: Brant. 6H 35
Wanlass Dr. HU16: Cott 5B 16
Wansbeck Rd. HU8: Hull 5D 20
Wansford Gro. HU9: Hull 5B 30
Ward Av. HU11: Bil 5G 21
Wareham Cl. HU7: Brans 6F 19
Warn Av. HU12: Hed 2E 49
Warneford Gdns. HU5: Hull 6F 27
Warrendale DN18: Bart H 4D 54
Warton Av. HU17: Bev 4G 7
Warton Dr. HU17: Wood 2C 10
Warwick Dr. DN18: Bart H. 5D 54
HU17: Bev 1D 6
Warwickshire Cl. HU5: Hull 5C 26
Warwick St. HU9: Hull 1E 45
Wascana Cl. HU4: Hull 5A 42
Wasdale Av. HU8: Hull 3E 31
Wasdale Grn. HU16: Cott 5A 16
Waseley Hill Way HU7: Brans 3G 19
Washington St. HU5: Hull 3A 28
Washington Vs. HU9: Hull. 6H 29
(off Rosmead St.)
Wassand St. HU3: Hull 4H 43
Waterdale HU7: Brans. 4B 18
Waterhouse La. HU1: Hull 3B 44 (5C 4)
Waterland Cl. HU12: Hed 3F 49
Water La. HU15: S'th C. 4C 34
Waterloo St. HU2: Hull 5B 28 (1C 4)
(not continuous)
Waterside Bus. Pk. HU13: Hess 2H 53
Waterside Rd. DN18: Bart H 1E 55
HU17: Bev 5G 7
Waterworks Ho's. HU6: Wood 1E 17
Waterworks La. HU11: Bil 6F 21
Watford Wlk. HU9: Hull 5F 31
Wath Gro. HU8: Hull 5F 29
Watkinson Cl. HU12: Prest 5F 33
Watmough's Arc. HU12: Hed. 2E 49
(off St Augustine's Ga.)
Watson Av. HU9: Hull 4D 30
Watson Dr. HU12: Hed. 2F 49
HU17: Bev 1E 9
Watson St. HU17: Bev 6G 19
Watton Gro. HU6: Hull 5G 17
Watts Rd. HU17: Bev 3E 7

Watt St. HU9: Hull 5H 29
Waudby Cl. HU17: Walk 5C 8
Wauldby Cl. HU10: Anla 1F 41
Wauldby Vw. HU14: Swan 3G 39
Waveney Rd. HU8: Hull. 1C 30
Waverley St. HU1: Hull 3B 44 (6A 4)
WAWNE 4A 12
Wawne Gro. HU5: Hull 3A 28
Wawne Lodge HU7: Brans. 6C 12
Wawne Rd. HU7: Brans 5C 12
Wayfbain HU12: Hed 2E 49
Weald Pk. HU7: King 1B 18
Weardale HU7: Brans 4C 18
Weaver Gro. HU8: Hull 5D 20
Webb Cl. DN18: Bart H 5D 54
Wednesday Mkt. HU17: Bev 5E 7
Weel Rd. HU17: Tick. 1H 7
Weelsby Way HU13: Hess. 6D 40
Weeton Cl. HU11: Bil 5H 21
Weeton Way HU10: Anla 1F 41
Weghill Rd. HU12: Prest 5F 33
Weighton Gro. HU6: Hull 1E 27
Weir, The HU13: Hess 1F 53
Welbeck St. HU5: Hull. 6G 27
Welbourn Wlk. HU4: Hull 2A 42
Welburn Gro. HU5: Hull 4D 26
Welburn Gro. HU9: Hull 4D 30
Welholme Vs. DN19: New H 2A 58
(off Barrow Rd.)
Welland Rd. HU8: Hull 5D 20
Wellesley Av. HU6: Hull 2A 28
HU9: Hull. 6G 29
(off Middleburg St.)
Wellington Ho. HU1: Hull 5B 4
Wellington La. HU3: Hull 6A 28
Wellington Rd. HU17: Bev 3E 7
Wellington St. HU1: Hull 3C 44 (6E 5)
Wellington St. W. HU1: Hull 3C 44 (6C 4)
Well La. HU10: Will. 4D 24
HU17: Bev (not continuous) 5E 7
Wells St. HU3: Hull 3F 43
Wellsted St. HU3: Hull 3H 43
Welshpool Cl. HU7: Brans. 5C 12
WELTON 5G 37
Welton Av. HU16: Cott. 6F 15
Welton Cl. DN18: Bart H 5E 55
HU17: Bev 2F 9
Welton Gro. HU6: Hull 1E 27
Welton Low Rd. HU15: Ello 4E 37
Welton Old Rd. HU14: Welt. 6A 38
HU15: Welt 5H 37
Welton Rd. HU15: Brou. 6C 36
Welton Wold Vw. HU14: Swan 3F 39
Welwyn Pk. Av. HU6: Hull 5H 17
Welwyn Pk. Dr. HU6: Hull 5A 18
Welwyn Pk. Rd. HU6: Hull 5H 17
Wembley Pk. Av. HU8: Hull 1H 29
Wendron Cl. HU7: Brans 5F 19
Wenlock Ct. HU3: Hull 2F 43
Wenlock St. HU3: Hull 1H 43
Wenlock Ter. HU9: Hull 5G 29
(off Rustenburg St.)
Wenning Gro. HU8: Hull 5E 21
Wensley Av. HU6: Hull 2D 26
Wensleydale HU7: Brans. 4C 18
Wentworth Cl. HU10: Will 6G 25
HU17: Bev 2E 9
Wentworth Cres. DN19: New H 2A 58
Wentworth Way HU9: Hull 1F 45
Wesley Cl. HU15: S'th C 3D 34
Wesley St. HU3: Hull. 3H 43
West Acridge DN18: Bart H 3D 54
Westborough Way HU4: Hull 2A 42
Westbourne Av. HU4: Hull. 5D 42
(off Gloucester St.)
HU5: Hull 5F 27
HU13: Hess 6F 41
Westbourne Av. W. HU5: Hull 5F 27
Westbourne Gro. HU13: Hess 6E 41
Westbourne St. HU3: Hull 4F 43
Westburn Av. DN19: New H 2A 58
WEST CARR (Bude Rd.). 5B 18
(Helsinki Rd.) 1C 28
W. Carr La. HU7: Hull (Copenhagen Rd.). 2C 28
HU7: Hull (Sutton Rd.). 6C 18
West Cl. HU17: Bev 2C 6
Westcott St. HU8: Hull. 4F 29
West Dock Av. HU3: Hull (not continuous) 4G 43
West Dock St. HU3: Hull 5G 43
WEST ELLA 1A 40
W. Ella Rd. HU10: Kir E 2H 39
W. Ella Way HU10: Kir E 1D 40
WEST END (Staithes Rd.). 5C 32
(Water La.) 4B 34
West End HU14: Swan 4F 39
HU15: S'th C 4B 34
HU17: Walk 6A 8
Westenders Way HU1: Hull 3B 44 (6C 4)
W. End Farm Cl. HU15: S'th C 4B 34
W. End Farm M. HU15: S'th C 4B 34
West End Rd. HU16: Cott 5G 15
Westerdale HU14: Swan 3F 39
Westerdale Gro. HU9: Hull 6H 29
Western Dr. DN18: Bart H 3D 54

Western Gailes Way
HU8: Hull. 6B 20
Western Vs. HU9: Hull 6H 29
(off Rosmead St.)
HU9: Hull 1F 45
(off Franklin St.)
Westfield Av. HU17: Bev 2C 6
Westfield Cl. HU16: Cott. 6G 15
Westfield Gth. HU17: Walk 5A 8
Westfield La. HU17: Prest. 5C 32
HU14: Swan. 4F 39
Westfield Pk. HU15: Ello. 5D 36
Westfield Ri. HU13: Hess 6E 41
Westfield Rd. DN18: Bart H 3A 54
DN19: Gox. 4D 58
HU4: Hull 2C 42
HU16: Cott 6G 15
HU16: Skid 3A 24
Westgarth Av. HU6: Hull 1E 27
Westgate HU15: N'th C 2A 34
West Grn. HU10: Kir E. 6A 24
HU16: Cott 6H 15
West Gro. DN18: Bart H 3D 54
HU4: Hull 4C 42
West Hall Gth. HU15: S'th C 4B 34
West Hann La. DN19: Bar H 2E 57
WEST HILL 2D 52
West Hill HU13: Hess 2D 52
Westland Rd. HU10: Kir E. 1C 40
Westlands Cl. HU12: Hed 3D 48
Westlands Dr. HU12: Hed 3D 48
Westlands Rd. HU5: Hull 6A 26
HU11: Sproat. 2E 23
HU12: Hed. 3D 48
West La. HU17: Hed 2D 48
Westleigh Cl. HU7: Brans 3D 18
W. Leys Pk. HU14: Swan 5F 39
W. Leys Rd. HU14: Swan. 5F 39
W. Marsh La. DN19: Bar H 1C 56
DN19: Gox. 1D 58
Westmeath Av. HU3: Hull 3G 43
Westminster Av. HU3: Hull 3H 29
W. Mill Ri. HU17: Walk. 6A 8
Westmoreland St. HU2: Hull 6C 28
Westoby La. DN19: Bar H 6E 57
Weston Ct. HU5: Hull. 6B 26
West Pde. HU3: Hull 1H 43
(not continuous)
HU7: Hull. 5G 19
W. Park Gro. HU3: Hull 2F 43
W. Parklands Dr. HU14: N'th F 1D 50
W. Point Trad. Pk. HU3: Hull 5F 43
West St. HU1: Hull 2B 44 (3C 4)
HU17: Bev 4H 7
West Ter. HU17: Bev 5F 7
West Vw. HU5: Hull 5A 28
HU14: N'th F 2E 51
Westway Av. HU6: Hull 6E 17
Westwick HU12: Hed 3E 49
West Wold HU14: Swan. 4F 39
Westwood HU17: Bev 6C 6
Westwood Cl. HU7: Hull 6F 19
Westwood Dr. HU4: Anla 2A 42
Westwood Ga. HU17: Bev 6D 6
Westwood Rd. HU17: Bev 5C 6
Westwood Way HU17: Bev 4C 6
Wetherby Cl. HU6: Hull 5E 17
Wexford Av. HU9: Hull 5F 31
Weymouth Cl. HU7: Brans 6E 19
Wharfedale HU5: Hull 4H 27
(off Goddard Av.)
Wharfedale Av. HU9: Hull 5H 29
Wharncliffe Rd. HU5: Hull 6F 27
Wharram St. HU2: Hull 5C 28
Wheatcroft Av. HU10: Will 4G 25
Wheatfield Cl. HU4: Hull 6C 42
Wheatlands Dr. HU17: Bev 2B 6
Wheatley Gdns. HU8: Hull 3G 29
Wheeldale Cl. HU8: Hull 5G 19
Wheeldale Rd. HU8: Hull 5G 19
Whernside Av. HU3: Hull 2E 43
Whernside Cl. HU7: Brans 1D 18
Whin Moor La. HU15: Brant 2A 36
Whins, The HU17: Bev. 6F 7
Whiston Way DN18: Bart H 3G 55
Whitby Av. HU8: Hull 6E 29
Whitby Gro. HU3: Hull 3E 43
(off Rhodes St.)
Whitby St. HU8: Hull 6E 29 (1H 5)
Whitebeam Cl. HU3: Hull 3A 44 (5H 5)
Whitecross St. DN18: Bart H 4F 55
Whitedale HU4: Hull 5D 42
(off Gloucester St.)
Whitefields Cl. HU17: Bev 1D 6
Whitefriargate HU1: Hull 2C 44 (4E 5)
Whitehall Gdns. HU5: Hull 5F 27
Whitehaven Av. HU5: Hull 4H 27
Whitehead Cl. HU17: Bev 5E 7
(off Hallgarth St.)
Whitehope Cl. HU7: Brans 1D 18
White Horn Way HU8: Hull 2G 29
White Ho. Cl. HU10: Will 4D 24
White Ho. Gth. HU14: N'th F 1D 50
Whitehouse M. HU14: N'th F 1D 50
Whitehouse Wlk. HU6: Wood 1F 17

Whitelees Ct. HU4: Hull 2C 42
White St. HU3: Hull 3E 43
White Wlk. HU10: Kir E (E. Ella Rd.) 2B 40
   HU10: Kir E (Mill La.). 2D 40
Whiting Cl. HU16: Cott 6H 15
Whiting Cl. HU13: Hess. 3E 53
Whitstable Cl. HU8: Hull 5H 19
Whitstone Cl. HU7: Brans 4C 18
Whittington Vs. HU9: Hull 6H 29
Whitworth St. HU9: Hull 4H 29
Wickenby Gth. HU7: Brans 4F 19
Wickwane Rd. HU17: Bev 2F 7
Wilbar Gro. HU5: Hull 4G 27
Wilberforce Cres. HU17: Bev 3F 7
Wilberforce Dr. HU1: Hull. 1C 44 (2E 5)
Wilberforce House Mus. 2D 44 (3F 5)
Wilberforce St. HU3: Hull 2A 44 (3A 4)
Wilberforce Vs. HU9: Hull. 6H 29
               (off Rosmead St.)
Wilbert Ct. HU17: Bev 4E 7
              (off Wilbert La.)
Wilbert Gro. HU17: Bev. 4E 7
Wilbert La. HU17: Bev 4E 7
Wilbert Pl. HU17: Bev 4E 7
             (off Wilbert Gro.)
Wilburn Ct. HU16: Cott 6H 15
Wilderspin Hgts. DN18: Bart H. 4D 54
              (off Furniss Ct.)
Wiles Ct. HU17: Bev 5F 7
Wifflete Ct. HU9: Hull 3C 30
WILLERBY 5E 25
Willerby Carr Cl. HU5: Hull. 5A 26
Willerby Hill Bus. Pk. HU10: Will. 2D 24
Willerby Low Rd. HU10: Will. 3D 24
   HU16: Cott 3D 24
Willerby Rd. HU5: Hull 6H 25
Willerby Shop. Pk. HU10: Will 4C 24
Willerby Sq. HU10: Will 5E 25
Willesden Cl. HU8: Hull 1A 30
Williamson St. HU9: Hull. 1E 45 (1H 5)
William St. HU1: Hull. 3B 44 (5B 4)
Willingham Gth. HU12: Thorn 6F 49
Willingham Way HU10: Kir E 5C 24
Willow Cotts. HU11: Bil. 6B 22
Willow Ct. HU10: Will 5F 25
   HU17: Bev 2B 6
Willowdale HU7: Brans 4C 18
Willow Dr. DN18: Bart H 3G 55
   HU10: Will 6F 25
   HU12: Thorn 6F 49
Willowfield HU6: Hull 6F 17
Willow Gdns. DN19: Bar H 4F 57
Willow Gro. HU5: Hull. 4H 27
             (off Prince's Rd.)
   HU17: Bev 4C 6
Willow La. DN19: Gox 3D 58
   HU17: Bev 1F 9
Willows Av. HU9: Hull 3A 30
Willows, The HU13: Hess 5F 41
Willow Tree Gth. HU17: Bev 1E 7
WILMINGTON 5D 28
Wilmington Cvn. Site HU8: Hull 5D 28
Wilson Cl. HU14: N'th F 2E 51
Wilson Row HU2: Hull 6C 28 (1E 5)
Wilson's Av. HU3: Hull 3E 43
             (off Rhodes St.)
Wilson St. HU9: Hull 1E 45 (2H 5)
   HU10: Anla. 2F 41
Wilton Av. HU9: Hull (off Holland St.) 6G 29
   HU9: Hull (off Franklin St.) 1F 45
Wilton St. HU8: Hull 1E 45 (1H 5)
Wiltshire Rd. HU4: Hull 4E 43
Wimbledon Cl. HU8: Hull 1B 30
Wimborne Cl. HU7: Brans 6F 19
Winchester Av. HU9: Hull 2C 30
   HU17: Bev 1F 9
Winchester Cl. HU9: Hull 2C 30
Wincolmlee HU1: Hull 1D 44 (2F 5)
   HU2: Hull 5C 28 (1F 5)

Windass Ct. HU13: Hess (off Hull Rd.). 1F 53
Windermere St. HU7: Brans 5C 18
Windham Cres. HU7: Waw 4B 12
Windle Av. HU6: Hull 5H 17
Windmill Wlk. HU17: Bev 4D 6
Windmill Way HU13: Hess 1G 53
Windsor Av. HU5: Hull. 3H 27
   HU9: Hull 1F 41
Windsor Cl. HU16: Cott 1A 26
   HU17: Bev 3G 7
Windsor Gro. DN19: Gox. 2E 59
Windsor Rd. HU5: Hull 4E 27
Winestead Gro. HU9: Hull. 4B 30
Wingfield Rd. HU9: Hull 4D 30
Wingfield Way HU17: Bev. 2D 8
Winscar Cft. HU8: Hull 5G 19
Winship Cl. HU3: Hull 3H 43
Winslade Cres. HU5: Hull 6F 27
              (off Perth St.)
Winston Dr. HU16: Cott. 1G 25
Winteringham Wlk. HU16: Cott 1H 25
            (not continuous)
Winthorpe Rd. HU13: Hess. 5G 41
Wintringham HU15: Ello 5E 37
Wise Cl. HU17: Bev. 1D 6
Wises Farm Rd. HU5: Hull. 5E 27
Wiske Av. HU15: Brou 6F 37
Wisteria Way HU8: Hull 5H 19
Wistow Gro. HU4: Hull 3C 42
Witham HU9: Hull 1D 44 (1G 5)
Withernsea St. HU8: Hull 5D 28
Witty St. HU3: Hull. 5F 43
Wivern Rd. HU9: Hull 3E 31
Woburn St. HU3: Hull 4E 43
Woldcarr Rd. HU3: Hull. 2E 43
Wold Hill HU15: N'th C 1B 34
Wold Rd. DN19: Bar H. 6E 57
   HU5: Hull. 5A 26
Wolds, The HU16: Cott 6F 15
Wold Vw. HU15: Ello 5E 37
   HU15: S'th C 3D 34
Wolfe Cl. HU16: Cott. 1G 25
WOLFRETON 1G 41
Wolfreton Ct. HU10: Anla (off Wolfreton Dr.). . . 2F 41
Wolfreton Dr. HU10: Anla 2G 41
Wolfreton Gth. HU10: Kir E 6E 25
Wolfreton La. HU10: Will 5G 25
Wolfreton Rd. HU10: Anla, Will. 1G 41
Wolfreton Vs. HU10: Anla 1G 41
Wolsey Dr. DN19: Bar H 6E 57
Wombwell Gro. HU8: Hull 5E 29
Woodbine Cl. HU2: Hull. 6B 28
Woodbine Vs. HU5: Hull. 4H 27
            (off Reynoldson St.)
Woodcock St. HU3: Hull. 4F 43
Woodcotes Cl. HU17: Bev 1E 7
Woodcroft Av. HU6: Hull 1E 27
Wood Dr. HU14: N'th F 2D 50
Woodfield La. HU13: Hess 1D 52
Woodford Leisure Cen. 3H 29
Woodgarth Vs. DN19: New H 2A 58
Woodgate La. HU5: Hull 6E 27
Woodgate Rd. HU5: Hull 6E 27
Woodgates Cl. HU14: N'th F 1E 51
Woodgates La. HU14: N'th F, Swan. 6E 39
Woodgates Mt. HU14: N'th F. 6E 39
Woodhall Dr. HU17: Bev 2C 6
Woodhall Pk. HU17: Bev 1C 6
Woodhall St. HU8: Hull 4D 28
Woodhall Way HU17: Bev. 1B 6
Woodhill Cl. HU10: Anla 1F 41
Woodhill Ri. HU13: Hess 6D 40
Wood Hill Way HU16: Cott 3D 14
Woodhouse St. HU9: Hull 1G 45
Woodland Av. HU15: Ello. 5E 37
Woodland Dr. HU10: Anla 3D 40
Woodland End HU4: Hull. 3B 42
Woodland Ri. HU11: Sproat 3F 23
Woodlands HU17: Bev. 4C 6

Woodlands Cl. DN19: Bar H 6E 57
Woodlands Dr. HU17: Bev. 4C 6
Woodlands La. HU15: Ello. 5E 37
Woodlands Ri. HU14: N'th F 1E 51
Woodlands Rd. HU5: Hull 6A 26
Woodlands, The HU5: Hull 4G 27
   HU12: Hed 2C 48
   HU16: Cott 5G 15
Woodland Vs. HU9: Hull 5G 29
            (off Rensburg St.)
Wood La. HU16: Cott. 1A 26
   HU17: Bev 4D 6
Woodleigh Dr. HU7: Hull. 1G 29
WOODMANSEY 2C 10
Woodmansey Mile HU17: Bev 6D 6
Woodmarketgate HU12: Hed 3E 49
Woodside HU13: Hess. 6E 41
   HU14: Swan 3H 39
Wood's La. HU1: Hull. 3B 44 (5C 4)
Woodstock Cl. HU16: Cott. 6G 15
Wood Vw. HU14: Swan 3G 39
Wool La. HU16: Cott 3A 26
Woolsheds Cl. HU5: Hull 5E 27
Woolsthorpe Gro. HU7: King 1C 18
Woolwich Dr. HU4: Hull. 6A 42
Worcester Rd. HU5: Hull. 5B 26
Worcestershire Cl. HU5: Hull 5C 26
Wordsworth St. HU8: Hull 4G 29
Workington Av. HU4: Hull (off Hull Rd.). . . . 2A 42
Worsborough Cl. HU9: Hull 5G 19
Worship St. HU2: Hull 1C 44 (1E 5)
Worthing St. HU5: Hull 3A 28
Wrawby La. HU12: Prest 3F 33
Wray Cl. HU17: Bev. 3E 7
Wright St. HU2: Hull. 1B 44 (2B 4)
Wrygarth Av. HU15: Brou 6D 36
Wyke Av. HU3: Hull 3F 43
Wykeham Cl. HU8: Hull 5G 19
Wykeland Ho. HU1: Hull 3D 44 (6F 5)
Wyke St. HU3: Hull 1G 45
Wylies Rd. HU17: Bev. 4D 6
Wymersley Rd. HU5: Hull 6H 25
Wynburg St. HU9: Hull 5G 29
Wyndham St. HU3: Hull 1H 43
Wyntryngham Cl. HU12: Hed 3G 49
Wytherstone HU7: King 1B 18
WYTON 5B 22
Wyton Gro. HU9: Hull 4B 30
Wyton Rd. HU12: Prest 1B 32

Y

Yarborough Ct. DN18: Bart H 5G 55
Yarmouth Av. HU4: Hull. 5H 41
Yatesbury Gth. HU7: Brans 3E 19
Yeadon Gth. HU7: Brans 4F 19
Yeoman Dr. HU17: Bev 1E 9
Yew Tree Dr. HU5: Hull 1A 42
Yiewsley Cl. HU8: Hull 6H 19
York Gdns. HU10: Will. 4D 24
York Rd. HU6: Hull. 5E 17
   HU17: Bev 4C 6
Yorkshire Cl. HU5: Hull 5C 26
Yorkshire Water Mus. 1H 41
York St. HU2: Hull 5D 28
York Ter. HU9: Hull (off Rustenburg St.) . . . 5G 29
York Way HU10: Will 4D 24

Z

Zeals Gth. HU7: Brans. 3E 19
Zeigfeld Ct. HU9: Hull 3B 30
Zetland St. HU3: Hull. 3F 43